REASONS AND PURPOSES

Reasons and Purposes

Human Rationality and the Teleological Explanation of Action

G. F. SCHUELER

CLARENDON PRESS · OXFORD

OXFORD
UNIVERSITY PRESS

Great Clarendon Street, Oxford OX2 6DP

Oxford University Press is a department of the University of Oxford.
It furthers the University's objective of excellence in research, scholarship,
and education by publishing worldwide in

Oxford New York

Auckland Bangkok Buenos Aires Cape Town Chennai
Dar es Salaam Delhi Hong Kong Istanbul Karachi Kolkata
Kuala Lumpur Madrid Melbourne Mexico City Mumbai Nairobi
São Paulo Shanghai Taipei Tokyo Toronto

Oxford is a registered trade mark of Oxford University Press
in the UK and in certain other countries

Published in the United States
by Oxford University Press Inc., New York

British Library Cataloguing in Publication Data

Data available

Library of Congress Cataloging in Publication Data
Schueler, G. F.
Reasons and purposes: human rationality and the teleological explanation of action/
G. F. Schueler.
p. cm.
Includes bibliographical references
1. Intentionality (Philosophy) 2. Practical reason. I. Title.
B105.I56 S39 2003 128'.4—dc21 2002034605
ISBN 0-19-925037-5

1 3 5 7 9 10 8 6 4 2

Typeset in Minion by
Cambrian Typesetters, Frimley, Surrey

Printed in Great Britain
on acid-free paper by
Biddles Ltd.
Guildford & King's Lynn

For Greg and Jason

Only a rational being has the power to act *in accordance with his idea* of laws—that is, in accordance with principles—and only so has he a *will*. Since *reason* is required in order to derive actions from laws, the will is nothing but practical reason.

Kant, Groundwork, 412

Preface

In the first sentence of 'Actions, Reasons and Causes' (1963), Donald Davidson asks, 'What is the relation between a reason and an action when the reason explains the action by giving the agent's reason for doing what he did?' This is the question that this book will address. However, the answer that will emerge in the course of the discussion is very different from the one that Davidson has been widely interpreted as defending in his paper.

Davidson's answer to this question, famously, consists of two claims. The first is that what he calls 'the agent's reason' always essentially involves a desire to perform (or what he calls a 'pro attitude' toward performing) an action with a certain property and a belief that the action she performed (under the description by which she conceived it) had that property. The second claim is that this desire and belief together are the cause of the action they explain, that is, that the explanation here is a causal one.[1] (Davidson's exact formulation of these two claims can be found in Section 1.2, below.)

In the years since Davidson's paper first appeared, some version of the idea that actions are explained causally in terms of the agent's 'desire–belief reasons' has come to be accepted by many, perhaps most, philosophers working in philosophy of action, philosophy of mind and connected areas, as well as by numerous social and behavioral scientists whose work bears on explanations of human action. And I think it is fair to say that even those who don't accept this answer have had a hard time agreeing on anything like a clear alternative answer to Davidson's question. So, even though deep problems have been raised about his answer to the question (for instance that it seems to commit him to epiphenomenalism[2]), to a large extent, Davidson's two claims still constitute for many philosophers the

---

[1] It has been argued, of course, that this second claim is itself really two distinct claims, that 'reasons are causes' and that the explanation involved is a causal one (see e.g. McGinn 1979). Hornsby (1997) argues that, while the explanations at issue are causal, it is not true—indeed, perhaps not intelligible—to hold that desires and beliefs are 'causes'. These and connected issues will be explored below.

[2] See e.g. Antony (1989), Kim (1993a), or Robinson (1999).

starting point for discussions of explanations of action (see e.g. Smith 1994, or Mele 1992). In spite of the difficulties they have encountered, they are something close to the 'received view' on these issues.

I think this is partly because of the brilliant job Davidson did in demolishing the most prominent objections to his two claims to be found in the philosophical literature at the time, perhaps most notably the objection that causes and their effects cannot stand in any sort of 'logical' relation. This and other objections to the causal view were so convincingly met that in the years since Davidson's paper the burden of proof has shifted completely. Whereas previously the philosophical climate of opinion seems rather to have favored the sort of anti-causal view advocated for instance by Ryle in *The Concept of Mind* (1949), currently anyone attacking the causal, desire–belief view of reasons is suspected of being guilty, at least until proven innocent, of making one or other of the mistakes exposed by Davidson. Beyond that, however, this general account of how these explanations of actions work has been understood to be consistent with, and very much in the spirit of, three widely accepted, and jointly reinforcing, doctrines.

The first, a consequence (or apparent consequence) of the 'fact–value distinction', is the view that no genuine explanation can involve in any essential way any *evaluation* on the part of the person doing the explaining. Genuine explanations are 'value-neutral', as it is sometimes put by the social and behavioral scientists who endorse this view. To explain an action is one thing, it is thought; to hold that it is right or wrong, or to offer any other evaluation of it, quite another.[3]

The second doctrine is an apparent corollary of the idea that all successful explanations of events must be causal. It is the view that so called 'belief–desire' explanations of actions must therefore be analyzed in terms of the causal interactions of these mental states (or the physical states that instantiate or 'realize' them). The thought is that genuinely *causal* explanations of events such as actions require reference to some other states or events as the relevant causal factors, 'the efficient causes', of which the actions are the effects. So, since

---

[3] I am referring here to how the belief–desire account of action explanation has been understood by many of its supporters. That Davidson *himself* would accept this 'value-neutral' point is not at all obvious, given his views about the role of 'radical interpretation' in explaining actions.

explanations of actions in terms of the agent's reasons are causal explanations, and a desire and belief are cited as the essential explanatory factors, the role of the desire and belief cited in the explanation must be that of the states or events that function as the efficient causes of the action in question.

There is also a third doctrine, with which Davidson's account as it is usually understood is compatible, and from which it may have gained some support. This is the doctrine that nature contains 'at bottom' no purposes, or at least none that cannot be completely explained in purely mechanical, causal terms. This is an apparent corollary of the view that all features of living organisms can be explained, directly or indirectly, by appeal to the sorts of mechanical causes that produce evolution, of which natural selection is the most important. As Richard Dawkins (1995, p. 85) colorfully puts this doctrine, 'The universe that we observe has precisely the properties we should expect if there is, at bottom, no design, no purpose, no evil and no good, nothing but pitiless indifference'.[4] Dawkins is discussing the sense of 'purpose' used by supporters of the argument from design, where one might for instance speak of the purpose of the cheetah's claws or the deer's antlers. But presumably if this doctrine is to be correct it has to apply to absolutely *all* of nature, and so to human purposes, such as Dawkins's own purpose in writing the article from which this quotation was taken.

In the pages that follow I will try to do two things. First, I will try to show that the sort of answer Davidson has been widely understood as giving to the question of how reasons explain actions is deeply problematic in ways that seem to make repair of this sort of answer impossible. While much of what I want to say on this issue builds on arguments made by others, I hope to show that, when set out fully, the case against the kind of answer Davidson has been understood as giving is decisive. (And as we will see, if I am right about this, it may well be that the answer that Davidson has been *understood* as giving is not in fact the answer he really gives at all.[5]) Second, I will try to

[4] Exactly how 'no evil and no good' got onto this list is not at all clear from what Dawkins says. Perhaps he is thinking that, if there is no God to provide any purposes, there will be no good or evil either. I will suggest below that at least some genuine purposes entail that there are genuine evaluations.

[5] As should be clear, I am discussing here the view that Davidson has been widely interpreted as giving in 'Actions, Reasons and Causes' (Davidson 1963). There is a strong case to be made that the so-called 'radical interpreter' view he gives in other, later papers (especially

construct an answer to Davidson's question that is sharply different
from this one, one that entails, among other things, that each of the
three doctrines just described is false.[6]

   Intentional actions are inherently purposive. At the same time, it
is an essential, one might say 'defining', feature of intentional actions
that they are done for reasons.[7] So the agent's reason or reasons for
performing some action of necessity always include the purpose or
purposes for which the action was performed. So far as I can tell,
these are not controversial points. It follows from them, however, that
any account of how the agent's reasons explain her actions must be,
or at least entail, an account of the purposiveness of the action being
explained. It is the inability of the causal, desire–belief view of agents'
reasons to provide such an account of the purposiveness of the action
that shows most clearly where this sort of view goes wrong. At the
same time, it gives an indication of how a better account can be
constructed.

when one thinks of its strong anti-reductionist element) is at least very different from, and
perhaps not even compatible with, the view he is often *understood* to be advocating in
'Actions, Reasons and Causes'. Though this book is not intended as an interpretation of
Davidson's views, the answer proposed below to the question of how reasons explain
actions seems to me at least compatible with much of what Davidson says in, e.g., 'Thought
and Talk' (Davidson 1975) and other papers, as well at least one way of reading 'Actions,
Reasons and Causes'. Perhaps that constitutes reason for thinking that the usual understanding of 'Actions, Reasons and Causes' needs to be reconsidered.

   [6] Deciding whether these doctrines are genuinely entailed by the views of which I have
said each is an 'apparent corollary' will have to wait for another time.

   [7] There is a difference of course between the intentional–unintentional distinction and
the voluntary–involuntary distinction. If I am absentmindedly tapping my foot while
reading a book, for instance, that is presumably voluntary (I wasn't forced against my will
and could stop if you told me it annoyed you) but not intentional (since, I would say, I am
not doing it for a reason—of course it isn't 'unintentional' either, presumably because there
is no description under which it is intentional). To start with, at least, it will be easiest to
focus on clear cases of actions that are both intentional and voluntary. We can deal with the
complications as they arise.

Acknowledgements

This book was started under a tree in my backyard in the summer of 1998. I don't know whether any good was done to the manuscript by its place of origin, but since that time it has certainly benefited from the comments, suggestions, and criticism (to say nothing of the epithets, jokes, and general bewilderment) of quite a lot of people. That fall the Philosophy Department at New Mexico State University kindly put up with my reading of an early version of part of Chapter 1. Along with their hospitality, Tim Cleveland, Richard Ketchem, Danny Socicia, and Jennifer Noonan all contributed very useful comments. A marginally more intelligible version of that same part of Chapter 1 was also delivered a bit later to participants in a conference on intentionality at the University of Oregon, organized by Bertram Malle, Louis Moses, and Dare Baldwin, where among others Bertram Malle, Joshua Knobe, and Al Mele tried valiantly to help me figure out what I was trying to say.

During the spring semester of 2000 I gave a seminar at the University of New Mexico based partly on the entire manuscript as it then was. The papers and discussion from the students in that seminar were a great help in the preparation of the next draft. Thanks are due in particular to Shelly Weinberg, Dan Gold, and Amy Lund. At about that same time Gordon Pinkham gave much of the manuscript a through editing job, which helped it greatly. Conversations about purposes and functions (and much else) with Aladdin Yaqub during that semester and at other times produced good results that showed up later at various places in the book. Other conversations with Rebecca Kukla, Amy Schmitter, Jennifer Nagel, and Sergio Tenenbaum helped me a lot in thinking about the issues discussed in Chapters 2 and 3.

Sergio Tenenbaum also read and made extensive comments on an early draft of the whole manuscript. His careful reading and insightful criticisms and suggestions were models of philosophical colleagueship. They saved me from countless mistakes and confusions. (In fact, his reading of the manuscript was so conscientious, and his comments on it so thorough, clear, and persuasive in helping

with the next draft, that I think that, to be completely fair here, I have
to say that in one way or another, either through omission or
commission, any mistakes and confusions that remain are really his
fault.)

In the fall of 2000 I was asked by Leslie Francis and Peggy Battin
to read what turned out to be a version of part of Chapter 3 at the
Virgil Aldrich Colloquium in the Philosophy Department of the
University of Utah as the Rod P. Dixon Lecturer. The questions and
comments of Michael Thompson, Michael Bratman, Elijah Mill-
gram, Bruce Landesman, Nick White, and several members of the
audience at that Colloquium have proved to be very helpful. Scott
Sehon, Jonathan Dancy, and Dugald Owen read versions of the entire
manuscript and provided extensive, and extremely useful, comments.
I am very grateful to them for their efforts, which improved the book
immensely. I hope they will each excuse me for not footnoting indi-
vidually the numerous places where their suggestions were used.

In addition, Sandy Robbins, Trish Aragon, and especially Peter
Momtchiloff deserve thanks for their help and unfailing good humor
through the whole time when this book was being prepared for
publication. Jessica Archibeque helped with the bibliography. Sue
Hughes did the copy editing.

Finally, I owe a huge debt of gratitude to my family, Karen, Greg,
and Jason Schueler. They have put up with an unconscionable
amount of muddled exposition, enthusiastic unclarity, and occasional actual philosophy from me over the years. Certainly this book
could never have been written without their love and support, and
even if it could have been, what would have been the point?

G.F.S.

Albuquerque, New Mexico

Contents

1

Purposes, Causes, and Reasons Explanations

It seems clear enough that intentional actions are inherently purposive; indeed, intentional human actions are paradigm examples of purposive behavior. There is always some point, aim, or goal to any intentional action. It is equally clear that our everyday explanations of actions in terms of the agent's reasons ('reasons explanations' for short) must always refer to that fact, that is to the purpose of the action, if only implicitly, on pain of not explaining the action at all.[1] If I tell you that my reason for sprinting toward the bus stop is that the last bus leaves in five minutes, you will take this as an explanation of my action only if you assume that my purpose is to catch the last bus (or anyway that it is something involving my being there at the same time the bus is—spray painting it with graffiti perhaps). Without some such addition, my reference to the time of the last bus simply won't 'connect' in the right sort of way to what I am doing, i.e. sprinting toward the bus stop, and my action won't have been explained.

When such a purpose is identified, then at least sometimes that lets you see what I am up to; that is, it really does sometimes explain my action. It does so when the purpose mentioned really is the one for which the action was performed. The issue we will be looking at in the chapters below, at the most general level, is simply how such explanations work. So to get our bearings we should begin by looking briefly at the question of what a 'purposive' explanation is.

---

[1] The claims that all intentional actions have some purpose and that all intentional actions are done for some reason both seem to me to be conceptually true. But nothing in what follows should *depend* on either claim as an assumption. So if one is doubtful of either claim one need only think of the arguments here as covering that subset of intentional actions that do have a purpose and are done for some reason. In the end, I hope, the arguments below will at least strongly suggest that both claims are true, and indeed are conceptual truths.

1.1 Purposes

An explanation is teleological, according to J. L. Mackie, 'if it makes some essential use of the notion that something—perhaps an event, or a state, or a fact—is an end or goal to which something else is, or is seen as, a means' (Mackie 1974, p. 279).[2] But it is important to notice that, within this broad definition, there is a sharp distinction to be drawn between purposive explanations, strictly so called, and functional explanations.

In this respect the term 'functionalism', as philosophers often use it, can be misleading. In philosophy of mind, for instance, it typically refers to accounts of *all* mental states in terms of their 'causal roles', that is in terms of their causal connections to other mental and non-mental states of the person. But authors of such functionalist theories of mind usually have little or nothing to say *in particular* about the specific states that embody the aims or purposes of the person (or mind) being explained. Apparently they assume that these notions will be sufficiently covered in the detailed expositions of the causal relations used to explain desire, hope, fear, and other such 'conative' states.[2] This is a small terminological oddity that can lead to confusion. 'Functionalist' theories of mental states usually give no special or separate account of an agent's purposes, simply lumping them in with all other mental states, even though in ordinary speech the term 'purpose' strongly overlaps with 'function' and purposive mental states would *contrast* with non-purposive ones such as belief. ('The function of the coffee mug on my desk is to hold my pencils' would, in ordinary speech, be taken to mean essentially the same as 'The purpose of the coffee mug on my desk is to hold my pencils'.)

In biology and philosophy of biology, however, this ordinary, 'purpose' sense of 'function' is of central importance. This is at least partly because of the naturalness of speaking of the function (or purpose) of organs, traits, or behavior of animals and plants, as when someone says that the function of eyes is to see, the function of hands

---

[2] Strictly speaking, of course, it is not at all clear that there *are* any genuine functionalist theories of mind, if by 'theory of mind' here one means something like an account of how some or all of the various sorts of mental states interact with each other, with perceptual input, and so on. What philosophers who discuss such theories do, rather, is discuss what features such theories would have to have if any were ever constructed. A clear sense of how difficult it would be to actually construct such a theory is given by Michael Smith in Smith (1994, pp. 44–55).

to grasp, or the function of green leaves to produce food for the plant to which they belong. So it is important for biologists to give an account of how eyes, hands, and green leaves can have functions or purposes, but to do so without making any reference to any person *with* that purpose, on pain of committing themselves to some sort of 'creationist' view, or at least to a view that allowed something to have a purpose only if some person had a purpose for it. Aristotle of course thought that things could have 'final causes' which were not the result of anyone's goals or ends. But it has been possible to explain how this could be so only since Darwin.

As they are understood in biology, an 'explanation in terms of the function' of, for instance, some trait of an organism explains the function of that trait by reference (roughly speaking) to the role the having of this trait played in the reproductive success of the ancestors of that organism.[3] That is, such functional explanations use natural selection, usually on the basis of the adaptive benefit to the ancestors of the organism, to make sense of the assignment of functions to traits (or organs, etc.). Since natural selection is a purely mechanical process, this also means that functional explanations require no reference to any person (or to God). As Elliot Sober puts it,

The theory of evolution allows us to answer . . . two conceptual questions about function . . . It makes sense of the idea that only some of the effects of a device are functions of the device ('the function of the heart is to pump blood, not to make noise'). The theory also shows how assigning a function to an object requires no illicit anthropomorphism; it does not require the pretense that organisms are artifacts. (Sober 1993, p. 83)

'Anthropomorphism' in such cases would be illicit just because (and just *if*) the actual explanation of the trait in question is not that someone (maybe God, maybe super-beings from outer space) constructed it for that purpose, but rather that this trait conferred an adaptive advantage of some sort on the organism's ancestors.[4] Anthropomorphism would not be illicit, of course, if the trait in question had *actually* been intentionally placed in the organism by

---

[3] Or else in terms of the causal role the trait plays in the explanation of the system in question. These two somewhat different senses of 'function' will be explained below.

[4] Or perhaps that it was a 'side effect' of some trait with an adaptive advantage, a 'spandrel', as Stephen Jay Gould calls it. I don't of course mean here to take a stand on any of the various controversies about the exact role of adaptation, genetic drift, group selection, etc. in evolution.

someone with some aim in mind. That is the case, for instance, when so-called 'genetic engineering' techniques are used to produce disease resistant strains of plants by placing bits of DNA into the plants' cells. In this sort of case, although the term 'artifact' may not be the appropriate one, it seems clear enough that the explanation of that particular trait of the organism is not correctly given in terms of natural selection and adaptive benefit, but rather in terms of the aim or intention of the scientists who planned the genetic engineering that resulted in the new DNA in the organism's genes, and hence in the new trait in the plant.

So we need to distinguish 'function', in the evolutionary or adaptive sense in which natural selection can be used to make sense of the function of some trait of an organism, from 'purpose' in its ordinary sense. To see why this is important, think for a moment about how *ordinary* purposive explanations work. Suppose you walk into my house and see a small nail sticking out of the wall. 'What is the purpose of that?' you ask, to which the reply is 'It is for holding up the new painting we just bought.' Such an answer, I want to say, entails that someone *assigned* this purpose to that nail, i.e. that *someone's* purpose *for* the nail was that it hold up the painting.

I am going to take examples of this sort as paradigmatic of the sense of 'purpose' on which I want to focus, though it is perhaps worth pointing out that events, as well as objects such as nails, can have purposes in this sense. ('The purpose of that explosion was to create shock waves for our instruments to detect.') In all such cases, there are really two distinct, logically connected, uses of the term 'purpose'. We can speak of 'the purpose of something' (object, event, etc.—here the nail in that wall), and we can speak of 'someone's purpose for something'. And clearly, in this sort of case at least, assigning a purpose *to* some object or event *entails* that someone had a purpose *for* it. This has the consequence that any analysis or definition of 'the purpose of something' that tries to do away with this entailment must be giving a different sense of 'purpose' from this one.

To mark this point, then, I will follow the practice of many philosophers of biology and use the term 'function' for those cases where speaking of the function (or 'purpose') of a thing does *not* entail that someone *had* a purpose for it. The term 'function' will then cover at least two sorts of case: (1) causal role analyses of 'systems', such as functionalism in philosophy of mind uses for mental states, and (2) explanations of traits or features of organisms in terms of the evolutionary history of the species in question. In the first sort of case functions are 'capacities or effects of components of systems, which are salient in the explanation of capacities of the larger system', as Peter Godfrey-Smith (1998, p. 16) puts it (following Cummins, 1975). In the second case, for something to be a function 'it must explain why the functionally characterized entity exists, and this explanation must involve some process of selection', as Godfrey-Smith says (1998, p. 16, following Wright, 1973).

The term 'purpose', on the other hand, will be used to cover cases analogous to the nail case mentioned above, where talk of *the purpose of something* entails that *someone had that purpose for it.* Roughly speaking, to talk of the purpose of something in this sense is to talk of the role the thing plays in someone's plan or project.

So one can figure out the *function* of a thing, in the sense of this term I am using here, either from what the thing actually is doing (its causal role) in the system of which it is a part, or from its evolutionary history, depending on which of the two sorts of function one is focusing on. Typically, in biology, where the second ('evolutionary') sense of 'function' is often the relevant one, once one has discovered what it was about some trait that gave the ancestors of an organism an adaptive advantage, one has figured out the function of that trait (in the Wright sense).

But this is not so for *purposes*. In the sense of 'purpose' I am focusing on here, no analysis or explanation of 'the purpose of something', in terms of the microstructure of the object or its causal connections to other things or its causal history, is possible. The purpose of something, in this sense at least, is necessarily *assigned* to it by someone. There are presumably various ways in which this can be done, but the point is that the notion of 'the purpose of something' is relational in the sense that reference is always implicitly made to someone (or some group, company, etc.) who has this purpose for this thing. So trying to give an analysis or explanation in terms of causal connections or microstructure or causal history of the thing itself, for this notion of 'the purpose of this thing', would be like trying to give an analysis in terms of microstructure or causal connections or causal history of some object for the property of 'being thought of by the Mayor of San Francisco'.

Another way to see this is to notice that things can fail, even fail *completely*, to serve or promote their purposes. Even though the purpose of that nail in my wall may indeed be to hold up our new painting, it might in fact be far too small to do so, with the result that it never does or even *could* actually hold up that painting. To say that something has a certain purpose is to say in part that it should do something, or is supposed to do something (i.e. according to the role it has been assigned in some plan or project someone has), not that it actually is doing that thing or even could do it. (So 'should' here doesn't imply 'can'.) Even though we have *assigned* that nail the role of holding up our new painting, and that is what it *should* do, it might still be that it cannot fulfill this role because, unbeknownst to us, it is simply too small to bear the weight of the painting we have. Evolutionary accounts of the function of some trait, such as the color of a flower, might *mimic* this feature of purposes (to some extent at least), as when one says that the sexual, reproductive function of the dandelion flower is (or at least was) to attract insects for pollination, but that this function is no longer served since dandelions now reproduce asexually. But by the same token, the fact that the dandelion flower no longer plays any role in reproduction seems to justify the conclusion that it no longer *has* any reproductive function. That nail, however, could still have the purpose of holding up our new painting, even if there is no possibility of its doing so given the weight of the painting.

Since the purpose of a thing, in the sense I am focusing on, always comes from someone's having a purpose for it, nothing about the thing itself (or what it is doing or even could do) determines what its purpose is or even that it has a purpose. And from this it follows that there is nothing at all about what a thing is actually doing, or how it got to be where it is, or the like, that determines, or in fact is even directly logically relevant to, the question of what its purpose is, what it should be doing.

Suppose for instance that, hours later and miles away, it finally dawns on me that that little nail in the wall is far too small to hold up our new, very heavy, painting. So I consult with my family and we decide instead to use it to hold up our little plastic thermometer, which we think it can indeed do. (True, we reason, the plastic thermometer won't look nearly as nice on our living room wall as the painting; but, on the other hand, we can use the thermometer to see at a glance what the temperature of the room is, something for which the painting was no help at all.) Once we make this decision, the nail's purpose now *becomes* holding up our thermometer, though absolutely nothing in the nail's microstructure or causal history or causal relations to the rest of the world has changed one bit. (Presumably there are some conditions on who gets to assign purposes to what, more or less analogous to what Austin (1962) called 'felicity conditions' for speech acts such as naming. Just as I can't name your baby, or christen your ship, at least not without your permission, you can't assign a purpose to the nail in my wall.[5] Since none of the issues to be discussed below turn on this, I won't pursue it.)

It might be worth mentioning here that the standard examples of objects with purposes—artifacts like pens or knives—are misleading in a significant way. It is true enough that artifacts have purposes only because people have purposes for them. So this is a case where 'purpose' and not merely 'function', is the appropriate term. But at the same time, it seems implausible to say that one can't simply 'see' or 'read off' the purpose of a ball-point pen, say, just by looking at it. So there would seem to be a question how this can be if, as I am arguing, there is nothing in the causal history or causal role of objects with purposes that determines what their purposes are. So it is important to be clear about how one's knowledge of the purposes of artifacts works.

One's knowledge of the purpose of, say, a ball-point pen comes not, or at least not merely, from a knowledge of its physical makeup or causal role or causal history alone, but from this *plus* one's knowledge of the human culture in which such pens are widely used, that is from knowledge of the fact that people have designed, constructed, and used objects of this shape and structure *for a certain purpose*. It is part of our knowledge of the causal history of pens that they are intentionally designed, produced, and used by people just so they will fill a certain causal role. In the terminology explained above, artifacts such as pens have the *function* they have (in either the causal role or causal history senses) partly because some people (primarily their designers and manufacturers but also partly their users) have constructed or adapted them to be used for certain *purposes*. Nothing changed (or at least nothing needed to change) in either the structure

---

[5] At the same time, purposes of things are relative to plans or projects someone has for them. So it could be that my wife's purpose for that nail is to hang our new painting, and mine to hang the thermometer. Simply to ask what 'the purpose of that nail' is would be to presuppose, perhaps falsely, that it has only one purpose.

or causal history of the goose quill that was first assigned the purpose of being a pen, though presumably whoever it was who assigned it that purpose did so largely because it had the structure it did, one that fitted it for a certain role, that is for a certain function.

1.2 Reasons and Causes

Let us turn now to intentional human actions, perhaps the most common examples of 'things that have purposes', in the sense of 'purpose' I have just set out.[6] Explanations of intentional actions in terms of the agent's reasons succeed in actually explaining the action in question, when they do explain it, partly by identifying the purpose or purposes for which the action was performed. That is the moral of the example at the beginning of this chapter of explaining my running toward the bus stop by citing my goal of catching the bus. At the same time, of course, intentional actions are events,[7] and thus fully inside the 'causal net'. So any explanation of these actions needs to accommodate that fact as well.

There are two theses about the explanation of actions in terms of the agent's reasons that, taken together, seem to many philosophers to cover both these points, that is to keep action explanations fully inside the causal net, while at the same time displaying their essential purposiveness. These theses are thus widely held jointly. The first is the thesis that such explanations of actions must always make essential reference to some desire the agent has in combination with a belief about how to satisfy it. (I'll call this 'belief–desire thesis', BD for short.) The second is the thesis that these explanations are causal explanations (the causal thesis, or CT for short). Both theses have been held by philosophers since (and indeed including) Aristotle.[8] In contemporary philosophy, however, these two theses have been most famously held by Donald Davidson, and since nothing I will say turns on any of the various 'fine-grained' variations of these two theses that

---

[6] Of course, there is one big difference between many 'things that have purposes', such as that nail in my wall, and at least most actions, namely that in understanding some event as an action one is necessarily understanding it as having some point or purpose, at least under some description.

[7] What exactly this means, and indeed whether it is true of all intentional actions, has of course been much debated. I won't try to add to that debate here.

[8] According to Aristotle, 'The origin of action—its efficient, not its final cause—is choice, and that of choice is desire and reasoning with a view to an end' (*Nicomachean Ethics*, 1139a, 31–32).

other philosophers have adopted, it makes sense simply to stick with Davidson's formulation of them. According to him, then,

> BD: R is a primary reason why an agent performed the action A under the description d only if R consists of a pro attitude of the agent towards actions with a certain property, and a belief of the agent that A, under the description d, has that property. (Davidson 1963, p. 687)
>
> CT: A primary reason for an action is its cause. (Davidson 1963, . 693)[9]

In the paper from which these formulations are taken ('Actions, Reasons and Causes') Davidson argues primarily against those who wanted to deny CT *because* they accepted BD, that is who accepted BD but thought they saw an incompatibility between BD and CT. So the bulk of his paper consists of attempts to show that various arguments that tried to use BD as a basis for denying CT were mistaken. I want to reopen this issue, since I think that, on the only reading of BD under which it is true, it really does make CT problematic, at least if it is understood as providing an account of the explanatory force of BD, as Davidson seems to have intended.

The first problem I face in doing this, however, is in showing that there really is an issue here at all. Davidson and other philosophers who have agreed with him on this topic have done such a spectacular job of demolishing earlier mistaken arguments against CT that many of these mistakes have acquired the status of textbook examples of bad philosophical reasoning. The result is that for many philosophers it is now almost impossible to see that there is any issue here, that is to see how anyone could sensibly, and without obvious confusion, think that accepting BD made it difficult to accept CT as simply solving the problem of how reasons explanations explain. So we need to start by spending some time trying to figure out whether there is a genuine issue here, and if so what it could be. There is no doubt that many of the arguments attacked by Davidson and others in this context really were bad ones. And I am certainly not going to try to resurrect, say, the 'logical connection' argument against CT.

The question though is whether there is any coherent position, or even any real issue, left once the confusions have been set aside. I will try to show that there really is an issue here, and I think that the best way to start is by setting out what I take to be the situation as reflected

---

[9] Davidson calls these two theses 'C1' and 'C2', names not easy to remember in the midst of a long argument or dozens of pages later.

in Davidson's own discussion. Clearly, there has been a great deal of work on these issues since Davidson's paper appeared, and I am certainly not going to try to retrace the twists and turns of these debates. Instead I will set out, in a rather summary way, what I take to be their upshot. They seem to me to point toward a need for more work to be done.

Since BD seems to be accepted by both sides, CT is the place to start. Doubts about CT are doubts about whether reasons explanations are causal explanations. And of course at least some of the most prominent of Davidson's targets, such as Ryle, explicitly claimed that reasons explanations of actions are not causal (Ryle 1949). So it makes sense to begin by examining the question of what really is being claimed when one holds that reasons explanations are 'causal explanations', and in particular what has been shown and what has been left open here. It is relevant to start by focusing on an apparent, and now well known, ambiguity of CT.

In the third sentence of the paper from which the above formulations are taken, Davidson says that he will defend the position that a reasons explanation of the sort described in BD (a 'rationalization' he calls it) 'is a species of causal explanation' (Davidson 1963, p. 685). So presumably CT is intended to express that thought. But in fact CT can be read rather differently, as Davidson makes clear—and exploits—in the course of his discussion. Explanations are intensional. So one thing explains another only 'under a description'. Though the sentence 'Oedipus married Jocasta' and the sentence 'Oedipus married his mother' describe the same event, the second goes a lot further than the first in explaining Oedipus's later behavior (Mackie 1974, p. 260). But Davidson also holds that causation relates events 'no matter how described'.[10] And CT itself merely says that a reason for an action, of the sort described in BD, 'is its cause'. So another reading of CT is possible. It can be read as merely asserting a causal relation between two *things* ('no matter how described'), a claim that *presumably* could be true even if the explanatory force of the explanation described in BD comes from something other than the causal connection referred to in CT.[11]

So there really are two possible readings of CT here, an 'intensional' one, which interprets it as claiming that reasons *explanations*

---

[10] See 'Mental Events', in Davidson (1980a, p. 215).
[11] See McGinn (1979). Hornsby (1997) contains an excellent discussion of this issue.

of the sort described in BD are 'causal explanations', and a non-intensional one, which simply claims that the *events* (or whatever they are) referred to in BD are related as cause and effect. But in fact, in this context one cannot read CT as asserting that the explanation described in BD is a causal explanation, as the first reading would have it, at least not without damage to Davidson's own argument. This is because it is the non-intensional, mere-relation-between-events reading that Davidson uses to defend against a major objection to his causal thesis. The objection is that causation requires laws, and there are no genuine laws governing reasons explanations. Davidson's reply is (in essence) that this is true but irrelevant, since causation is a relation between events, however they happen to be described, and hence the only requirement is that the relevant events are governed by some laws or other, not necessarily ones using the terms of the explanation described in BD.[12]

But this reply, though it defends CT, defends the wrong reading of it. On the resulting view, though reasons remain as causes, reasons *explanations* of the sort described in BD might still not be causal explanations.[13] Worse than that, holding that the events described in BD and CT can really, in the end, *only* be explained under some *other* descriptions than 'reasons' (or 'beliefs' and 'desires') and 'action', seems to entail that 'explanations' of the sort described in BD are not really explanations at all. Though reasons will be causes, the *explanatory force* of reasons explanations will be completely unaccounted for. The agent's beliefs and desires will then appear to be mere 'epiphenomena' that can do no 'explanatory work', that is can contribute nothing to the explanation in which they are cited.[14] They would be like the meanings of the words the soprano sings ('Break, O you wine glass') when it is actually the pitch and strength of her voice that

[12] According to Davidson, 'The principle of the nomological character of causality must be read carefully: it says that when events are related as cause and effect, they have descriptions that instantiate a law. It does not say that every true singular statement of causality instantiates a law' Davidson (1980a, p. 215).

[13] This would be the case if for instance causal explanations really did require laws that are formulated in the same terms as the explanation, or perhaps terms that can be used to directly reduce the terms of the explanation.

[14] Those familiar with the contemporary literature on this issue will realize that I am summing up, and taking a side on, a very vigorous debate. My point here is not to engage in that debate. Rather, as I said above, my goal is to see whether there is any coherent position 'on the other side', that is, a position that is not simply demolished by the pro-'causalist' arguments Davidson and others have given. For some of the details of this debate, see the papers in Heil and Mele (1993).

causes the wine glass to break.[15] So if one wants to defend the idea that reasons explanations are causal explanations, something needs to be changed.

One might of course try to drop one or both of the two assumptions that led Davidson into this move in the first place, i.e. the assumption that causal explanation requires laws and the assumption that there are no genuine laws governing reasons explanations. Dropping the second of these seems hopeless for all the familiar reasons, the most telling of which is that, whatever set of beliefs and desires one tries to connect 'by causal law' to some action, it is always possible (and usually easy) to specify a further belief or desire which, if the agent has it, will lead to some other action or to none at all, thus refuting the supposed 'causal law'.[16]

So it seems that the first assumption, that causation requires laws, will have to be the one to go if Davidson's defense is to avoid the above ambiguity, and the attendant threat of epiphenomenalism. Davidson's attempt to keep that assumption, by reading CT as referring to a mere relation between events, doesn't work, since it leaves him without an account of the explanatory force of explanations of the sort described in BD. Dropping that assumption, however, raises even more sharply the question of what the issue really *is* between those who hold and those who deny that reasons explanations are 'causal'. After all, if one thinks that causation requires laws, then there will be at least one very sharp issue between those who hold and those who deny that reasons explanations are causal explanations: namely, whether there really are laws in reasons explanations. If that is not the real issue, and it seems it can't be, given the obvious implausibility of holding that reasons explanations are actually lawlike (not to mention the fact that Davidson himself, famously, holds a view that entails this, the 'anomalousness of the mental'), then what is? Is there perhaps some other thesis about causation or

---

[15] This is Dretske's example (see Dretske 1988, p. 7).

[16] Here again, I am summarizing and taking a stand on a vigorously discussed contemporary issue. For a good discussion of the more or less current 'state of play' in this debate, see Kim (1996, 32–35).

An anonymous reader of an earlier version of this book suggested to me that, in fact, the issue here is simply the local manifestation of the problem of *ceteris paribus* clauses, without which no scientific 'law' would work. Following out this thought, however, would take us off the track here. Whatever the merits of this idea in general, it provides no help in understanding the question of whether to accept CT. This should become clearer in the next chapter, especially Sect. 2.2.

causal explanations that divides the two sides here? To answer this question, we need to take a brief look at what it means to say that one thing causes another or that an explanation is a causal explanation.

1.3 Causes and Causal Explanations

What are 'causal' explanations? Not (or at least not merely) explanations that make essential use of the term 'cause'. Genuine causal explanations seem frequently to get along quite well without ever actually using the *word* 'cause' or any of its cognates.[17]

Here is a brief (but I think perfectly accurate) causal explanation of why water comes out of the tap in my kitchen when I turn the cold water faucet handle to the right. A few miles from where I live, the city water department has pumped quite a lot of water into large storage tanks which are situated at some of the highest locations in the city, right up against the mountains. The water in these tanks is connected by underground pipes to virtually every part of the city, including my house. Since the tanks are higher than my house, there is positive water pressure in my pipes. When I turn the cold water tap to the right far enough, some holes in the faucet line up, allowing the water to flow out in much the same way as if one removed a plug from the bottom of a large bucket filled with water.

Of course there is plenty of 'causal terminology' in this little explanation. 'Pumped', 'turn' and so on refer to causal processes, certainly. But there is no reason to think that we would need to use *the term* 'cause' or any of its cognates in explaining these processes either. Just the reverse in fact, since presumably what would be wanted in the end would be (in the ideal case at least) very general physical laws and sets of initial conditions, period. Finding, in such an explanation, a sentence to the effect that one thing 'caused' another would lead us to think that there was more explaining to be done. How did it do this causing?

On the other hand, if I simply tell you that one thing has caused another, though I may have given you quite a bit of information, maybe even very useful information, I may not have done much, or even anything, to actually *explain* the effect in terms of the thing that

---

[17] A point made by Bertrand Russell in Russell (1953). Russell thought we should do away with the idea of 'cause'.

caused it.[18] It has been known for many decades that smoking causes lung cancer, but the actual mechanism by which this happens is only now being discovered. And there was quite a bit of evidence for the claim that smoking does indeed cause lung cancer (for instance, from comparison studies with matched groups of smokers and non-smokers) before there was *any* real idea of how the causal mechanism worked. So a straightforward way to put this situation would be to say that, while it has been known for quite awhile *that* smoking causes lung cancer, the actual causal *explanation* of how this happens is only now being worked out.

What both these points suggest is that our ordinary use of the term 'cause' would seem to be a sort of 'minimal' use, where the claim that one thing caused another amounts to nothing more than saying that the second happened *because* of the first, that is, *that* the one explains the other, period, with no information at all about how this explanation works. The word 'because', I would say, is a (or even *the*) minimal explanatory term in this sense, applying to anything that can be explained at all but *in itself* giving no content whatever to the explanatory claim. As J. L. Mackie puts this point, 'It is especially where we are inclined to ask why-questions that we will be ready to accept because-statements as answers to them, and we are particularly ready to call causes those items that can be described by clauses introduced by "because" ' (Mackie 1974, p. 156). The term 'because' cites *the fact that* there is an explanatory story connecting two things, but by itself actually *tells* none of that story at all. And, as Mackie says, there is an ordinary use of 'cause' too where nothing more than that happens, though one might want to add that 'cause' seems a bit more restricted in the sorts of things to which it can apply (roughly, events, states, facts, etc.) than 'because'.[19]

---

[18] Of course, much depends on how minimal one's conditions are on what counts as an 'explanation'. David Lewis holds that something is a causal explanation of an event if it gives *any* information about the causal history of that event. Given this account of 'causal explanation', then, correctly claiming that something was the cause of some event, even in the minimal sense of 'cause' explained below, would count as a causal explanation if reference to 'the cause' turned out to give any information about the causal history of the event (see Lewis 1973).

[19] We can say '7 is the square root of 49 because 7 times 7 gives 49', but not 'The fact that 7 times 7 gives 49 causes 7 to be the square root of 49'. On the other hand, as Sergio Tenenbaum pointed out to me, mathematicians say things like 'The behavior of this number in these equations is caused by the fact that it is divisible by . . .' Presumably this is metaphorical. Aristotle's discussion of the four kinds of cause—formal, material, efficient,

Mackie's own analysis of our ordinary concept of a cause provides a well known account which is a good example of what I am calling the minimal sense of the term 'cause'.[20] His account turns on the thought that something is said to be a cause if, given the assumed background circumstances, the effect would not have happened had not the cause happened—that is, that the cause is necessary for the effect (though he also allows that we frequently think of causes as sufficient for their effects). Beyond this, however, he wants to add the idea that in this ordinary use a cause is 'causally prior' to its effect, which he explains not as temporal priority, since he doesn't think the ordinary concept rules out the logical possibility of simultaneity between cause and effect, or even temporally reverse causation, but as the cause being 'fixed' when the effect is not. He holds though that 'The distinguishing feature of causal sequence is the conjunction of necessity-in-the-circumstances with causal priority'(Mackie 1974, p. 51). It is a feature of Mackie's account of ordinary singular causal claims that they involve conditionals (of the form 'If C had not happened, E would not have happened'), and hence that (as Hume also held) causation is not directly observable. '[T]he distinguishing feature of causal sequences . . . is not something that can be observed in any of those sequences' (p. 54).[21]

Whether or not one accepts Mackie's analysis of our ordinary concept of 'cause' (and of course I am giving only the barest of a bare bones description of it here), it is important to see that this analysis, like any plausible analysis of this ordinary, minimal concept, must *leave completely open* the question of what the *ground* is for the causal claim, what 'makes it true'.[22] That is not part of such a causal claim at all. It may be that, as many have thought, there is always some sort of regularity involved to back up any true causal claim (though Mackie

and final—might be held to employ a somewhat analogous, 'minimal' sense of 'cause' to mean something like 'explanatory factor'.

[20] Nothing here turns on accepting Mackie's analysis. Of course, there are deep problems about causation and causal explanation, and these have received a lot of discussion since Mackie's book. For more recent discussion of some of these problems, see Hitchcock (2001).

[21] Since he also holds that the conditionals involved are non-material, which he argues are simply 'suppositions', they will frequently be neither true nor false, since the suppositions will not obtain.

[22] Or 'makes it acceptable' on Mackie's account, since, given the 'suppositional' nature of such claims, they will frequently be neither true nor false, according to him (Mackie 1974, pp. 53–54).

himself rejects this). If so, that would ground those singular causal claims which reflected such a regularity. But in any case the question of what it is that *makes* the causal claim true is a completely different question from whether it *is* true. Saying that one thing *can be explained* in terms of another, which is what any such singular causal claim says, though perhaps useful and informative, is not the same as *giving* an explanation, at least in any but the most minimal sense.[23] It is more like a promissory note that says that this factor (event, state, fact) being cited will prove to be the most interesting (or important, or relevant to your purposes) in the full explanatory story, when and if it comes out. But having a promissory note, even if it is as solid as solid can be, is not the same as having whatever it is that is promised. If I promise to return the camera I borrowed from you, then, assuming I am a trustworthy person, in one sense that is as good as actually having it back. You can quite safely list it among your possessions in your will, for instance. But it is still not really the same has having it back. You can't take any actual photographs with my promise to return your camera. Similarly, saying that one thing caused another, though it might be useful in all sorts of ways (e.g. in the search for an explanation of the second thing), tells us nothing yet about how this 'causing' got done.

This minimal account of our ordinary concept of 'cause' makes sense of Davidson's statement that causes are relations between events no matter how described, which can be understood as simply making this point concisely and dramatically. To say that one thing caused another, in this minimal sense of 'cause', is really not to *give* a substantive explanation of the one in terms of the other: it is to *claim* that there is such an explanation to be had, and that these events, described in some way or other, will be referred to in that explanation. Explanations, as I said, are intensional. The content of the descriptions they contain makes all the difference. Not so in the ordinary, minimal sense of 'cause', where the only claim is *that* the one explains the other (on Mackie's analysis, that without the one the other would not have happened), and for this, how they are *described* makes no difference.

It is easy to overlook this, because the information we get in ordinary life from finding out that one thing caused another comes from

---

[23] Though this seems to be close to what David Lewis has in mind for the minimum of a 'causal explanation': see Lewis (1973).

the fact that the *actual descriptions* of the 'things' tend to be ones that interest us (compare 'The event that took place at 1:28 pm at latitude *X* and longitude *Y* caused the event that took place at 1:29 pm . . .' with 'Your son threw a rock that broke my plate glass window'). And sometimes, in addition, it comes from the fact that picking out one specific thing as the cause serves to pin down one among a small number of possible explanatory factors. (It was the rock that broke the window, not the high note from the opera singer, not the earth-quake.)

This way of understanding the claim that one thing caused another (i.e. the minimal or 'promissory note' account as exemplified by Mackie's analysis) has the advantage of demystifying claims about causation such as Davidson's. It is not that 'causation' is some myste-rious, metaphysically primary, relation between events on this view. (Or at least on this account, making causal claims doesn't *commit* one to there being such a mysterious relation.) Saying that one thing caused another, on this account, is simply claiming *that there is* an explanation to be had of the second in which the first will figure importantly. At the same time, however, and for this very reason, this raises more sharply the question of what the issue could possibly be between those who claim and those who deny that reasons explana-tions are 'causal explanations.'

On the minimal, 'promissory note' view of 'cause' just described, it will certainly be true that his reason for standing on his head (he thought it would impress her) caused him to do it. In this minimal sense of 'cause', at least, such a claim says nothing more than that the state (or event or thought or whatever it is) referred to by the phrase 'his reason for doing it' will figure in the explanation, whatever it turns out to be, of the event referred to by the phrase 'his standing on his head'. On Mackie's account, for instance, this will be to say that he would not have stood on his head had he not thought it would impress her (and his thinking this was 'causally prior' to his standing on his head). Since it is hard to see that anyone would deny this, it is also implausible that this is the issue that separates Davidson and other defenders of CT from those they are defending it against. If this minimal claim were all that Davidson *et al.* wanted to make with CT, it would make sense of why they took this to show that explanations of the sort described in BD are 'causal' (and of Davidson's own defense of CT, as I said above). But it would make deeply mysterious why anyone would want to deny it.

So we still have a puzzle here. On the minimal, promissory note, account of 'cause' (which I am claiming is simply the ordinary use of this term), reasons explanations of actions will be causal because *any* explanation of actions will be causal. Reasons explanations fit Mackie's analysis of 'cause' just fine. So there could hardly be an issue about whether 'reasons are causes' in this sense. And on at least one common, stronger view—the view that causal explanations, to be true, require laws (or 'lawlike connections'), as I have been arguing—it is also hard to see what the issue could be, since it seems that virtually no one who thinks 'reasons are causes' has wanted to base this view on the implausible claim that reasons explanations involve laws. Certainly Davidson, the defender of 'anomalous monism', hasn't wanted to do this.

So what *is* the issue? The suggestion I will defend below is that the real issue here is not whether 'reasons are causes'. In the ordinary (minimal) sense, of course they are. Rather, the issue is whether reasons explanations, which *on their face* always involve goals or purposes, i.e. are 'teleological' in Mackie's sense,[24] are completely analyzable in terms of *efficient* causes which make no essential reference to any goals or purposes, e.g. perhaps in something like the way I argued above that functions are. It is easy to get confused here, because the term 'cause' seems often to be used by philosophers to apply to what are in fact efficient causes. So it is easy to think that in the ordinary, minimal sense 'cause' really *means* 'efficient cause'. If that were so, then of course showing that reasons are causes in the ordinary sense would be showing that they are efficient causes, and holding that reasons explanations are essentially teleological would entail that they are not 'causal' explanations. But, as I have been arguing, this is not so. The ordinary sense of 'cause' is a minimal, promissory note, sense which allows that reasons are causes *whatever* turns out to be the correct account of how reasons explanations work.

A brief look at how Mackie's analysis of our ordinary notion of cause deals with teleological explanations might help make my claim clear here. Mackie holds, as was mentioned above, that 'The distinguishing feature of causal sequence is the conjunction of necessity-in-the-circumstances with causal priority.' At the same time,

---

[24] Mackie's account of when an explanation is teleological is given on p. 2 above, and restated on p. 19 below..

according to him, an explanation is teleological 'if it makes some essential use of the notion that something—perhaps an event, or a state, or a fact—is an end or goal to which something else is, or is seen as, a means'. The most 'extreme' teleological claim, he says, would be where some future event or state—the 'goal'—simply determined a present or past event or state through some sort of time-reversed causal process.

Now if there were such a case, we could call the later event an end or goal, simply in virtue of its relative temporal position, rather than (as we have been doing) a time-reversed cause. And then this would be in a very clear sense a case of teleology or final causation: the 'end' would indeed be responsible for the coming about of the 'means', and any adequate explanation of these earlier-occurring items would have to refer to this end. (Mackie 1974, p. 274)

So there is no doubt that the ordinary term 'cause', as Mackie analyzes it, would apply to this sort of case, though it would simply be time-reversed efficient causation. 'The only trouble', he says, 'is that such cases never seem to occur' (Mackie 1974, pp. 274–5).

Two of the other three sorts of teleological explanation that Mackie distinguishes—animal behavior and 'goal-seeking and feedback mechanisms'—also involve efficient causation, he argues, and can be explained, without reference to any goals, in terms of evolution or various 'feedback' mechanism; that is, they will be explained using what I have above called 'functional' explanations (Mackie 1974, pp. 277–9). So here too, though these processes are causal in the ordinary sense he explains, there is a strong reason to think that the mechanisms that explain them involve only efficient causation.

On the other hand, for the third sort of teleological explanation, involving conscious human purposive actions, Mackie argues that there is no reason to think that such underlying efficient causal explanations will be found:

[C]onscious purposive action which calls for the kind of explanatory causal account suggested does seem to involve a distinct *species* of efficient causation. . . . It *might* be that this teleological sort of account could be reduced to a more basic causal account which eliminated what I am here calling the teleological form; but there is no obvious reason why this should be possible. (Mackie 1974, p. 295)

Mackie is here using the term 'efficient causation', as he makes clear, to refer to 'the genus that covers all actual laws of working and perhaps all processes by which things come about' (p. 296). That is, he is using this to mean, in essence, what I have been calling the minimal or promissory note sense of 'cause'.

This use of the term 'efficient cause' is a bit misleading, I think, since it leaves Mackie saying that an irreducibly *teleological* form of causal explanation, which one would have thought would count as a paradigm of 'final causation' and hence be in sharp *contrast* to efficient causation, is still a 'species' of efficient causation. It would be clearer, I think, to say that, within 'the genus that covers all actual laws of working [or] . . . processes by which things come about', there might be causes of an irreducibly teleological sort, different from other, efficient, causes. This is I suppose just a linguistic quibble, but I think that ignoring it can lead to philosophers who in fact *agree* saying what look like very different things. For example, if I understand him, Michael Smith is making exactly the same point that I am (and that I claim Mackie is) when he says that reasons explanations may *not* be 'causal' at all. When he says that 'there is nothing in the debate about the theory of motivation *per se* that forces us to suppose that motivating reasons are causally, rather than merely teleologically, explanatory' (Smith 1994, p. 103), he is restricting 'causal' explanations to those using efficient causes; but he is certainly not at all denying that 'motivating reasons' are an essential explanatory factor in the way actions are brought about, that is that they are 'causes' in the minimal sense I have been describing.

If I am right then, the real issue here is not whether 'reasons are causes' in the ordinary (that is, minimal) sense of 'cause'. They are indeed. Rather, the issue is whether what Mackie says 'might' happen does in fact happen, that is whether reasons explanations, which certainly seem to make *essential* reference to goals and purposes, can—or even must—have their explanatory force explained without any such reference. This is the view of what the essential issue is here that I will try to support in the next chapter.

2

Non-teleological Explanations of Actions

We have been looking for a clear understanding of whether there is really a substantive issue between, on the one side, those who follow Davidson in accepting both the belief–desire account of reasons explanations (BD) and the thesis that such explanations are causal (CT) and, on the other, those against whom Davidson and other advocates of these two claims are arguing. And I have been claiming that it is hard to find any thesis about the nature of causation, or of causal explanations, that can be plausibly held to divide the two sides here. Of course, as was noted, Ryle, in *The Concept of Mind* (1949), explicitly says that reasons explanations are not causal.[1] The problem is that, on the clearest analysis of 'causal' in which this seems true, where causal explanations must involve strict laws (stated in the same terms as the explanation), Davidson and other advocates of BD and CT explicitly accept it. So if this were someone's only reason for thinking there was a conflict between BD and CT, this opposition would indeed be based on a confusion, or at least a misunderstanding. Both sides would be in agreement on the issue of whether reasons explanations allowed strict laws stated in the terms of those explanations (i.e. would agree that they do not). At the same time, as I argued above, it is hard to see that either side would deny that CT is true under the much more minimal, 'promissory note' reading which I suggested is the ordinary sense of 'cause'.

So we still have a question concerning whether there is a genuine, coherent position opposed to the one held by the advocates of BD and CT. I think the answer to that question is 'yes'. But I think that the issue as it is often formulated, and as I have formulated it so far—the

[1] And of course, as Davidson himself noted, many other philosophers have said things that seem to entail this.

issue of whether CT is true—is not really what is in dispute. Of course, merely examining a few of the numerous suggestions philosophers have made for understanding what a 'causal explanation' is, even ones that seem fairly far apart on the spectrum, is not enough to show conclusively that this is so.[2] It leaves the possibility that some other notion of causal explanation is the one over which the two sides divide. But I want to explore a different possibility, namely that the real issue that divides the two sides (assuming I am right in thinking that there is one) is not simply over whether CT is true in some sense of 'cause', i.e. over whether reasons explanations are or are not 'causal' in some sense. If that is right, then it is no surprise that we have not found a way of understanding CT where the sides disagree as to its truth or falsity.

To find the real issue here, I suggest, we will need to shift gears and look at the argument offered for holding the other of the two claims Davidson makes: BD, the claim that reasons explanations of actions always and essentially involve reference to some desire, or 'pro attitude' (as Davidson calls it), of the agent (plus a belief about how to satisfy that desire). I will argue that in fact the real issue is over how to understand BD.

2.1 The Argument for 'The Humean Theory of Motivation'

Perhaps the most straightforward way of understanding BD is as a statement of what Michael Smith calls 'the Humean Theory of Motivation' (Smith 1994, chapter 4). Hume himself famously summed up his view on this issue by saying that 'Reason is, and ought only to be the slave of the passions, and can never pretend to any other office than to serve and obey them' (Hume 1888, p. 415). Put more prosaically, this has been taken to boil down to the thought that, since no one would intentionally or knowingly do anything that they did not want to do, there must be a desire to motivate any action that actually gets performed. Beliefs alone will never be enough. As Simon Blackburn puts it, 'Beliefs do not normally explain actions: it takes in addition a desire or concern, a caring for whatever the belief describes' (Blackburn 1998, p. 90). So the thought is this. It is a necessary condition of my doing anything intentionally that in *some* sense I want to do it, otherwise I wouldn't have done it intentionally. So it

---

[2] A good bibliography for other accounts is contained in Sosa and Tooley (1993).

would seem that, if I really have no desire to do something, then I won't do it intentionally. So a desire would always seem to be required to motivate any intentional action.

This thought is frequently used as an assumption in arguments supposed to support one form of 'internalism' in ethics, the form that holds that moral or ethical commitments or beliefs must always somehow include a desire or other similar motivating factor.[3] Roughly speaking the argument is that someone with a moral belief cannot just be neutral with respect to acting on that belief; someone who really has some moral belief must be inclined to act on it, at least in some circumstances. That is what it means to say that moral beliefs are 'practical' in a way that other beliefs are not. Combined with the thought that a desire is always required to motivate any intentional action, the conclusion seems to follow that 'wants' of some sort must somehow always back up or even be part of genuine moral beliefs.

Simon Blackburn uses this argument to support his version of 'expressivism' about moral thoughts. This fact (that wants are always required to actually move us), according to Blackburn, puts an 'insuperable obstacle' in the path of what he calls 'keeping ethics under the rule of Apollo', that is, roughly, accounting for moral motivation in terms of nothing but the agent's beliefs and how she reasons about them. It does this by certifying replies, in the form of arguments with a 'zigzag structure', as he puts it, to the claim that beliefs by themselves can explain actions. Each appeal to a belief to explain some act (e.g. her belief that removing the piano from his foot would lessen his pain) is met with the response that this belief will explain the act only if the agent *cares* about the thing in question (here, lessening his pain). And if it is said that the agent believes it is morally right to lessen pain, the reply will be that she must then care about doing what is morally right. And so on (Blackburn 1998).

But it is important to notice here that an argument of the sort Blackburn makes employs the claim that proper desires are always

---

[3] The term 'internalism' can also be taken simply to mean that genuine moral beliefs must be capable of motivating those who hold them (that is, while remaining uncommitted about how this motivation takes place). As John Deigh puts it in *The Cambridge Dictionary of Philosophy*, '[M]otivational internalists hold that if one sees that one has a duty to do a certain action or that it would be right to do it, then necessarily one has a motive to do it' (Audi, 1995, p. 514). That is a slightly weaker (hence more plausible) thesis than the one I am referring to here, which is the stronger view that this motivation must come via proper desires.

required for the explanation of action *as an assumption*. The zigzag structure Blackburn cites, by itself, is completely consistent with genuine beliefs motivating actions *all by themselves* if we distinguish proper desires, such as cravings and urges, from 'pro attitudes', understood simply as '[any] mental states that move us', and understand 'caring' about something in terms of the latter.[4]

A 'proper' desire is one where it makes sense to say that someone acted even though she had no desire *at all*, in *this* sense, to do so, as I might attend what I know will be a really boring meeting even though I had no real (i.e. 'proper') desire to go. Of course if I attended that meeting of my own free will, even if only because I regarded it as my duty to attend, then there is a *sense* in which I *must* have wanted to go. That sense of 'want' is what I am calling the 'pro attitude' sense. Here the term 'want', in this 'pro attitude' sense, simply means (something like) 'a mental state that can lead me to promote whatever it is an attitude toward'. So a proper desire, such as a craving for guacamole, might be a pro attitude, but so might a belief that something is my duty. It *follows* from the fact that I did something intentionally that I had a pro attitude toward doing it (or whatever I thought it would achieve); that is, it follows that there was *some* mental state of mine that led me to do it. That is part, at least, of what makes it an intentional action *of mine*. (This is why, if I did it intentionally, then I *must* have wanted to do it in this sense of 'want'.) But it doesn't follow that this pro attitude *consisted of* anything other than my belief that I had a contractual duty to do it.

Suppose that my thought that it would be morally right to lessen your pain was my reason for moving the piano off your foot. It follows that I wanted to do what was morally right (in the pro attitude sense of 'want'). But it doesn't follow *at all* from this that what moved me was some *independent* mental state, a proper desire (craving, yen, urge) to do what was morally right (or to lessen your pain). We can get to this conclusion only if we tack on as an extra assumption the Humean Theory of Motivation, that is if we tack on (one way

---

[4] This terminology comes from Schueler (1995a) pp. 29–38, following Davidson (1963). It is worth repeating that Davidson, when he uses the term 'pro attitude', seems pretty clearly to draw it broadly enough to cover any mental state that could possibly be held to move anyone, that is to be using it essentially in the sense I am. That means (as Dugald Owen pointed out to me) that Davidson himself, in advocating BD, is not *in fact* committed to 'the Humean Theory of Motivation', since, as I will argue below, it is only if we understand BD as referring to proper desires that it is a version of the Humean Theory.

of understanding) BD itself, i.e. the assumption that such desires are always needed. That is the only way we arrive at the conclusion that moral beliefs for instance can't move us by themselves, that is aren't perfectly good pro attitudes all by themselves. But of course assuming something is not a way of arguing for it. Blackburn's 'zigzag' argument *uses* BD (understood as referring to proper desires) to argue for expressivism. It is not an argument *for* BD itself. This is not clear, I think, unless one keeps in mind the distinction between proper desires and pro attitudes.

That same distinction, I want to argue, is just as crucial for seeing the weakness in the support for this way of understanding BD itself, that is as a statement of the Humean Theory of Motivation. The main contemporary argument for this theory turns on the idea that desires and beliefs have different 'directions of fit'.[5] According to Michael Smith, the Humean Theory is entailed by the following three premises:

(a) Having a motivating reason [for some action] is, *inter alia*, having a goal;
(b) Having a goal is being in a state with which the world must fit; and
(c) Being in a state with which the world must fit is desiring. (Smith 1994, p. 116)[6]

James Lenman spells this out as follows:

Intentional action is goal-directed: it seeks the realization of some state of the world conceived not as actual but as sought after. In this respect, to act intentionally (or merely to have some intention or desire on which one may not act) is to be in a state of mind with *world–word direction of fit*. A state of mind is said to have such direction of fit if the onus of match between the content of the thought involved and the world lies on the world and not the thought. Thus if I find a thought of mine with word–world direction of fit, i.e. a belief, failing to match the world, the thought is at fault and subject to revision. But if a thought with word–world direction of fit fails to match the world it is rather the world that has let us down. So if I wish to be driving toward Cambridge . . . but find I am not, I change not my attitude but my direction of travel and match is attained . . . Generally, the concern implicated in a thought with word–world direction of fit is that the thought be had only if

---

[5] This is what Jay Wallace has called 'the teleological argument' (see Wallace 1990). But since, as I will argue, this argument is aimed at, in essence, explaining *away* the appearance of genuine teleology in reasons explanations, this is a somewhat misleading label.

[6] In giving his version of BD (which he labels 'P1'), Smith references Davidson's version but substitutes the term 'motivating reason' for Davidson's 'primary reason' (Smith 1994, p. 92).

its content is true. The concern implicated in a thought with world–word direction of fit is that the world be such as to match its content.

Thoughts of the latter kind—*desires*—contrast with those whose direction of fit is word–world: with *beliefs* whereby the thought content is supposed to match the world. The two are quite distinct: it is one thing to have beliefs about how things are in the world, another to care how they are. There is no belief to which we might not, in principle, be indifferent. . . .

We may take world–word direction of fit as a defining characteristic of desires thus generously understood. The central claim is then that intending to phi, in virtue of being a goal-directed state, involves having a thought of this kind: so that anyone who intentionally phi's necessarily has some desire, presumably at least the desire to phi (under some description). So, given that belief and desire are distinct, any purely cognitive understanding of the reasons that motivate us to action appears fatally incomplete. (Lehman 1996, pp. 291–292)

The argument here, I think, comes down to this. (1) Intentional actions are goal-directed; that is, they involve 'desires' in the broad sense. (2) Desires have as their defining or essential characteristic a world-to-word direction of fit. (3) Nothing with a word-to-world direction of fit (that is, no belief) can also have a world-to-word direction of fit.[7] So, it is concluded, reasons explanations of actions must always involve desires, which is what BD says.

There is a very tempting way of reading this argument in which one might wonder why the two extra, middle premises ((2) and (3) in my version, or (b) and (c) in Smith's) are inserted here. This is because it is easy to understand the conclusion, BD, so that it obviously follows directly from the first, central, assumption that intentional actions always involve desires broadly conceived, i.e. that they are goal-directed. But I think this would miss the crucial point, that is contained in those extra premises. The real point of this argument must be to give an *account* of 'being goal-directed' in terms of being in one of two distinct kinds of mental or psychological state, one with a world-to-word direction of fit.[8] That is, the thought must be that the direction of fit of the mental state more commonly called a 'desire' is *the* central explanatory fact of being goal-directed.

---

[7] Smith doesn't state this in the brief version of his argument that I quoted, but he argues for it explicitly (Smith 1994, pp. 120–125).

[8] I think it would be clearer to use the term 'world-to-*mind*' direction of fit, but since I will be discussing Lenman's version of this argument I will try to stay closer to his terminology.

Lenman himself succumbs (or nearly succumbs) to the temptation just described when he calls world-to-word direction of fit the 'defining characteristic' of goal directedness. That comes dangerously close to merely using the term 'world-to-word direction of fit' to *mean* 'goal-directed'. That would merely be to give a stipulative definition about the usage of this invented term. And if that is all that is happening, the argument could not possibly yield any conclusion that couldn't be attained with the concept of being goal-directed by itself. It could not for instance, yield the conclusion that, as Lenman says, 'any purely cognitive understanding of the reasons that motivate us to action appears fatally incomplete'.

It is not, after all, contentious that actions involve purposes ('being goal-directed')—that is the first assumption of this argument and is not itself under dispute. And it is hardly less obvious that having a goal is different from having a garden variety factual belief. So if advocates of this direction of fit argument are doing anything beyond repeating uncontentious truisms in a contorted terminology—as they must be, since their conclusion is certainly *not* uncontentious— they must be proposing an *explanation* of *why* being goal-directed is different from merely having any sort of belief and is required for every action, an explanation in terms of psychological states that can have one, and only one, of two possible 'directions of fit'.

In itself, there is nothing *philosophically* objectionable about the 'direction of fit' terminology if it is simply used as a stylistic variant of terms such as 'belief' and 'goal-directed'.[9] But by the same token, if that were all this argument were doing, i.e. substituting some made-up terms for some ordinary ones, then it would not really be an argument at all. It could, under this way of understanding, arrive at no conclusion that is not available *without* using the 'direction of fit' terminology. And in particular, it could not reach the main conclusion being sought, that beliefs alone are never enough to explain actions. So it seems to me that, if we want to understand the direction of fit argument as it is intended, that is as actually supporting the Humean Theory of Motivation (and supporting BD as a statement of this theory), as a genuine argument for it, we have to understand the phrase 'world-to-word direction of fit' as a technical term referring to some feature of mental states that provides an explanation or account

[9] Though of course one might still have stylistic objections; see Strunk and White (1959, Rule 21).

of goal directedness. It cannot merely be another way of referring to goal directedness.

Another way to see that this is the way the direction of fit argument is intended comes from the fact that, while it is held to be a feature of what is called 'direction of fit' that mental states can have one or the other direction of fit, having *both* is explicitly ruled out. Beliefs in particular, which are paradigm examples of states with word-to-world direction of fit, are forbidden from having world-to-word direction of fit. But that is certainly *not* the case for pro attitudes, as this term is understood apart from this argument. As I explained it above, a pro attitude is any mental state that moves one to act. This follows Davidson's explanation. He mentions as examples of pro attitudes, along with 'desires, wantings, urges', and 'promptings', 'a great variety of moral views, aesthetic principles, economic prejudices, social conventions and public and private goals and values' (Davidson 1963, pp. 685–6). So if we were to understand 'world-to-word direction of fit' as *simply* applying to all the cases covered by the term 'pro attitude', it would be false that some beliefs, e.g. moral beliefs, could not have world-to-word direction of fit. And of course BD would then not look like a version of the Humean Theory of Motivation.

We can put this in terms of the distinction explained above between proper desires and pro attitudes. In order to understand the direction of fit argument as supporting the idea that beliefs by themselves can never explain actions, we cannot understand the term 'world-to-word direction of fit' as simply referring to goal directedness (purposiveness). That could at best get us to the conclusion that a pro attitude is always required for any action, and without some further argument there is nothing to say that pro attitudes (that is, mental states that can lead one to promote whatever they are attitudes toward) cannot be, say, moral beliefs. Nor can we understand 'world-to-word direction of fit' as merely referring to proper desires, since then there is a gap between the conclusion and the initial, crucial premise, that all intentional actions are goal-directed. There could still be (goal-directed) actions not motivated by proper desires. Actions performed from the thought that it is one's duty, for instance, might simply not stem from any proper desires.

So we have to understand 'world-to-word direction of fit' as referring to some feature of proper desires, which in the end, according to the argument Smith and Lenman propose, turns out to be what *accounts for* or explains goal directness. So in the end, according to this argument, the *apparent* possibility that a belief, such as a moral belief, by itself could move one to act turns out to be only apparent, not a real possibility. In short, the direction of fit argument purports to support, as a conclusion, the claim that proper desires (plus the relevant belief) are required to explain any action (that is, to support the Humean theory of Motivation) by arguing that all actions are purposive and that only mental states with a certain feature, one found *only* in proper desires, namely a world-to-word direction of fit, can explain purposiveness. As Smith puts it, 'Desires are . . . the only states that can constitute our motivating reasons' (Smith 1994, p. 125).

If this is right, then of course it is very important—crucial, in fact—for this argument that the explanations given of this feature of psychological states (direction of fit) be neither metaphorical nor circular, as they clearly are in Lenman's version of this argument quoted above. If this feature of psychological states is to *explain* what being goal directed *is*, then we need some clear way of understanding direction of fit that is *independent* of notions such as purpose, intention, and the like. This does not happen in Lenman's discussion.

To explain world-to-word direction of fit by saying that 'the onus of match between the content of the thought involved and the world lies on the world and not the thought' is to give a misleading moral or legal metaphor, as if it is the world's job or duty to match my world-to-word psychological states. ('The world has let us down' if there is no match, Lenman says.) So taking this metaphor seriously, one would get the idea that when I have a world-to-word psychological state the world somehow thereby becomes duty-bound to shape up and reorganize itself so as to match the content of my psychological state, which is obviously not what Lenman means.

Likewise, explaining the claim that '[t]he concern implicated in a thought with world–word direction of fit is that the world be such as to match its content' by a *wish* to get to Cambridge which leads me to change the direction in which I am driving, rather than to change my belief about it, if we take it seriously as an explanation, seems plainly circular. Wishes are just the sorts of things that are supposed to be *explained by* the idea that they have a world-to-word direction of fit. So, though this can serve as an example of a goal-directed state, it gets us nowhere as an actual explanation. (Anyway, if I discover that I am not going where I wish to be going, I can, after all, achieve a match between the direction in which I wish to travel and my actual direction *either* by changing my direction of travel *or* by changing where I wish to go.)

Other philosophers, including certainly Smith himself, have tried to be more careful in explaining the idea of 'direction of fit' of psychological states.[10] I will consider Smith's account below. In general, though, there would seem to be only two forms that such an account can take which are of relevance to the argument we are considering here. That is because the idea must be to give an account or explanation of the difference between these two sorts of mental state which isn't either circular or question-begging in the argument supporting the Humean Theory of Motivation (and so as supporting this way of understanding BD).

One form would be to give an explanation of direction of fit in terms of something like the inherent shape or structure (or other inherent features) of the two proposed psychological states themselves (where as a minimum these 'inherent' features will of course have to be fully understood without reference to concepts such as 'purpose' or 'pro attitude' that they are intended to explain).[11] That is what the 'direction of fit' metaphor suggests, and it would be the most straightforward account that a defender of this argument for the Humean Theory could give. The other form would be to give a functionalist account in terms not of the inherent features of these states, but of their causal connections to each other. Let us look first at the sort of account that understands the two different directions of fit in terms of the inherent structure of the two psychological states.

One difficulty that arises at once is that it is hard to see why such a way of understanding 'direction of fit' wouldn't mean that there are after all laws involved in reasons explanations of actions. That is because BD would be true, on this 'inherent structure' account of mental states, only as a result of the actual interactions of these states, for instance in something like the way certain chemicals interact in chemical reactions. And then it certainly looks as if these mental state 'interactions' would themselves be describable in terms of laws, just

---

[10] See Smith (1987; and 1994, chap. 4). Zangwill (1998) gives an excellent summary and a devastating critique of all these.

[11] Such an explanation would not have to be 'reductive' in the definitional sense, of course. It could as well be a matter of explaining what such terms as 'belief' or 'desire' actually refer to, e.g. in the way early chemists figured out what molecule the term 'water' actually referred to. As J. J. C. Smart (1959) put it long ago, the identities here would be 'contingent' ones.

as the chemical interactions are. It is hard to see why this wouldn't be the case, for instance, if specific mental states (types) were simply identified with brain states (types).

So on this sort of account BD itself would be a very general causal law to the effect that a certain sort of event—actions—is caused only by complexes of psychological states which include at least one state with a certain sort of inherent structure, i.e. a world-to-word direction of fit. Such an account would thus support a full-blown, 'causal law' reading of CT (rather than the minimal, mere-causal-connection or 'promissory note' reading), because it would go well beyond the minimal claim that there is *some* explanation of actions to be had in terms of reasons. It would propose a substantive, underlying, lawful connection between the *sorts* of events involved, described in terms of their inherent structures. But all this is clearly in conflict with the thought that there simply are no such psychological laws.

There are two other serious difficulties for this sort of account of these psychological states. The first is that (so far as I know) there simply are no plausible (non-circular) accounts of beliefs and desires (or 'cognitive' and 'conative' states) in terms of anything that could plausibly be called their inherent features, such as the configuration of neurons in which they are realized in the brain. Even decades ago, when type–type identity theories of mind still had fairly wide support, philosophers typically did no more than wave their hands in the direction of 'states of the central nervous system' when asked for inherent features of beliefs and other mental states. And in recent years, with defenders of type identity between mental states and brain states very few and far between, there seems not to be even this much.

The other difficulty for this sort of account is even worse, I would say, because it gives a very plausible explanation for why type–type identity theories seem so problematic. It is now widely regarded by many philosophers as a virtual truism that human mental states can only be understood as a whole, in the sense that it makes no sense to try to understand one kind of mental state, such as a desire, in isolation from most or all of the other kinds.[12] It is this 'holistic' feature of mental states, among other things, that led to the popularity of functionalism as an account of these states. According to that view, each mental state is to be understood in

---

[12] For a contrary view, see Fodor and LaPore (1992).

terms not of its inherent structure, but of its causal interconnections with other mental and physical states of the person who has these states. Anything with the right set of interconnections is the state in question, no matter what its inherent structure turns out to be. The 'holism of the mental' entails that it is not possible to understand individual mental states, or even kinds of mental states, in terms of their inherent features. Functionalist accounts, which explain mental states in terms of the relations between different states, are consistent with this fact.

So here is another reason for thinking that the first way of explaining the direction of fit of mental states, i.e. in terms of their inherent features, is ruled out. Not only are there no actual explanations of mental states of this sort in the offing, but any non-question-begging form of such a view would seem to entail that reasons explanations of actions would indeed be describable in terms of laws, something that certainly seems false—and is in fact false if it is true that mental states can be described 'as a whole' only in some sense. That is, the holism of the mental requires reading BD much more like a conceptual truth than like the description of a causal regularity, and hence pressures us toward reading CT as about mere causal connections between events, however described (what I am calling the 'minimal' or 'promissory note' reading), rather than as saying that BD describes some sort of substantive, law-like regularity. To put it another way, understanding CT as saying that reasons explanations of the sort described in BD involve causal *laws*, as the 'inherent structure' analysis of 'direction of fit' seems to require, runs into the problem that it is always possible to refute any such alleged 'law' by thinking up another desire or belief the agent might have which would not lead to the action in question. And presumably this *is* always possible, at least partly because of the holism of the mental.

This brings us to the second general way in which supporters of reading BD as a statement of the Humean Theory of Motivation might try to explain 'direction of fit', the one that does not try to give accounts of the two 'directions' in terms of the inherent features of these mental states but somehow takes account of the holism of the mental. This would involve giving 'functionalist' accounts of beliefs and desires, or cognitive and conative mental states generally, in terms of their causal interconnections with each other and with other mental and physical states, including of course actions. As Smith puts it, on such an account 'desires are states that have a certain functional role' (Smith 1994, p. 113).[13] Unlike an account of direction of fit in terms of the inherent structure of mental states, such a set of functionalist definitions would not, or at least not obviously, entail that reasons explanations would allow for general laws (in the terms in which they were stated), since the connections among mental states would be conceptual or definitional.[14]

It is going to be very difficult actually to construct anything like such a full set of definitions in any detail, of course, if only because of the huge number of interconnections one would need to find and specify for each of the actual mental states being explained. The point of holism is that to do one mental state we will need to do all, or at least many. But I don't want to pursue this sort of difficulty. It is already very familiar from the many discussions of functionalism; and, who knows, perhaps supporters of the direction-of-fit argument can side-step at least some difficulties of this sort by aiming their analyses squarely at the two very general features of mental states (the two directions of fit) that they are interested in.

This is in essence what Smith tries to do by explaining the two directions of fit in terms of the different dispositions each state involves, that is (so to speak) by focusing only on the specific functional roles of states with each of the two directions of fit. According to him,

[T]he difference between beliefs and desires in terms of direction of fit can be seen to amount to a difference in the functional roles of belief and desire. Very roughly, and simplifying somewhat, it amounts, *inter alia*, to a difference in the counterfactual dependence of a belief that p and a desire that p on a perception with the content that not p: a belief that p tends to go out of existence in the presence of a perception with the content that not p, whereas a desire that p tends to endure, disposing the subject in that state to bring it about that p. (Smith 1994, p. 115)

---

[13] At the same time, though, Smith says that his account can 'remain neutral about whether desires are causes' (1994, p. 113), though he doesn't say how this can be done. Even if, as I suggested in the previous chapter, Smith can be best understood as using the term 'cause' to mean 'efficient cause', things remain a bit unclear. On the relevant sense of 'function', functional accounts of mental states will be in terms of the causal role these states play, where 'causal roles' are understood in terms of efficient causes.

[14] Though it is hard to see why this wouldn't just push the issue back one stage, since it would leave the question of how there could be states of the sorts that had these conceptual interconnections unless they were realized in underlying physically describable states connected by causal laws. And since there could hardly be an infinite number of such physically describable states, why wouldn't there be laws connecting reasons and actions?

There are a number of questions one might raise about this account as is stands. For instance, it is not clear how it can deal with desires for things in the past, such as my current desire that (it be true that) I turned off the lawn sprinklers in my backyard before I left for campus this morning. There is nothing I can *now* do to make it the case that I did this. So it is hard to see what it could mean to say that I am somehow disposed to make it the case that I did it. More generally, there are plenty of desires that have as objects things utterly outside the agent's control. Desires about the past are only one kind of example of this larger class.[15] More generally still, why should the contents of desires and beliefs be restricted to the sorts of things that can plausibly be said to be possible contents of perceptions? It is hard to see how the sort of account that Smith gives could replace 'perception' with 'belief' or some cognate without becoming plainly circular. But then, how will this account deal with imperceptible things, for instance with someone's desire that some version of Rawlsian liberalism be the morally best political theory? It might seem odd to have such a desire (though why?), but it doesn't look impossible.

But there is a bigger problem for the sort of functional account of direction of fit that Smith proposes, a problem that comes not from the implausibility of the account itself, but from the role it is supposed to play in the argument we are considering. It is important to remember that the whole direction-of-fit account is supposed to provide *support* for a particular way of understanding BD (for 'the Humean Theory of Motivation' as Smith calls it). And it is an essential feature of BD, on this way of understanding it, that the 'desire' referred to is a *proper* desire. Lenman puts this by saying that his 'concern is with the Humean claim that no purely cognitive state could, in combination with appropriate other beliefs, but *with nothing else*, originate a process of rational motivation' (Lenman

---

[15] I have discussed this problem with Smith's account, as it appeared in Smith (1987), in Schueler (1991). Smith's response is at Smith (1994, pp. 208–209), where he says that a 'more accurate and fully general characterization of the functional role of desire' would be to say 'A desire that p is a state that disposes a subject to make certain sorts of bets when faced with lotteries where the outcome is *inter alia* that p.' But, while this does at least allow Smith's account to *apply to* desires whose objects are outside the agent's control, it seems to me to do so only at the cost of the plausibility of this account. This 'more accurate and fully general' version doesn't seem to work when applied the garden variety cases that made the earlier version superficially plausible. Does Smith really want to say that my desire for a beer, when combined with my belief that there is one in the fridge, disposes me to make a certain sort of *bet*?

1996, p. 291). And, as was explained above, it is an assumption of this argument that '[i]ntentional action is goal directed' (p. 291). So this argument is supposed to show (or at least argue for, provide some reason to think) that the only way actions can be purposive, that is can *be* 'goal directed', is for the agent to be motivated by what I have called a 'proper desire', which is what Smith and Lenman propose to explain as a psychological state with world-to-word direction of fit.

But how could a functional account of direction of fit possibly do this? Any functional account of mental states, or of features of mental states, will have to take as data, as the evidential starting point on which to build the functional account, a detailed story about the roles of these states *vis à vis* all the other states in question. That story will be the basis on which it is decided which dispositions get built into which mental states. But this means that the truth or falsity of the Humean Theory of Motivation will have to be decided *before* any such functional theory gets written, that is before we can figure out which dispositions get attached to which mental states. It cannot be used to support the Humean Theory (i.e. BD understood in this way).

Consider again Blackburn's example of the person who moves the piano off someone's foot because she believes it is the morally right thing to do. If we take this at face value, it looks like this means that this *belief* was what moved this agent, and so that *it* had the disposition to produce such an action, and thus that any functional account of its 'direction of fit' will have to register this fact. But of course this would *not* support the 'Humean Theory' that Smith and Lenman want to support—just the reverse. It says that this belief can move someone to act *without* any proper desire being required. Presumably supporters of the Humean Theory will say that we should not take this example at face value. We should say that there was also a proper desire to do what is right (or to lessen the pain or the like). I will argue that this is not so, but in any case the point here is that, since this and other contentious examples are the *data* on which any dispositional/functional account of 'direction of fit' will have to be based, there is no way in which such an account can be used to support the Humean Theory. We have to decide how to describe such examples, and that includes deciding whether this Humean Theory reading of BD is correct, before we can decide which states have which dispositional connections, i.e. which directions of fit.

It is easy to miss this point, I think, because it is so easy to shift unwittingly from speaking of proper desires and the (Humean Theory of Motivation) reading of BD, which understands it as saying that a proper desire is always needed to move anyone to act, to speaking merely of pro attitudes, which refer only to *whatever* moved the agent to act and so could include, say, moral or other beliefs. I think this is just what happens in Smith's own defense of the Humean Theory in terms of a functional account of direction of fit. In considering what to do with mental states such as wishes, which don't seem to be exactly the same as full-blown desires, Smith says that 'if "desire" is not a suitably broad category of mental state to encompass all of those states with the appropriate direction of fit, then the Humean may simply define the term "pro-attitude" to mean "psychological state with which the world must fit", and then claim that motivating reasons are constituted, *inter alia*, by pro-attitudes' (Smith 1994, p. 117). And he cites at this point Davidson's account of 'pro attitude'.

But this doesn't so much defend the Humean Theory reading of BD as utterly abandon it. As was pointed out above, Davidson explicitly includes 'moral views' under the category of 'pro attitudes'. So to adopt Smith's suggested definition here would be in essence to decide the 'data' issue represented by Blackburn's piano example *against* the Humean Theory reading of BD. It would entail that any accurate functional account of mental states of the sort Smith is proposing would have to allow that the belief that it was the right thing to do could, all by itself, move someone to move that piano off Blackburn's foot, which is just what the Humean Theory of Motivation denies.

So it seems to me that any attempt to defend the Humean Theory of Motivation by appealing to a functional account of the mental states that can lead to action faces an insuperable dilemma, though perhaps one that becomes clear only after we distinguish proper desires and pro attitudes. It can simply build into the account of proper desires (and nothing else) that they cause actions when combined with appropriate word-to-world states (that is, beliefs), and of course can build into the corresponding account of actions that they are caused in this way. Such a functional account will simply and flatly beg the question here. It will just assert, or assume without argument, that the contentious cases that provide apparent counter-examples to this account are decided in its favor. Alternatively, if such a functional account tries to include such states as moral beliefs in the group with world-to-word direction of fit, perhaps by being expanded so as to apply not only to proper desires but to pro attitudes generally, it simply doesn't support the Humean Theory of Motivation.

So this second, functionalist, account of direction of fit seems of no more help than the first in actually *arguing for* this 'Humean Theory' reading of BD. If I am right that these really are the only two general ways of explaining direction of fit, in terms of the inherent features of the mental states in question or in terms of their causal (functional) roles in the network of mental and physical states and actions to be explained, then it looks like the direction of fit argument gets nowhere as a way of supporting this reading of BD.

It might be questioned whether I am right, of course. My reason for thinking that these are the only two ways possible comes from the generality of what the direction of fit argument is being called on to do, namely support the idea that proper desires are required for all intentional actions by starting from the premise that all intentional actions are goal-directed. That certainly seems to entail that the argument needs an account of the psychological state with what is called world-to-word direction of fit (that is, proper desires), which can be used to *explain* goal directedness in a way that does not itself make use of notions that already involve goal directedness. And *that* seems to restrict this argument to the two sorts of accounts I have specified, in terms of the inherent structure of mental states and in terms of their functional interconnections. These are the only two *sorts* of accounts of mental states that I can think of that even *seem* to have the potential not to involve this argument in circularity by using purposive notions as part of the explanation. If there are other sorts of accounts possible, of course, they will need to be looked at.

The point of examining the direction of fit argument, and more generally the Humean Theory it is supposed to support, was to try to discover why someone who accepted BD might think this led him to deny CT or at least question whether it accounted for the explanatory force of reasons explanations of actions. That is what Davidson and the other defenders of the idea that BD and CT can be held jointly are concerned to show. Though it may not be obvious, I think we now have the elements for answering this question. The direction of fit argument purported to support a specific 'reading' of BD, one that understands what Davidson calls a 'pro attitude' as a proper desire. This is to understand BD as stating what Smith calls 'the Humean Theory of Motivation'. As we have seen, reading BD in this way requires direction of fit theorists to provide an account of world-to-word direction of fit (that is of 'proper desires') which, since it is intended to *explain* 'being goal directed', cannot make essential use of purposive or 'goal-directed' notions, on pain of circularity. So direction of fit theorists are forced to use some sort of causally based account, or at least an account that does not use purposive notions, which means either one that cites the inherent structure of the mental states at issue, or some sort of functionalist account.

It is this issue, I believe, that separates those who think it important to hold BD and CT *jointly* from those who accept BD but question CT. I have already argued that the issue is not (directly anyway) what counts as a 'causal explanation', or whether explanations of the sort cited in BD are causal. Rather, I believe, the issue is whether in the end explanations of the sort described in BD, reasons explanations of actions, must themselves be explained in terms of non-purposive notions of the sort that 'direction of fit' is supposed to be or, alternatively, whether unanalyzed purposive notions such as 'having a goal' or 'having a purpose' can do the required explanatory work. The former alternative would require that the explanatory force of reasons explanations of the sort described in BD come from something *other* (and presumably 'deeper') than the goal-directed notions employed in BD itself, hence presumably from some underlying causal regularities. That was what the direction of fit defense of the Humean Theory of Motivation was supposed to provide.

But there is another possible reading of BD, different from the one that understands it as referring to mental states such as proper desires, which could have identifying features like 'direction of fit', a reading different from the Humean Theory of Motivation that Smith and Lenman take as the *conclusion* of their argument. This is the reading of BD that both Smith and Lenman occasionally (though I think unwittingly) shift to. Instead of reading BD as referring to proper desires which, when understood, can be used to provide an *explanation* of the fact that actions are always goal-directed, we might read it as simply a slightly different, somewhat more detailed, way of saying the same thing: namely that actions *are* purposive or 'goal-directed'. This would be to understand BD as the *assumption* from which the direction of fit argument as described above begins, rather than as its conclusion. This reading of BD, I will argue, though it provides no argument against CT, also provides no support for it (in anything beyond the minimal reading of it, which is uncontentious).

It is compatible with either the truth or the falsity of any reading of CT beyond the minimal one. (I'll return to this point below.)

If this is right, then the issue is not whether some specific reading of CT (beyond the minimal one) is correct. Rather, the issue is *whether there must be* a (correct) version of CT which goes beyond the minimal one. That is, the issue is whether reasons explanations of actions of the sort described in BD, which certainly on their face make use of purposive concepts, must be somehow explainable or analyzable in terms that do not involve such concepts. That is what the 'direction of fit' terminology is supposed to do, provide a terminology with which to understand the explanatory force of reasons explanations but which itself involves no purposive concepts.

One thing that I think has made it easy to miss this issue is that it is not difficult to be misled by the fact that there really are *three* distinct ways to read BD. That there are at least two ways is entailed by the thought that the direction of fit argument is really an argument, rather than merely a restatement of the obvious in technical terms, since BD can be understood as either a restatement of the main premise of this argument or as its conclusion. But there is no very convenient terminology for stating even these two readings so as to make clear which is which. Neither ordinary terms such as 'want' or 'desire' nor philosophical jargon such as 'pro attitude' or 'desire very broadly understood' naturally sort out the two readings of BD that I am pointing to. So, before getting to the third possible reading of BD, it will be worthwhile restating carefully exactly what these first two readings are.

BD can be read as simply restating in a bit more detail the unexceptional and uncontroversial thought that reasons explanations give the purpose or goal for which the agent performed the action in question, which is then specified in the content of the pro attitude mentioned in BD. In this sense of the relevant term ('want', 'desire', 'pro attitude', etc.), it *follows* from the fact that the action was performed intentionally that the agent had some attitude of this sort. As Thomas Nagel puts it, 'That I have the appropriate desire simply follows from the fact that [some] considerations motivate me; if the likelihood that an act will promote my future happiness motivates me to perform it now, then it is appropriate to ascribe to me a desire for my own future happiness' (T. Nagel 1970, p. 29). So, to put another way, this way of reading BD simply takes it as saying that having a purpose or having a pro attitude toward something is a necessary feature of intentional action. In the now disfavored terminology, BD, on this way of reading it, is a conceptual or analytic truth. That is because, in the terminology of 'proper desires' verses 'pro attitudes' explained above, on this reading BD merely says that a pro attitude is required for any intentional action, where a 'pro attitude' is understood simply as 'a mental state that can lead one to promote whatever it is an attitude toward'.

This is in contrast to the reading of BD that I have been attributing to the defenders of the direction of fit argument, where BD, though intended to be completely general, is not analytic. This is to understand BD as a statement of what Smith calls the Humean Theory of Motivation. On this reading, the essential term of BD ('pro attitude', 'want', 'desire', etc.) refers to a *proper* desire and marks a feature of mental states whose explanatory role in action explanations can be set out fully only in totally non-purposive language, such as 'direction of fit' is supposed to be. BD on this reading records a general fact about actions that is itself then open to and in need of (I would say very badly in need of) further explanation. And since this feature is intended to *account for* the 'surface' or apparent purposiveness of BD, it will not be, or use, a purposive notion itself. That is why, on this reading of BD, CT, which claims that reasons explanations are 'causal', is called on to carry real explanatory weight, to go beyond the minimal sense of 'cause'. The purposive notions in BD itself, on this reading, do not really carry that weight. They need to be explained in terms of some further feature of proper desires, which is what direction of fit is supposed to do.

That there is a third reading of BD which gets confused with the other two can be seen by looking at some of the conclusions which defenders of the teleological argument have claimed it supports. Lenman, for instance, considering the reasoning 'I know how much this person is suffering so I want to help', says: 'When we describe any process that simply lurches inexplicably, as in [this example], from belief to a desire, we . . . tell a story that may indeed be a true account of a causal process but it is not plausibly held to be a story about a piece of practical reasoning (Lenman 1996, p. 295). This certainly seems to suggest that he thinks the direction of fit argument supports some account of practical *reasoning*, and presumably not merely a descriptive account, since there is no reason to think that people do not in fact sometimes reason exactly as described, as Lenman says.

So the thought would seem to be that only proper desires count as *good* reasons for acting, i.e. that, unless one has a proper desire of some sort for some end promoted by the action one performed, one has no good reason for doing what one did. '[T]he governing norm of practical reasoning is, at least arguably, *that one's desires be satisfied . . .*', Lenman says (1996, p. 296). But whether or not he really wants to suggest that the direction of fit argument actually *yields conclusions* about what are and are not good reasons for acting (and some other things he says seem to indicate he does not), other philosophers have held not only that we must understand an agent's reasons for her action in terms of her proper desires (i.e. the second, Humean Theory, reading of BD above), but also that only desires can provide *good* reasons for acting, which is quite a different thought.[16]

So this is a third, normative, reading of BD. We can understand the term 'reason' in BD as 'good reason', and then BD becomes a 'governing norm of practical reasoning' to the effect that, if you don't have some sort of desire or pro attitude toward doing something, then you have no good reason to do it. However plausible or implausible one finds this idea in itself, though, I hope it is clear that it is quite a different claim from either of the two embodied in the first two readings of BD already distinguished and not at all supported by any of the considerations we have been looking at so far. It is one thing to say that actions are always of necessity purposive (the first reading of BD), or that purposiveness can be explained in terms of proper desires with a feature such as world-to-word direction of fit that connects them causally to actions (the second reading), quite another to hold that one has a *good reason* to do something only if it contributes to the satisfaction of some desire or the achieving of some goal.

After all, *each* of the first two readings of BD, if true, *presupposes* that there are no actions performed for reasons in which the agent fails to have a 'pro attitude' of the sort described in BD. If there are such actions, they will constitute counterexamples to BD, understood in either of these two ways. But people sometimes act for reasons that are not good ones. So to understand BD as a *norm* of practical reason means that we have to allow that people sometimes actually do (or at least can do) things they do not have a pro attitude towards doing, in the sense of 'pro attitude' that is implicit in this third way of reading

---

[16] Smith of course explicitly denies that we should accept such a 'Humean' account of what he calls 'normative reasons': see Smith (1994 chap. 5).

BD. Otherwise, why have a norm forbidding this or recommending against it? But then this third reading of BD will specify a principle that looks incompatible with either of the first two readings. According to either of the first two readings of BD, there can never be cases where agents act for reasons where they fail to have a pro attitude of the relevant sort.[17] So for the purposes of this discussion we may simply set this third reading aside. The doctrine embodied in it is simply a different one from the one we are exploring. (It is also false, I want to say, but we will get to this issue latter.)

2.2 Are 'Causal' Explanations Unavoidable?

I suspect that much of the popularity of the doctrine embodied in the third, normative, reading of BD rests on confusing it with one of the other two readings. And I have been arguing that the second, Humean Theory of Motivation, reading of BD, once it is clearly distinguished from the first reading, seems at least unsupported. I don't, of course, think that anything argued above 'refutes' the second way of reading BD, only that it lets us see why advocates of this reading are committed to a less-than-minimal, and hence problematic, reading of CT. They are committed to finding the explanatory force of reasons explanations in the underlying, non-purposive, features of proper desires and their accompanying beliefs. That is at the heart of the thought that only proper desires generate purposes. Finding such a reading of CT that is plausible will not be easy. This is why I suspect that much—perhaps all—of the popularity of the second, Humean Theory, reading BD stems simply from failure to see that there is an alternative. So we need to look at the sort of explanation of action we get when we stick with the first, merely purposive, reading.

On this reading, BD is to be understood simply as a somewhat more detailed way of saying that human intentional actions are purposive, that is that the agent always has some purpose or goal in performing them, a purpose specified, or at least referred to, in the content of the description of the action under which the agent has the pro attitude toward it. Such a way of understanding BD commits its defenders to no more than the minimal reading of CT because it commits them to no further analysis or account of 'purpose'. Defenders of the direction of fit argument, since they are committed

---

[17] This is argued at greater length in Schueler (1995*a*).

to giving an analysis or account of proper desires in terms that are not themselves purposive ('causal' terms for short, though I hope it is now clear why using this shorthand can be misleading), must hold out for some substantive, less than minimal, way of understanding CT, the claim that 'reasons are causes'. That is, on this sort of view, the purposive terms used in BD have explanatory force only because of some other, presumably 'causal', features in terms of which they can be analyzed. Proper desires, on this view, are the generators of human purposes, but they do this only by way of some underlying features which themselves are not to be explained in purposive terms. So this sort of view is committed to giving some substantive, non-minimal, and non-teleological account of what these features are and how they work.

The reading of BD I am going to be advocating here understands it as saying nothing more than that actions are performed for purposes, while leaving 'purpose' unanalyzed. Defenders of this reading are of course still committed to the minimal reading of CT. But the explanatory force of explanations of the sort described in BD will come from the fact that they are essentially purposive. There may (or may not) be a further analysis of 'purpose' or 'reason' which is plausible, but accepting the 'purposive' reading of BD by itself commits one to no position on the issue of whether there must be some further account in non-purposive terms. If I am right, therefore, in thinking that this is what really separates the two sides of the 'Are reasons causes?' debate, then, as was said, this issue has been somewhat ill-stated. It is not that one side asserts and the other side denies that reasons are causes. It is rather that one side, including defenders of the direction of fit argument, is committed to an account of the explanatory force of purposive or goal-directed explanations of intentional actions in non-purposive (hence presumably substantive causal) terms, while the other side is not.

What I have been calling the 'first' reading of BD claims that reasons explanations of actions are purposive in the sense of 'purpose' explained in Chapter 1 above, the sense in which, in order for something to have a purpose, someone must have a purpose for it. One consequence of this way of reading BD is thus that it includes an essential reference to the *person* who has the purpose specified in the description of the pro attitude mentioned in BD. This might seem a small point, but in fact it marks a sharp difference between the purposive and the Humean Theory readings of BD. Though BD itself of course refers to 'the agent' who has the pro attitude and belief in question, the direction of fit account of proper desires understands the explanation involved in such a way as to make no essential use of this reference except to identify which set of beliefs and desires to describe. All the explanatory work, so to speak, on this reading of BD is supposed to get done by whatever account is given of the supposedly causal interactions of the relevant desires and beliefs themselves (or the physical states in which they are realized) in virtue of their different 'directions of fit'. (Or at least that is the hope; that is what would be so if defenders of this sort of view could find a plausible account of direction of fit.) So accepting the direction of fit account of proper desires entails an account of how reasons explanations work, which constitutes a shift to an essentially non-purposive or non-teleological form of explanation.[18] Or rather, it constitutes a *commitment* to a shift to this form of explanation, a commitment to the thought that it is in the causal interactions of the relevant features of desires and beliefs that an explanation of the action in question will be found.[19]

By contrast, according to the first, purposive, reading of BD, the explanatory mechanism of the explanations being described becomes—or rather remains—teleological, since essential use is made of 'purpose' in the sense in which, for something to have a purpose, *someone* must have a purpose for it. So this reading of BD understands the action being explained as something for which the agent has a purpose, which purpose itself gets specified, or at least

[18] One might I think describe this as a shift to what Hornsby, following Dennett, calls the 'subpersonal' level (see Hornsby, 1997, esp. pp. 157–167, and Dennett, 1987, 43–68). Hornsby describes the personal level as 'a level at which mention of persons is essential, and . . . commonsense psychological explanations are indigenous to that level' (p. 161). She has an excellent discussion of some of the ramifications of the personal–subpersonal distinction, but for our purposes I think it is enough to say that the 'subpersonal level' of explanation is one at which no essential reference to a person is made and the explanations are not 'commonsense psychological explanations'. Explanations of behavior in terms of the interactions of brain states would thus be paradigm examples of subpersonal explanations. That would be one way of trying to explicate the interactions of proper desires with beliefs, but perhaps not the only such way. If it is not the only way, then perhaps the 'personal–subpersonal' terminology will not always apply to the sort of shift I am describing.

[19] Of course, as long as we refer to the states in question as 'desires' and 'beliefs', we are still at the 'personal' level, since every desire or belief is always a desire or belief *of someone*. But at the same time, the explanatory apparatus that is being proposed, since it will operate only in terms of the interactions of these states with other such states, will itself require no such reference to a person.

referred to, in the description of the content of the pro attitude and belief mentioned.

What this means, I think, is that according to this reading of BD explanations of actions must involve at least two elements: first, the agent's actual reasons (as she understood them, typically), including her actual reasoning, if any, and, second, the relevant features of the agent, that is the person, who did this reasoning and had these reasons (including such things as character traits, intelligence, reasoning ability, strength of will, and so on). Unsurprisingly, these are just the things that so-called 'folk psychology' does use to explain actions (see e.g. Malle 2001).

So we may seem to have come more or less full circle here. For many philosophers at least, the whole excursion into a non-purposive analysis of BD, one part of which we have been examining, has been motivated by the thought that there is something deeply unsatisfactory, or at least very puzzling, about ordinary, so-called 'folk psychological' explanations of actions in terms of the agent's reasons, *unless* we regard them as explainable in non-purposive, causal terms, that is unless we give a reading of CT in such terms beyond the minimal one. That is presumably why not being committed to any reading of CT of this non-purposive sort, as what I am calling the purposive reading of BD is not, is thought to be an untenable position. If this view is correct, then whether or not the direction of fit argument is successful in explaining direction of fit so as to specify a plausible non-minimal reading of CT, that is a plausible non-teleological account of how such explanations work, we would still know in advance that *some* such way of understanding reasons explanations of actions must be right. So, before going on to look at how reasons explanations work if we simply stick to the purposive reading of BD, we need to face directly the question of whether they really do work at all, unless we presuppose some sort of underlying, non-purposive, causal mechanism (yet to be explained of course) between the agent's reasons and the actions they produce.

I have been arguing that each of Davidson's two claims, BD and CT, can be understood in two very different ways, in what might be called an uncontentious way and a contentious way. The uncontentious reading of BD understands it as saying nothing more than that what I have called a pro attitude is always involved in any intentional action, i.e. merely that the agent had some purpose in doing what she did. The contentious reading understands BD as an expression of what Smith calls the Humean Theory of Motivation, i.e. as claiming that what I have called a proper desire is required to motivate any intentional action, that beliefs alone are never enough. The uncontentious, or what I have been calling the minimal, reading of CT is simply that whatever ends up being referred to by the term 'the agent's reason' is an essential explanatory factor in explaining her action, however, this explanation ends up working. So this reading is consistent even with irreducibly teleological explanations. The contentious reading of CT understands it as saying that the agent's reason has to be the efficient cause of her action.[20]

In Chapter 1 I argued that there *is* an uncontentious, 'minimal', reading of CT. On that reading, even someone who holds that reasons explanations are essentially teleological can accept it, i.e. can agree that 'reasons are causes' in a perfectly ordinary sense. In this chapter I have been arguing that the contentious reading of BD, the Humean Theory of Motivation, has not been established. At the same time, though, it could be that we can understand purposive explanations, at bottom, only *as explanations* in non-purposive terms. The fact that there *is* an uncontentious or minimal reading of CT, that CT makes sense when understood in this way, doesn't show that this is the correct reading, i.e. that we are not for some reason still required to understand CT as saying that reasons must be efficient causes. And of course, if we *are*, then it looks like we cannot stay with merely the uncontentious reading of BD, the purposive or pro attitude reading. That will not tell the whole explanatory story if in fact reasons must be efficient causes. So we still need to consider the arguments that seem to show directly that they must be.

The arguments for this view that I will consider here also come from Davidson (1963), who gives two positive arguments in favor of it, or perhaps two and a half. The 'half' argument is the thought that the position that explanations of actions in terms of the agent's reasons are 'a species of causal explanation' is 'the ancient—and commonsense—position'. That is, one might understand Davidson as holding that the causal account of reasons explanations is, so to speak, the 'default' position of common sense. This would be a

---

[20] It is perhaps worth adding here that, on the argument I have been making, Davidson's own explanations of BD and CT seem most plausibly read as supporting in each case the *uncontentious* reading of these claims, though this itself may be a somewhat contentious claim.

'burden of proof' point and would make sense of the structure of the paper from which this view is taken, which as I said above consists almost entirely of refutations of attacks on the position that reasons explanations are causal explanations (as opposed to giving positive reasons for supporting this claim). The idea would be that, unless there is a successful attack on this position, it stands as acceptable without a need, so to speak, of independent argument in its support.

This is only 'half' an argument because it is never explicitly spelled out by Davidson (and so, perhaps, is not actually one he would want to make). Once it is spelled out, though, it does not look very plausible. Granting that in some sense the commonsense position on a topic is always the 'default' position (de facto at least), it is not at all obvious that the position in question here, i.e. one that involves a substantive, non-minimal reading of CT in non-purposive terms, is the commonsense position on this issue. We certainly do give commonsense explanations of actions in terms of the agent's reasons, and sometimes at least these are explicitly her desires and beliefs. But does 'common sense' also have a position on the philosophical question of the *nature* of the explanation thus given?

We do of course say such things as 'She is leaving the meeting early because she wants to catch the 5.45 bus'. But it would be a mistake to think that the use of 'because' here somehow commits the speaker to an analysis of the nature of this explanation. As was argued in Section 1.3 above, 'because' simply serves to cite the important explanatory feature and is not itself 'an explanation', still less an account of how this explanation works. Its use here is merely to say that this (her desire to catch the bus) is what explains her action; that is, at most it commits 'common sense' to what I have been calling the minimal reading of CT. That would perhaps argue against any philosopher who wanted to deny that reasons were causes *at all*. But as an argument for, say, the Humean Theory of Motivation, so far as I can see, this 'default position' argument looks plausible only if one confuses the fact that commonsense or folk psychology does indeed *explain* actions in terms of agents' reasons (or tries to), and so of course entails acceptance of the minimal reading of CT, with something very different—a commitment to a further, substantive analysis in causal terms of how such explanations work.

The first (real) argument Davidson makes for the causal position is this. Discussing the view, which he attributes to followers of the later Wittgenstein, that reasons explain actions by placing them into a pattern or context in which they become intelligible, he says:

[T]alk of patterns and contexts does not answer the question of how reasons explain actions, since the relevant pattern or context contains both reason and action. One way we can explain an event is by placing it in the context of its cause; cause and effect form the sort of pattern that explains the effect, in a sense of 'explain' that we understand as well as any. If reason and action illustrate a different pattern of explanation, that pattern must be identified. (Davidson 1963, p. 692).

And two paragraphs later, after explaining Hampshire's rejection of Aristotle's claim that wanting is 'a causal factor' in producing actions, Davidson says:

But I would urge that, failing a satisfactory alternative, the best argument for a scheme like Aristotle's is that it alone promises to give an account of [what Hampshire called] the 'mysterious connection' between reasons and actions. (Davidson 1963, p. 693)

So the point here is simply that no viable alternatives have been suggested to a (substantive, non-minimal) causal account of reasons explanations. The argument would then proceed as follows. (1) Reasons explanations of actions do explain them. (2) The only viable account of how any events, including actions, are explained is in terms of cause and effect. Hence (3) reasons explanations must be a variety of cause–effect explanations. This is one of the two main positive arguments for the causal position that Davidson presents in this paper. It clearly depends on showing two things, the first of which is that the causal position is not disqualified as an account of reasons explanations in any of the ways its opponents have urged. So Davidson spends the whole final section of his paper arguing against such disqualifying claims, for example the claim that reasons couldn't be causes because there is (alleged to be) a 'logical' connection between reason and action.

This argument also depends on showing, second, that there are no *other* viable accounts of how reasons explain actions. That is why Davidson is concerned to refute, for instance, the 'placing-in-a-larger-pattern' account of reasons explanations. He argues that, unless this 'larger pattern' is a cause–effect pattern, it is hard to see that the action has actually been explained. But obviously, an argument of this sort, i.e. one that holds that there is really only one viable account on the table, is only as good as the actual refutations of the alleged alternative accounts that accompany it. It has no independent force of its own against any alternatives not specifically considered. It can be safely ignored, therefore, in considering the alternative account that will be presented below, which is not one that Davidson discussed.

This is not so clearly the case with the other argument in favor of a substantive reading of CT that Davidson gives, however. In discussing the justifying role of reasons, a role that causes, or at least other causes, seem not to have, Davidson says:

> [I]t is necessary to decide what is being included under justification. It could be taken to cover only what is called for by [BD]: that the agent have certain beliefs and attitudes in the light of which the action is reasonable. But then something essential has certainly been left out, for a person can have a reason for an action, and perform the action, and yet this reason not be the reason why he did it. Central to the relation between a reason and an action it explains is the idea that the agent performed the action *because* he had the reason. Of course, we can include this idea too in justification; but then the notion of justification becomes as dark as the notion of reason until we can account for the force of that 'because'. (Davidson 1963, p. 691)

If I understand it, this is intended to be an argument against any account of reasons explanations that doesn't rest the explanatory force of these explanations on an underlying causal mechanism. And on its face, it seems different merely from the claim that there are no alternatives to a causal account. The argument is this. It is agreed that reasons explanations operate in terms of the agent's desires and beliefs, and of course that they really do explain the action in question. But together, these two points commit us to a substantive causal account. After all, agents will frequently have lots of desires, some of which may require different actions for their satisfaction and some of which may be satisfied by the same action. Suppose, for instance, that I want to see my friend, want to have some coffee, want to get out of my office, and want some exercise. A different action might satisfy each of these desires, but it could also be that a single action—say, walking to the coffee house—might satisfy all of them. Still, it could be that when I do walk to the coffee house *my reason* for doing so is that I want to see my friend, and not that I want exercise or that I want to get out of my office, etc., even though I do in fact have these other desires as well. But then, how can we make sense of this unless we say that it was my desire to see my friend, and not one of these other desires, that *caused* me to act?

So it looks as if explanations of actions in terms of agents' reasons will have to be causal if they are to actually *explain*. Only causation will pick out the actual explanatory factor from the list of potential explanatory factors. Thomas Nagel makes what I think is the same point in his discussion of autonomy except that, since he wants to deny that autonomous choices are causally explainable, he reaches the conclusion that reasons (or what he calls 'intentional') explanations can not really explain actions. He says:

When someone makes an autonomous choice such as whether to accept a job, and there are reasons on both sides of the issue, we are supposed to be able to explain what he did by pointing to his reasons for accepting it. But we could equally have explained his refusing the job, if he had refused, by refer-ring to the reasons on the other side—and he could have refused for those other reasons: that is the essential claim of autonomy. It applies even if one choice is significantly more reasonable than the other. Bad reasons are reasons too. Intentional explanation, if there is such a thing, can explain either choice in terms of the appropriate reasons, since either choice would be intelligible if it occurred. But for this very reason it cannot explain why the person accepted the job for the reasons in favor instead of refusing it for the reasons against. (Nagel 1990, pp. 115–116)

So Nagel's point here seems the same as Davidson's: unless reasons are causes, reasons explanations do not really explain at all. Davidson thinks these explanations do really explain; hence he thinks reasons must be causes. Nagel thinks that reasons explanations are not causal (since they apply to autonomous choices); hence he thinks reasons explanations do not really explain. Since I want to say that reasons explanations do really explain but that this fact does not *require* analysis in substantively causal terms, this argument needs to be examined.

We may begin by setting out in slightly more detail the exciting story of my trip to the coffee house. Let's suppose that I have several desires that will be satisfied by going to the coffee house (the ones mentioned above—I want some coffee, want to see my friend, etc.), several others that will be frustrated by doing so (e.g. I don't want to spend any more money today; I want to get some more work done), and many that will be neither satisfied nor frustrated (e.g. I want to get home in time for dinner; I want to write a note to my sister; I want our football team to win their next game). In the end I walk to the coffee house, and my reason for doing so is that I want to see my friend.

The Davidson–Nagel point here is that, unless we say that my desire to see my friend *caused* me to head for the coffee house, we can't make sense of the thought that this is what moved me, that this was my real reason for going, rather than, say, my desire to get out of my office. Likewise, we can't makes sense of the fact that I went rather than stayed, since, after all, I had reasons for staying too; e.g., I wanted to get some more work done. I have this whole set of desires, some of which will be satisfied by going to the coffee house and some of which will be frustrated by this action (and some neither, of course). So the explanatory tools available at the level of reasons don't seem sufficient to actually explain my action. So if, as we are supposing, it is only my desire to see my friend that *is* my real reason for going, there must be something different about this desire that provides it with the explanatory force it has, and what can that be except that it caused me to act where the others did not? To find an explanation, we seem forced to say that this was the cause of my action. This is what Alfred R. Mele calls 'Davidson's Challenge' to anyone who wants to deny that reasons explanations are 'causal': ' If you hold that when we act intentionally we act for reasons, provide an account of the reasons for which we act that does not treat (our having) those reasons as figuring in the causation of the relevant behavior (or, one might add, as realized in physical causes of the behavior)!' (Mele 2000, pp. 279–80). This challenge, Mele adds, is 'particularly acute' when, as in the cases we are discussing, the agent has more than one reason for doing something but in fact does it for only some of those reasons.

This argument might look as if it clinches the case for the position that holds that there must be some substantive causal connection between desires and the actions they explain that is doing the explanatory work here. (It looked that way to me for quite a long time.) In fact, though, I want to say that this argument does no actual work at all in support of the view that the explanatory force of reasons explanations *must* come from some substantive, causal regularities, of a non-teleological kind, among the states and events in question. Its appearance of plausibility turns on the same ambiguity between a minimal and substantive reading of 'cause' explained in Section 1.3 above.

I am assuming here, as Davidson does, that reasons explanations really do explain actions. And the question is how exactly do they do that; how exactly do such explanations work? The Davidson–Nagel point is that, when we cite something as 'my reason' for my action (here: my desire to see my friend), it can't just be the fact that this reason 'justifies' my action (that is makes it reasonable) that does the explanatory job, since there are plenty of other things (which we are of course assuming that I am aware of and so on) that would also make my action reasonable, as well as things, such as my desire to get some more work done, that would make it reasonable for me not to perform this action. So there must be something *else* about the thing cited as my reason, beyond the fact that it makes my action reasonable, that lets it do its explanatory work. And what else could this be but the fact that this thing *causes* me to act?

Putting it this way should let us see that at least *part* of the force of this second argument against other possible accounts of reasons explanations is really no different from Davidson's earlier argument, the one that claims in essence that reasons explanations must 'be causal', that is must get their explanatory force from some substantive causal regularities among the events and states in question, because there are no other accounts available except such causal ones. The justifying feature (or reasonableness-making feature) of my reason for acting is not enough in itself to account for the explanatory power that citing my reason has to explain my action. So there must be something else. And what can this be except that my reason caused me to act? This is just the same as the earlier argument, and, as before, offers no genuine counter to any other account on its own. I'll suggest below an answer to the question of what else it could be.

Mele's description of this argument as a 'challenge' suggests that he thinks this is all this argument comes to. But is that so? The Davidson–Nagel point *seems* to offer more than that earlier argument since it seems to suggest that calling my reason 'the cause' of my action *does* do the explanatory work needed to get beyond the merely justifying feature of my reason, and, more importantly, that there is no other way to do this. If that is right, the claim here is not only that there are no *other* accounts 'on the table' for consideration that make sense of the explanatory force of citing 'my reason', but also a much stronger claim, that a substantive causal account is the *only* way to make sense of it. This extra claim, though, whether or not Davidson or Nagel actually intend to make it, is unsupported by this argument.

Consider (yet again) my walk to the coffee house. We are supposing that I had various desires (to have some coffee, to see my friend, to get some more work done, etc.) *each* of which was there, in place, so to speak, and would have made my action reasonable, had I acted on it. That was why some further feature was needed to set apart my desire to see my friend as 'my reason', that is some feature that would account for the explanatory force of this particular desire when compared with the others. But just saying that my desire to see my friend *caused* me to go to the coffee house, so far at least, does not do this.

After all, any of these other desires, had I acted on it, would have been my reason for going (or not going), just as any of them would presumably have made going (or not going) reasonable. They are all the sorts of things, desires, that any causal account will have to claim to have the causal power to produce actions. So if the fact that each desire, had I acted on it, would have made my going reasonable shows the need for some further explanatory factor to set apart one of them as 'my reason', endowing *each* of them with the causal power to produce action, as of course any causal position does, doesn't get us any further. Exactly the same question, now in 'causal' terms, arises again: Why did *this* desire, my desire to see my friend, cause me to act, rather than one of my other desires?

There is nothing at all in the bare claim that the connection between my desire and my action is a 'causal connection' which picks out this particular desire over the other ones I have; that is, there is nothing in this bare claim that solves the puzzle that Davidson and Nagel present, the puzzle of how such explanations really work. The bare causal claim in fact is simply the minimal reading of CT (which is presumably why Nagel, who says that reasons explanations do not in fact explain actions at all, doesn't endorse it). What would be needed here is not just the minimal causal claim that this factor is what explains my going, but *both* a genuine, substantive causal explanation that shows exactly why it does, something like the direction of fit argument was supposed to provide, *and* an explanation of why such an account in terms of efficient causation is the only way to answer this puzzle. The last part will be needed if this Davidson–Nagel argument is to do anything more than offer the 'challenge' described by Mele: if it isn't efficient causation, what is it?

Saying that my desire to see my friend *caused* me to go to the coffee house is just a way of saying that this is what *explains* my going; in addition, of course, any substantive causal position will add the claim that the actual explanation, when we finally figure out what it is, will be 'causal' in some substantive way that goes beyond the minimal reading of CT. The first part, that this explains my action, is of course already contained in saying that this is my reason for going; i.e., it adds nothing toward solving the puzzle of *why* this particular desire was the one I acted on, or of how this explanation actually works. That is, by itself this is simply the usual promissory note in the minimal reading of CT, with the addition, as yet unsupported, that the promised explanation will be substantively causal. But even if one thinks that this promise can be fulfilled in efficient causal terms, that still doesn't show that this is the *only* way to do it, i.e. that 'Davidson's Challenge' can't (also?) be met by some purposive or teleological explanation.

Saying that X caused Y in the standard, minimal sense of 'cause', as I said above, sometimes *does* give us very useful information about how Y came about (X did it—Y would not have occurred had X not occurred), and so *in just that sense* will count as 'an explanation' of Y. It does that when the question at issue is *what* explains Y, that is, when the question is what the central (or relevant, or interesting, etc.) explanatory factor is. 'It was the sign saying "Free Lunch Here Today", not the cross above the door, that caused all those people to line up outside that church';[21] or 'It was the dog bounding into the room, not the weight of the extra card you put on it, that caused the house of cards you were building to fall.' So saying, in some contexts, that some particular potential reason was what caused someone to act might be very informative in just this way.

But that is not the issue here. We already know it was the desire to see my friend that got me to go to the coffee house. The issue here is what *sort* of explanation this is and how it works. And, beyond that, we want to know whether an explanation in terms of efficient causes is all that will do the required job. To say that my desire caused my action in this context, where the question is how such an explanation works, is simply to say that *there is* an explanation that will pick out this desire as the central explanatory factor, not to actually *give* such an explanation, let alone take a stand on the philosophical question of what the nature of that explanation will have to be. The puzzle explained by Davidson and Nagel of why exactly this reason, rather than any of the other reasons available to me, was acted on is not addressed by my saying that it was this particular desire that caused me to go. In the minimal sense of 'cause', that is only to say that this desire will figure centrally in the full explanation, which we already

---

[21] This example comes from Dennett (1987). It is cited by Hornsby (1997).

know. The further, implicit claim that the full explanation *must* be substantively causal is still unsupported.

The point here, I should underline, is not that the question raised by Davidson and Nagel of how to account for the explanatory force of my reason, when I had other reasons on which I could equally have acted, is not a puzzle. It *is* a puzzle. In fact, it is the very puzzle of how reasons explanations manage to explain. The point is that saying in this context that my reason 'caused' my action is not a *solution* to this puzzle. In the minimal sense of 'cause' explained above, it is simply the claim that this factor (called 'my reason') will figure centrally in whatever the full explanation turns out to be. It is, as I said, a promise about what that full explanation will involve. To think that such a claim supports a *substantive* causal account is to think both that this promise can be redeemed in substantive causal terms and that it can be redeemed in no other way. Even if one thinks, perhaps on other grounds, that the first of these is true, by itself the Davidson–Nagel point doesn't support it. And in any case it is the *second* conclusion— that the promissory note here can be cashed *only* in efficient causal terms—that would be needed to cast doubt on understanding reasons explanations in terms of the purposive or uncontentious reading of BD.

3

Teleological Explanations of Actions

Explanations of actions in terms of the agent's reasons, I want to claim, work by citing the purpose or purposes for which the person who performed that action actually acted. In one sense this is hardly news. The commonsense or 'folk psychological' explanations of action, which have been very widely discussed by philosophers for quite awhile, obviously work by citing the agents' purposes. But what I have been suggesting is that reference both to the purpose in question and to the person who has it are not further analyzable, and need not be further analyzed, in the context of these explanations. That is, explanations of actions work as, and so should be understood as, teleological explanations. They don't depend on any account of desires and beliefs in non-teleological terms.[1] It can hardly be doubted that commonsense reasons explanations of actions really do 'work' in the sense of genuinely explaining, at least sometimes, the actions they are intended to explain. The question is how they do it. Advocates of the Humean Theory of Motivation hold that such explanations must depend on (perhaps implicit) reference to proper desires, and that in the end the 'motivational force' of such desires is itself to be explained in non-teleological terms, e.g. as the direction of fit argument tries to do. If the argument I have been making is correct, though, nothing forces us into such a 'Humean Theory' reading of BD. In fact, I think, it goes the other way. The Humean Theory reading seems plausible only because it covertly assumes the purposive or teleological reading.

---

[1] If I understand her, Jennifer Hornsby (1997) is defending a view very similar to this, though her terminology is different.

3.1 The Need for Teleological Explanations

The strategy of the direction of fit argument, a non-teleological strategy, was to understand the agent's reasons in terms of the mental states (desires and beliefs, roughly speaking) that contained them and then to look for some causal mechanism by which these states would interact so as to produce the action in question. This is a non-teleological strategy because it tries to account for the explanatory force of what certainly seem to be teleological explanations by reference to the non-teleological, causal interactions of these mental states. I will sometimes refer to this strategy as involving the 'non-teleological, belief–desire explanatory strategy', meaning by this not ordinary or commonsense reasons explanations of actions (which in fact rarely explicitly cite the beliefs and desires of the agent, even when these terms are 'broadly understood'), but the sort of non-teleological *account* of these explanations exemplified by the direction of fit argument (at least as I have interpreted it). This sort of strategy has the effect of doing *away* with any reference to the purposes or goals of the person in question, in favor of causal interactions among her mental states. The strategy I want to pursue, in contrast, leaves references to both the person and her purposes in the explanation—indeed, requires that there are such references.

One way of seeing that this latter sort of strategy is preferable can be found by noticing that the phrase 'the agent's reason' is ambiguous. It can refer to the *mental state* an observer would ordinarily cite in explaining someone's action, such as desires and beliefs. ('He clearly wanted to impress her with what a cool guy he is and thought that he could do so by standing on his head.') But it can also refer to the *contents* of this state, that is to what the agent himself would say or think were his reasons. ('It would be terrible if she thought I was a complete stuffed shirt; so it is important that I do something to let her see what a cool guy I am.') A 'third person' observing this action might describe the agent's reason as his desire to impress her. The agent himself, however, might describe the same thing—his reason for standing on his head—by referring to how *important* it is that she be impressed.

Advocates of the non-teleological belief–desire explanatory strategy stick firmly to the first of these two. This is partly, I think, on the grounds that the truths (even assuming they are truths) that constitute the contents of these mental states cannot by themselves explain anything. Truths, and falsehoods as well of course, are timeless, abstract entities. So, the reasoning goes, they cannot enter into explanations of actions 'by themselves', but only via the agent's awareness of them (or via some other propositional attitude the agent takes toward them). It must, therefore, be the *things* ('mental states') that *have* these true or false contents that do the explaining.

This doesn't by itself get one all the way to the non-teleological belief–desire explanatory strategy as I have characterized it, of course, since there is nothing in sticking to the observer's point of view by itself that requires understanding reasons explanations in terms of causal interactions of mental states or the like. But by the same token, someone who already thought that only causal interactions of some sort or other could serve to make sense of the explanatory success of reasons explanations would quite naturally stick to the observer's point of view here.

It would clearly be a mistake to think that, because the external or observer's description of the agent's reasons can include reference to mental states such as desires and beliefs, the *contents* of these states must refer to these desires and beliefs as well. This sort of shift from the observer's point of view on agent's reasons to the content of these reasons may be what has led some philosophers into what I called the third or normative reading of BD, that is to the thought that only if one has a desire to do something does one have a good reason to do it.[2] It would do that by illicitly shifting from a description of the person performing the action as having certain desires and beliefs to the thought that this person must take these desires and beliefs, rather than their contents, as what gives her reason to act. This confusion would be engendered by failure to notice that the term 'want' and its cognates can refer either to 'proper desires', such as a craving for attention, or simply to *whatever* moved one, that is to 'pro attitudes' generally, and then shifting from the true claim that an agent wanted something in the pro attitude sense to the thought that she must have taken the fact that she wanted it, that is had a proper desire for it, as her reason.

The agent who thinks that it is important that someone regard him as a cool guy, and takes that as his reason for standing on his head in her presence, can be correctly described by an observer (or

---

[2] I have argued elsewhere that at least some explanations of the practical syllogism make essentially this error: see Schueler (1995a, pp. 97–107).

for that matter by the head-stander himself) as *wanting* her to think that he is a cool guy. He has, that is, a pro attitude toward her thinking this. That follows from the fact that this is what moved him to stand on his head. But it could be a misdescription of this agent's reason for standing on his head to say that its *content* was 'I want her to think I am a cool guy', as if so to speak he had acted on the basis of what he took to be a proper desire he had that she think this. (And as I have explained this example, it would in fact be a misdescription, given the content of his reason. As just stated, his reason was that it is *important* that she think him a cool guy, not that he *wants* her to think this. He might after all think that her believing him a cool guy is crucial to achieving something of great value, such as world peace. That is quite different than his merely having a proper desire, a yen say, that she think this.[3]) A less trivial example should make this point clear.

Suppose I think it important, a good thing, that we have state subsidized day care, and that this is my reason for voting for a tax increase on which such day care depends. It would then be correct of an observer to say of me that I want us to have state subsidized day care. (I must have such a pro attitude since I was moved to actually vote in this way.) It would be correct for me to say this of myself too, though this might not be the natural way for me to describe things. In fact, it could be rather misleading. This is because it could well be false that I would take *the fact that* I want us to have state subsidized day care as a reason for voting for this tax increase, any more than I would think *the fact that* I value state subsidized day care would be. I might not be that self centered. I might not think that the fact that *I want* us (our city, state, country) to have something, or the fact that *I believe* something valuable, is by itself a reason for anyone, me included, to support a tax increase to get it. Rather, it is that *it is important* (that is, is valuable in

---

[3] The difference between wanting and valuing is explored by Gary Watson (1975). Watson holds that both can be sources of motivation, which entails, I think, treating 'valuing something' as at least involving (roughly) 'giving this thing weight in one's practical deliberations' rather than merely 'believing it to be of value'. This will be discussed much more fully below. Watson is responding to Harry Frankfurt's suggestion that freedom of the will is best understood in terms of second order desires that one's first-order desires be effective (see Frankfurt 1971). One would be free, or not, (roughly) depending on whether these second-order desires endorsed the first-order desires that actually moved one. Whatever one thinks of this as an account of freedom of will (and to me Watson's critique looks convincing), it seems a non-starter as a possible account of 'believing good', since it explicitly starts from first-order desires (that is desires that are at least potential determinants of action). So it provides no mechanism for explaining 'cool' evaluative beliefs, i.e. ones not connected to such desires.

some way) that we have subsidized day care that (I think) constitutes good reason to support a tax increase needed to get it.

So one very significant difference between these two points of view on the agent's reasons—that of the agent herself and that of some external observer—is the loss, in the shift from the former to the latter, of any normative or evaluative claims. That is just because the 'external observer' is using the pro attitude sense of 'want', which records only the *fact* of the motivation while ignoring its source, which could just as well be a carefully thought out evaluative judgment as a proper desire that welled up in the agent. In the former case, what to the agent who is doing the practical deliberation is an evaluation to the effect that subsidized day care is important or valuable is also correctly describable (and would in many circumstances be naturally described by the external observer) merely as 'his wanting subsidized day care'. But confusion arises if we take this to mean that he has and was moved by a *proper desire* for subsidized day care, as if so to speak the *content* of his judgment was that *he wanted* subsidized day care. (It would be a strictly analogous mistake to think that the *content* of the judgment of someone who was moved by her positive evaluation of subsidized day care was *that she judged* it to be a good thing.)

This should help make clear why this sort of case, where an evaluative belief is involved, presents a problem for the Humean Theory of Motivation. It is crucial to the Humean Theory that a *proper* desire is always required for motivation. And the direction of fit argument is supposed to support this thought by showing why it is so. 'World-to-word' and 'word-to-world' directions of fit are supposed to track desires and beliefs respectively (each 'broadly understood') *and to explain why the former is always needed* for any intentional action. But in a case of the sort just described, it certainly looks as if what is required is only a pro attitude, not a proper desire. The question is how the Humean Theory can deal with this sort of case.

It would make the Humean Theory much more plausible if the *contents* of desires and beliefs were always simply descriptions of how things are or might be ('that she think I am cool' or 'that our team wins', etc.), descriptions that is of how 'external reality' is or might be.[4] The thought that this is so, even if only implicit, would give the

---

[4] The original example Anscombe used to illustrate the difference between the two 'directions of fit' was of a shopping list, which could be seen as what was wanted, from the point of view of the shopper, or as a description of what was bought, from the point of view of someone recording what the shopper purchased (Anscombe 1963, p. 56).

Humean Theory of Motivation an unearned plausibility. If *these* are the only two candidates, then of course it is much more plausible to think that proper desires are always needed, since plain, factual beliefs hardly seem enough to make sense of even the simplest motivation to action.

But these are certainly not the only two candidates, as the current example shows. What of my *belief* that subsidized day care would be a good thing? It is possible to ignore the role of such a belief in motivation if one makes the mistake about content described above, since someone who votes for that tax increase on the basis of this belief does indeed want, that is has a pro attitude toward, subsidized day care. But it should now be clear that this does the Humean Theory no good, since the having of this pro attitude is perfectly compatible with the claim that the agent here had no proper desire for subsidized day care. So what can the Humean Theory, and the supporting direction of fit argument, do with cases of this sort, where my reason for voting for that tax increase is that the subsidized day care it will fund is a good thing? Clearly, simply insisting here that I *must* also have some sort of proper desire, toward doing good things or toward subsidized day care, is simply *assuming* the Humean Theory, not arguing for it.

One might think that, given the way this belief functions in getting me to vote for the tax increase, the direction of fit argument could come to the rescue by just saying that this belief also has 'world-to-word' direction of fit, that is that it is in fact some sort of desire. Agreeing that it really is a *belief*, with word-to-world direction of fit, would simply abandon the essential point of the Humean Theory, which, as we saw, was to establish that mental states with this (belief-like) direction of fit could not, by themselves, lead to actions. But in fact, I would say, simply *relabeling* my belief here as a desire, with world-to-word direction of fit, would be only a slightly less obvious way of abandoning the same point. It would disable this argument from supporting the Humean Theory, since it would now allow the very items the Humean Theory wants to rule out—ones ordinarily called 'beliefs'—as having world-to-word (i.e. desire-like) direction of fit. A big part of the original idea of this strategy, after all, was to explain in non-teleological, causal terms why desires, or more generally desire-like or desire-entailing mental states (such as wishes, hopes, fears, and so on), were always required for the explanation of actions, and why mere beliefs, by themselves, could never do the job.

If it is now allowed that what (up until now anyway) have always been thought of as *beliefs* also 'count as' desires, it certainly looks as if the essential point has been given up. *Of course*, if we simply *include under the label* 'desire broadly understood' all the items that ever move us, including beliefs about the value or worth of things, while restricting 'beliefs' to (roughly) factual beliefs, then it is hardly surprising that 'desires' in *this* sense are always required. In fact, this sort of move would just be to relable whatever mental state moves one to act as having world-to-word direction of fit; that is, it would in essence give up defending the Humean Theory in favor of the other, uncontentious reading of BD. So it could get nowhere as a way of actually arguing that a proper desire is always needed to move us to act, which was an essential feature of the Humean Theory of Motivation.

But even independently of this, so to speak, 'strategic' problem, assigning this belief world-to-word direction of fit is deeply implausible, though it is worth saying exactly why. For one thing, it leaves the annoying question of what to say of my neighbor's proper *desire* that subsidized day care be a good thing (which he has because he is such a committed liberal that he wants every bit of its moral outlook to be true, even though in this case he can't quite believe it). If my *belief* that subsidized day care is a good thing has world-to-word direction of fit, then it would seem that his *desire* that it be a good thing is rather left out in the cold. Giving my belief world-to-word direction of fit makes this desire and belief in essence the same thing, it would seem, which they clearly are not. In any case, this makes it very hard to see how they could differ, which clearly they do. And giving his desire (that subsidized day care be a good thing) the other (word-to-world) direction of fit classifies it with beliefs, which seems completely absurd. So not only does the direction of fit argument seem much more plausible if it implicitly ignores the fact that one can have beliefs (and desires) about what is good, important, worthwhile, valuable, and the like, as well as about 'facts',[5] such beliefs and desires present it with what seem to be insuperable problems.

There is another, superficially more plausible, way for the defender

[5] I suppose there must be a story to be told here about the connection between this sort of view and the logical positivist analysis of moral assertions as 'non-cognitive'. Without some such background, it is hard to see why anyone would accept so easily the implicit collapse of evaluative beliefs into forms of desire that the direction of fit metaphor entails. But I will leave this story for someone who is more qualified to tell it.

of the Humean Theory to try to deal with this problem.[6] She might say that my belief that subsidized day care is a good thing *causes* me to have a proper desire to promote subsidized day care (which then causes me to vote as I do, and so on). If I understand him, this is in essence the view that Michael Smith supports. As discussed above, on his account of how reasons produce actions, actions are explained (as the Humean Theory reading of BD says) by reference to the agent's (proper) desire to perform an action of a certain kind, plus her belief that the action in question is of that kind. And according to Smith's account of what he calls 'normative reasons', an agent has a *good* reason to phi when it would be rational for that agent to have a desire to phi. Of course, an agent may or may not actually be rational, but if she is, either she already has the desire to do what she has reason to do, or else her realization that she has reason to do it (as, say, when I see that casting my vote for that tax increase would help get something good, e.g. subsidized day care) *produces in her* a desire to do it. As Smith puts it, '[W]hen we deliberate, we try to decide what we have reason to do, and to the extent that we are rational we will either already have corresponding desires or our beliefs about what we have reason to do will cause us to have corresponding desires . . .' (Smith 1994, p. 180)

Smith argues that this allows him to hold onto the Humean Theory claim that '[a]ll actions are indeed produced by desires' (p. 179), while still giving an account of when something is a *good* reason that does not involve or refer to actual desires, only hypothetical ones. Since he admits though that 'some of these desires [that is, the desires that explain actions on his account] are themselves produced by the agent's beliefs about the reasons she has, beliefs she acquires through rational deliberation', (p. 179), it is not clear just how 'Humean' this account really is. It was an essential part of the Humean Theory of Motivation that beliefs alone are not able to move us to act. This is a feature that Smith seems to be giving up when he holds that some of the desires that explain actions are themselves directly produced by rational deliberation. In terms of the distinction between proper desires and pro attitudes, it looks as if Smith is able to maintain that a proper desire is involved in the explanation of every action only by holding that such a desire appears just in those cases where the agent had a pro attitude toward whatever it was she was trying to achieve.

---

[6] The argument of this and the next few paragraphs is adapted from Schueler (1996).

The status of the such proper desires produced by deliberation is therefore problematic. If nothing else, it is a bit difficult to see much substantive difference between a view which says that deliberation (sometimes) produces action all by itself, without the need for any proper desires, and one such as Smith's which says that deliberation (sometimes) produces a proper desire that produces action. In fact, if the desire supposed to be produced by deliberation exists only, so to speak, by courtesy of the fact that, once the agent performs the act in question it will be correct to say of her that she wanted to do it (i.e. that she had a pro attitude toward doing it), then Smith's deliberation-produces-desire–produces-action account will be only a terminological variant of the idea that deliberation produces action directly, the very view supposed to be opposed to the Humean Theory. Setting this aside, however, how plausible is the idea that Smith is advocating, i.e. that, in a rational person, deliberation of the sort that might lead me to the belief that voting for that tax increase will lead to something good at least sometimes *causally produces* a new, proper, desire to perform the act in question?

Consider a different case. I am at my desk, working away, with a mug of coffee within easy reach. At some point I am struck by a desire to have another swig. There was no deliberation; the craving just hit me, perhaps because the aroma of coffee wafted my way just at that moment. But I don't just immediately proceed to have another swig. I deliberate about it. I weigh the fact that I do indeed want another swig against the fact that I have already had several cups of coffee today, the fact that I know more coffee would make me jittery, and so forth. In the end I decide that my original craving for another swig is quite good enough reason to have another swig. So I do.

How exactly does Smith want us to understand this process? In particular, how are we to understand the 'so' here? Smith's view would seem to be that the belief that results from my deliberation, the belief that I have good enough reason to have another swig, causes in me a proper desire to have another swig (which then causes me to have another swig). But of course, I *already* want to have another swig, that was what my deliberation led me to think gave me good enough reason to have another swig. Read this way Smith's view seems to give us one desire too many here.

What Smith actually says is that if I am rational *either* I will already have the appropriate desire, *or* my belief about what I have reason to do will cause me to have such a desire (Smith 1994, p. 180). So perhaps what he wants to say is that in a case of this sort my original desire for another swig takes over, so to speak, and no second desire gets generated. But this can't be right either, since what is required for deliberation here is not an *actual* desire for another swig but merely my *belief* that I have such a desire. My deliberation should go the same way, and have the same result, whether or not that belief is correct (difficult as it might be to imagine it being false in this case). And in any case, there is nothing 'rational' about my original craving for another swig of coffee, even if I am right in deciding that, once I have it, it gives me a reason to have another swig.

What seems needed here is just the distinction between a proper desire (here, my original craving for another swig of coffee, caused perhaps by the aroma of coffee from the mug) and a pro attitude (here, the 'desire' supposed to actually move me to take another swig). But it is far from clear that Smith can allow this distinction. The problem is that, once one allows that deliberation by itself can 'generate' desires, that is desires that are *explained by reference to the reasoning that produces them* and which are thus quite *unlike* the cravings, yens, urges, and the like *on the basis of which* we sometimes reason (and which we can, if we think it best, decide just to ignore), it is difficult to see that there is any real substance left to the claim that a desire of the latter sort is involved in the explanation of every action.

So it seems to me that Smith's defense here really gives up the (or an) essential point of the Humean Theory. The idea that a desire-like mental state is always required for the explanation of any action will turn out to be compatible with the view that was originally being opposed, i.e. that beliefs themselves can lead to actions, since now certain sorts of beliefs can *by themselves* cause the relevant desire-like states. At the same time, the original, proper desire (the craving for another swig) does no work at all in the explanation when the agent actually deliberates. So it certainly seems that at least one of the original motives behind the Humean Theory—that there must always be some element in motivation that is outside our rational control (that, in Hume's famous phrase, 'reason is the slave of the passions')—will have to be dropped. The proper desire recruited by Smith to save the letter of the Humean Theory will get inserted between evaluative belief and action only by a kind of accounting trick that gives up the substance. There is no evidence for the existence of such a desire beyond the fact that the agent actually acts on the basis of her deliberation; and in any case this new desire will do no real work in the explanation since it will itself be completely explained by the evaluative belief that produces it (cf. Nagel 1970, p. 29).

It is worth pointing out here as well that it is very hard to see how such a desire could be defended by the non-teleological belief–desire strategy. It seems to just abandon the point of that strategy, which was to give a *non-teleological* account, presumably causal, of the purposive or goal-directed nature of action explanation, strictly in terms of structural, non-purposive features of certain mental states, proper desires. Once one allows beliefs about what is good and the like to determine whether or not a desire is present, this project is abandoned. This would not be an issue if advocates of the non-teleological desire–belief strategy had an independent account of how mental states (propositional attitudes of certain sorts) with certain inherent or structural features (certain 'directions of fit') interact so as to produce actions and then discovered, so to speak, that our ordinary psychological explanations in terms of agents' reasons can be subsumed as instances of these. We have seen though that no such independent account seems available.

The other example we have been considering seems boringly ordinary: I think it important, and a good thing, that we have state subsidized day care, and this is my reason for voting for a tax increase on which such day care depends. But we have seen that, unless defenders of the Humean Theory of Motivation simply beg the question by insisting that I *must* also have a proper desire to promote good things or the like (i.e. in essence by denying that such a case as I have described is really possible), it is extremely unclear that they can deal with this case. Holding that my belief that state subsidized day care is a good thing is itself some form of desire (with world-to-word direction of fit) both gives up the main point and is anyway totally implausible. And Smith's suggestion, that my belief here itself causes me to have the required proper desire, fares no better.

There is though another difficulty which this sort of example creates for the Humean Theory, one that seems to me more illuminating about why both the Humean Theory reading of BD and the attempt to defend it with the non-teleological belief–desire strategy won't work. This difficulty is also created by the difference between how the agent understands her reasons and how an observer could describe them. It applies independently of how one deals with the sort of difficulty we have been examining, which we might describe as whether the Humean Theory and its supporting direction of fit argument can assign *any* plausible role in the explanation of my vote to my belief that subsidized day care is a good thing. However one decides to deal with that problem, the fact remains that what the non-teleological explanatory strategy has to regard as a proper desire is (or is caused by) something understood by the agent herself as an evaluative belief, at least in cases like the one we have just been considering. The problem is that the only way we can *tell* what exactly the supposed proper desire is here is by *first* figuring out how the agent understands it and whether or not it actually moves her, that is (in the optimum case) how it features in the agent's reasoning about how to act.

This means that the 'direction of explanation' points, so to speak, the wrong way. It is not really that we explain my action by reference to my desire for subsidized day care (or for good things), but rather that we *ascribe* this desire to me by reference to my belief that subsidized day care is a good thing, together with my regarding this belief as a reason—indeed as reason enough—to vote for the tax increase. To put this another way, what I have been calling the observer's point of view on 'the agent's reason', the one in which it is correct to speak of what the agent wants, necessarily *follows* what I have been calling the agent's point of view, the one in which the agent understands herself as reasoning about, for instance, which course of action makes more sense, which has more to be said for it and the like, in deciding what action to perform. The agent's point of view is always prior. It is only once we know how an agent understands the considerations she regards as relevant, which ones she holds more important, etc. (including, very importantly, how she decides to act), that we can figure out which, if any, pro attitudes to ascribe to her.

The general point here seems obvious enough. Clearly, in order to understand some set of movements that someone engages in as the intentional action of 'voting for a tax increase', we have to ascribe various thoughts to her, that is, to see it from her point of view. Unless she has at least most of a very large and probably indefinite set of beliefs, about her physical surroundings, what 'voting' is, and so on, she can't have been intentionally voting for a tax increase, no matter how hard she pushed the button, or pulled the lever or whatever, in the voting booth. Similarly, I want to say, for any explanations in terms of her reasons for *why* she voted as she did. For any intentional action, what the agent did necessarily includes the point or purpose of her action as she sees it, i.e. why she did it.

There is a huge difference between someone who votes for a tax increase because she thinks that all government is evil and that tax increases will eventually so disgust the populace that they will rise up in revolt, and someone who thinks that subsidized day care a good thing and believes this tax increase is required to achieve it. By the same token, there is a difference between this latter person and someone who, say, thinks subsidized day care will benefit her family because it will save them money, or someone who just likes day care centers because they always have such cute names.

In each of these cases, except the first (where the motive is to bring down the government), it will be true that the person in question has a pro attitude toward subsidized day care. But what makes this true in each case will be quite unique. And the only way to establish in any such case *that* there is a pro attitude toward subsidized day care will be to somehow figure out what the person's actual thoughts are on this issue and which of them constituted her reasons for doing what she did. That is the only way to rule out cases like the first one, for instance, or cases where the person hates all subsidies but mistakenly thinks a 'yes' vote on this issue will kill off this one.

What this means is that, whatever other problems the non-teleological belief–desire explanatory strategy has, and I have been arguing that it has plenty, it in any case *presupposes* exactly the sort of purposive explanations that it is supposed to explain. So there is no possibility that it can succeed at its main goal. It is very easy to overlook this, I think, partly because it is easy to misunderstand exactly what the non-teleological belief–desire strategy really *is*, and partly because the lack of any clear terminology for marking off the Humean Theory reading of BD from the purposive reading has allowed advocates of the Humean Theory and the non-teleological belief–desire strategy freely to help themselves to the ordinary, everyday terminology of reasons explanations without noticing that, in the context of the view they are supporting, doing so is illegitimate. It flatly begs the question by making essential use of exactly the sorts of purposive terminology the non-teleological belief–desire strategy is supposed to explain.

3.2 Character Traits[7]

> Just bidin' my time,
> 'Cause that's the kinda guy I'm.
>
> —Ira Gershwin

How then do explanations of actions in terms of the agent's reasons work when we take their purposive nature seriously? As I have already suggested, there are two essential features. The actual purpose or purposes for which the agent acted must be explained and the relevant traits of character of the person who has those purposes have to be set out, if only implicitly. Neither of these should be at all surprising, since we use them all the time. And the first especially has been widely discussed by philosophers under the heading of 'folk psychology', though sometimes these discussions have been offered under the mistaken impression that they somehow support the non-teleological belief–desire strategy. I will discuss below a different account of how such purposive explanations really work. First, however, I want to focus on two other features of this form of explanation: the necessity of the reference to the *character*[8] of the person whose actions are being explained, and the *essentially normative* element of this sort of explanation.

First, character. To stick with the example we have been using, let's suppose that, in deciding whether to vote for that tax increase, I reason as follows:

1. Subsidized day care is a good thing [I say to myself].
2. This proposed tax increase is necessary if there is to be subsidized day care in my community.
3. At the same time, it will cost me some money, which I would like to use elsewhere, if this tax increase is passed.
4. Still, it is more important that my community have subsidized day care than that I keep for my own use the few dollars it will cost me each year.
5. So, I should vote for this tax increase.

---

[7] A somewhat different version of the argument of this section appears in Schueler (2003).

[8] As will become clear below, there is no assumption here that all character traits have a moral element. Some, such as honesty or selfishness, certainly do, but others, such as stubbornness or impulsiveness, do not seem to.

On the basis of this reasoning, let's suppose, I do indeed vote for the tax increase. My neighbor, who votes against this tax increase, accepts word for word the first three premises here (again, let's suppose) but reverses the weight she assigns each of the two facts (or whatever they are) described in the first and third premises. So the forth premise she accepts is not the one above but

　4′.　It is more important that I keep for my own use the few dollars it will cost me each year than that my community have subsidized day care.

What explains the difference in our reasoning (and hence the difference in our votes)? One possibility of course is that our circumstances are different. It could be that her need for those 'few dollars' the tax increase will cost each of us is very much greater than mine. So it could be that, given the difference in our circumstances, each of us reasoned correctly. (This raises the question of whether, for this to happen, the two different fourth premises, 4 and 4′, wouldn't need to be relativized to the two different agents. Does 'more important' here mean 'more important for me' or 'more important, period' so to speak? Let's just set this issue aside for the moment. We can return to it below.)

But let's suppose that our circumstances are relevantly similar, with incomes, expenses, and so forth that don't differ importantly. And to keep it straightforward, let's also suppose that neither of us misjudges our circumstances or how much extra tax we will have to pay. In short, let's suppose that, in our life circumstances, moral views (other than that contested fourth premise), and knowledge of whatever we regard as relevant to this issue, the two of us are essentially the same.[9] The only place we differ is about how to weigh the public good of subsidized day care against our own private interest, that is on the forth premise of the two pieces of reasoning described above.

In this circumstance, it would seem that the obvious explanation for the difference in our reasoning, and hence the difference in our

---

[9] All this agreement is intended to rule out, along with much else, any 'ideological' differences about whether it would be better to have only privately funded day care rather than publicly funded facilities, for instance. More importantly, though, this example is intended to be a 'two-person' analogue of Nagel's 'one-person', example, described in Section 2.2 above, of the person who takes the job for the reasons in favor rather than rejecting it for the reasons against. So of course differences have to be kept to a minimum. This should become clearer below.

votes, is that we are somewhat different kinds of people, with different values or priorities, that is that, really, we have somewhat different characters. I am *the sort of person* who is willing to put aside my own interest, at least when it is a relatively minor one like this, in favor of what I think is a public good (sterling fellow that I am), while my neighbor is not. That is, what this sort of comparison between my neighbor's vote and mine suggests is that, to understand either one of us, we must refer to more than just the considerations each of us acts on. We must also bring in a reference to the kinds of people we are, people who weigh up the same considerations in different ways.

One reason it is easy to miss this point is that the usual account of the agent's reasons as consisting of desires and beliefs invites the idea that this reasoning can be understood in terms of the traditional practical syllogism. As Colin McGinn puts it, 'Whenever someone acts for a reason we can assume some such reasoning [as is represented in the practical syllogism] to have occurred. We can thus say that an action is a bodily movement issuing from such practical reasoning as is codified in the practical syllogism' (McGinn 1979).[10] The problem is that understanding practical reasoning in this way simply ignores the countervailing considerations that agents typically consider when they deliberate. Instead, it focuses only on the single factor that the agent in question ends up regarding as the one to act on.[11] This is a problem inherited by some discussions of BD and of 'folk psychology' as well. On this sort of account, my reasoning in the case we are considering gets transfigured into something like this:

1'. Subsidized day care is a good thing [I say to myself].
2'. This proposed tax increase is necessary if there is to be subsidized day care in my community.
3'. So, I should vote for this tax increase.

By the same token, my neighbor's reasoning gets represented as follows:

1''. It will cost me some money, which I would like to use elsewhere, if this tax increase is passed.

---

[10] As McGinn makes clear (1979, p. 24), this is of course not to say that agents always engage in explicit reasoning whenever they act. They obviously do not.
[11] These problems with the practical syllogism were pointed out long ago by Davidson; see 'How is Weakness of will Possible' in Davidson (1980a).

2″. The only thing I can do toward stopping this tax increase is to vote against it.

3″. So, I should vote against this tax increase.

If taken literally, either as accounts of the reasoning my neighbor and I *actually* used or as accounts of the reasoning we *should* have used, both of these syllogisms are simply inaccurate, given the way I have described things here. Each leaves out any reference to the consideration on which we did not act, and also any description of the weight or evaluation each of us gave the two factors we considered (which I am representing in the two different versions of the fourth premise in the two pieces of reasoning described on pp. 69–70.). Understanding practical reasoning in terms of the practical syllogism thus can easily lead one to ignore completely the possibility that two agents can each be aware of exactly the same set of considerations—moral and factual—and yet, from differences in character, weigh these considerations differently (a situation that in ordinary life seems rather common).

One might say that, except for the simplest of cases, the practical syllogism accurately describes the practical reasoning only of the very narrow minded or the very badly informed. But even this is too generous, since practical reasoning occurs, makes sense in fact, only where a choice is possible, and as we have seen, the practical syllogism in its traditional form is incapable of giving any account of the weighing up of pros and cons that is the essence of deliberating about how to choose. (We will examine much more fully below the question of what is the correct account of practical reasoning, the one with which to replace the practical syllogism.)

A second, perhaps less obvious, reason why it is easy to miss the importance of referring to the agent's character in explaining her actions is that it is easy to make the mistake of understanding either my or my neighbor's version of the fourth premise in our reasoning as referring to 'what is important *to me*' rather than simply to 'what is important. That would be a variety of the mistake that we already noted above for the other premises in discussing the belief–desire strategy, as well as the mistake that seems to lead to the third or 'normative' reading of BD. It is the mistake of reading the third-person/observer's point of view, where reference is made to the pro attitudes of the agent, into the *content* of the reasoning as it appears to the agent.

Someone who weighs the public good of subsidized day care against her own interest in retaining the few extra dollars this would cost her and then decides that the former is more important (or that the latter is) is *already* thereby weighing her own concerns against those of the public at large. The version of the fourth premise that I accept (4 above), or rather the fact that I accept it, shows that I am the sort of person who regards the public interest in this situation as more important than my own interest in those extra few dollars, *not* that I am the sort of person who regards the public interest as more important *to me*.

That would be a different thought, a *factual* belief about the sort of person I am (or about what I regard as important), rather than an *evaluative* belief about the relative importance of subsidized day care and my having a few extra dollars each year. The public interest *is* more important to me (at least in this case). That is shown by the fact that I accept and act on premise 4 above. People of course sometimes hold that their own concerns are more important than those of the public generally; that is how I am portraying my neighbor in this example. But to understand the two people who reason in terms of the two versions of the fourth premise above as necessarily referring (at least implicitly) to what is important 'to them' is to misstate the difference between my neighbor and myself. It would be to mistake what I have been calling an external or observer's description of our attitudes (which would indeed be that having subsidized day care is more important to me, that is something I want more, than having those few extra dollars, and vice versa for my neighbor) for the *content* of our reasoning (which, in my case, is that having subsidized day care is more important than those few extra dollars). What makes the external description true, in my case, is that I think subsidized day care for our community is more important than my having those few extra dollars, and that thought is what moves me to vote as I do.

It is, I hope, clear enough how understanding practical reasoning in terms of the practical syllogism covers up the importance of referring to the character of the person doing the reasoning. In the case we are discussing, it does this by ignoring the need to refer to different versions of the fourth premise in the reasoning my neighbor and I engage in. But the second sort of mistake just described also covers up the importance of referring to the character of the reasoner by making it seem as if both of us look only at *our own* concerns in deciding how to vote. Reading 'importance' in the two versions of the fourth premises of our reasoning as 'importance for me' makes it seem as if all practical reasoning is necessarily egocentric or self centered, in the sense that the only thing anyone considers, or even can possibly consider, is her own interests and concerns.

Speaking of differences in character in such a situation will then seem quite disingenuous. Everyone will appear as profoundly, indeed *necessarily*, focused only on their own concerns. But in fact, as I hope is clear, this is a mistake. Neither of us, in the reasoning I described, looks *only* at our own concerns. Each of us weighs, that is evaluates the importance of, our own concerns, in this case represented by premise 3, against the public good of subsidized day care, which each of us also evaluates positively.

To understand the two versions of the fourth premise in this reasoning as referring for each agent to what is important *to that agent* would be to make both of the original two pieces of reasoning described above automatically and obviously fallacious. In fact, if accepted generally, it would seem to make any sort of non-fallacious practical reasoning impossible. As stated above, the premises of the original two arguments at least appear to support the conclusions drawn—and do in fact support it, I want to say. But if 'more important' is understood as 'more important for me' in each case, each piece of reasoning becomes an example of the fallacy traditionally known as *ignoratio elenchi*.[12] This is because the fourth premise in each piece of reasoning would now no longer evaluate the importance of the first and third considerations, and hence if true provide reason to accept the conclusion. Each version of the fourth premise now would simply report a fact about the person doing the reasoning and as such would become flatly irrelevant to the question of which way she or I *should* vote.

Genuinely evaluative premises, of the sort represented by the two versions of the fourth premise in the two pieces of practical reasoning we have been looking at, are essential to practical reasoning. (Or at least so I claim. We will examine this issue more carefully below). Accounts of practical reasoning that leave such premises out, as the standard 'practical syllogism' account does, according to some ways

---

[12] On the assumption that I am not the only one for whom 'Intro Logic' (not to mention first-year Latin) is only a distant memory, this is the fallacy more prosaically called 'irrelevant conclusion'. It sounds better in Latin though.

of understanding it,[13] or that distort evaluations into factual claims about the interests, attitudes or psychology of the person doing the reasoning, as reading 'important' to mean 'important to me' would do, make genuine, non-fallacious practical rationality impossible. Such accounts thus help clear the way for the sort of non-teleological, causal accounts criticized above. They make it seem that the actual reasoning agents use to decide what to do isn't worth looking at, since it is really never any good. Worse, they give a false account of explanations of actions in terms of the agent's reasons. They make it seem, one might say, that even the agents themselves are not so much *doing* the reasoning as observing or describing themselves doing it. (I will, as I said, return to this issue below.)

It is possible, of course, to describe the facts about the characters of my neighbor and myself that are revealed in our acceptance of the two different versions of the fourth premise externally, so to speak, in terms of different pro attitudes we have, or perhaps in terms of different strengths of these pro attitudes. By itself there is nothing objectionable in this unless we mistakenly think that this is the whole story. This is what the non-teleological belief–desire strategy would have us do, as a precondition for giving an account of the two different votes in terms of the different interactions of our different sets of desires. That is, what seem to me and to my neighbor to be actions *based on* reasoning involving different judgments about the relative importance of a public good and our own interests will be interpreted by the non-teleological belief–desire strategy, externally, in terms of 'pro attitudes' and then will be explained as being caused by different desires, or perhaps by the interaction of desires of different strengths, toward the public good and self-interest.

Describing these different votes and the reasoning behind them in terms of different pro attitudes is not false. It is one way to describe the difference between my neighbor and myself, from an observer's point of view so to speak. But this can be a source of confusion if it is taken to somehow support the non-teleological belief–desire strategy, which it does not. The same problems discussed in the previous section arise here. For instance, the contents of the judgments made by me and by my neighbor get distorted by the shift from our evaluative beliefs to 'pro attitudes' in the way described above. Similarly,

---

[13] See e.g. Robert Audi's discussion of the practical syllogism in Audi (1989, p. 99). Audi's account will be discussed below.

for reasons already given, reference to our pro attitudes and their strengths cannot be used to explain accounts in terms of our reasons, since such accounts are logically prior to pro attitude descriptions. In the case we are examining, the only evidence an observer could have that I *have* a pro attitude toward publicly subsidized day care is that my belief that it is a good thing is used by me in the reasoning described above as a reason for voting for that tax increase.

But there is an additional point to be made beyond these earlier ones. The reference to the *character traits* of the person acting on the basis of this reasoning is simply not eliminable in favor of some set of pro attitudes and beliefs. References to character traits as elements of explanations of actions will seem deeply problematic, of course, if one thinks of them the way Ryle for instance often seems to, as *nothing but* 'propensities', that is if one thinks of the names of character traits as standing for nothing but dispositions to behave in certain ways. (Ryle 1949, chapter 4).

It is hard to see how dispositions of *this* sort could be used to explain the behavior at issue in any but the 'virtus dormativa' sense of 'explain'. On this account of character traits, we would 'explain' the fact that someone acted impulsively, say, by referring to the fact that he was disposed to be impulsive. This problem seems to force anyone who wants to include character traits in the account of explanations of actions into giving an analysis of these traits in terms of their underlying features, on the model of an account in terms of molecular structure of the dispositional property some objects have of being water soluble. And what more obvious underlying features for analyzing character traits than some sets of pro attitudes (a thought that would allow character traits to dovetail nicely with the non-teleological desire–belief strategy)? But I want to argue that neither the 'plain' (Ryle-like) 'dispositional' account nor any 'set of pro attitudes' account of character traits gets them right. This will perhaps be clearer if we shift to a different case and a different character trait.

Suppose I know a generous person. By seeing that this person has this character trait, I am able to understand, give an explanation of, why, in certain circumstances, he acts and reasons as he does. Of course, for any particular action in which this character trait plays a role, I will be able, if I know enough of the details, to describe his action in terms of his factual beliefs and 'pro attitudes' (some of which, I hope it is now clear, may really just be evaluative beliefs of course). But knowing that he is generous, I will also be able to see *why* he has some of these evaluative beliefs and other pro attitudes.

It might seem possible that we could, if we worked at it, spell out what it is to be generous in terms of some set of pro attitudes (and perhaps the relevant factual beliefs). But even if we got this completely right, in the sense of describing a set of attitudes that fit all (and only those) people who were generous (above some minimum), it would be a mistake to think that we had somehow done away with the need to refer to generosity itself, the character trait. People after all sometimes do generous things, and thus have the relevant particular pro attitude, but not from generosity. There is a difference between someone who does something generous, say gives some of her money to someone who needs it, on a whim or from a momentary feeling of generosity or to impress a friend or salve her conscience, and someone who gives this money *out of simple generosity*.[14]

So, even if we could set out completely the set of beliefs and attitudes that are in some sense extensionally equivalent to the character trait of generosity, we would lose something in explaining some act only by reference to some members of this set of attitudes and beliefs. We would still need to know why this particular set of beliefs and attitudes hang together as a unit, so to speak, and how that unit *itself* figured in explaining the action in question (when it did), before we could get from explaining some particular action on the basis of one or a few of these attitudes and beliefs to seeing it in terms of the whole set, that is in terms of the character trait.

Suppose I discover that you gave your neighbor's son your old car. I find out something of why you did this when I find out that you wanted, or perhaps thought it important, to do something to help him out and he needed a car (as opposed to wanting to get that eyesore out of your driveway, for instance). But your pro attitude toward doing something that would help him out, by itself, connects to nothing further, even if I know that you also have the other attitudes and beliefs in the extensionally described set supposed to be coextensive with generosity. The mere fact that you *have* all these

---

[14] There might be cases where we were inclined to say that someone had acted 'out of generosity' even though she wasn't 'a generous person', that is where she did not have the character trait of generosity. She acts 'out of character', as we say. This and numerous other cases raise the issue of the exact nature of the explanation being offered when a reference is made to character traits in these ways.

other attitudes and beliefs in this set by itself does nothing to explain this particular act of yours. All those other pro attitudes and beliefs in this set are, so far at least, simply idle as far as this explanation is concerned. There is still the question: why did you want (or think it important) to help him out? And the mere fact that you have all those other attitudes and beliefs that are supposed to constitute or be coextensive with generosity, by itself, does nothing to answer that question.

There may of course be a further attitude or belief that explains this one: perhaps you wanted him to be in your debt. If that really was your reason for wanting to help him out, then your action doesn't look quite so generous after all. That particular attitude—desire to put someone in your debt—probably isn't a member of the relevant set (the one supposed to be coextensive with the character trait of generosity). But, whether or not there is a further reason of yours to explain why you wanted to help him out, any such explanations will come to an end somewhere, and I want to say that one such place that lets us make sense of the explanation is in a character trait such as generosity. It could be for instance that you don't have any further reason, such as a desire to put him in your debt, to explain why you wanted to help him out. It could be that you wanted to help him out simply because you are a generous person.

So there are two points here. Reference to a character trait such as generosity *explains* (or certainly seems to explain) the having of certain beliefs and attitudes in a way that merely citing the fact that the attitude in question is a member of some extensionally described set cannot. At the same time, reference to a character trait moves outside the 'chain of reasons', and so doesn't leave the explanation hanging, so to speak, in the way that explaining one attitude in terms of another that constitutes your reason for having it does. If we find out that you wanted to help out your neighbor's son because you wanted to put him in your debt, we are left with the question of why you wanted to put him in your debt. That is, we are left with the same *sort* of question all over again, in a way that we are not when we find that you wanted to help him out because you are a generous person.

The difference here is that attitudes such as wanting to help someone out and wanting to put someone in your debt are things that can themselves be explained in terms of the agent's reasons for having them. So when we explain your wanting to help him out in terms of your wanting to put him in your debt, we are explaining one thing for which you can have a reason—your wanting to help him out—by citing another thing for which you can have a reason—your wanting put him in your debt. That clearly leaves us with the question of what your reason was for having that second attitude, i.e. of wanting to put him in your debt. And this sort of question will arise whether or not the second attitude is a member of the appropriate extensionally described set. Nothing about the fact that the second attitude is (or is not) a member of that set means that you couldn't have it 'for a reason' as well.

But character traits are typically not things that one has for a reason, at least in anything like the same way. Though you may well have a reason for wanting to put someone into your debt, and then give him your old car for that reason, it doesn't seem likely that you are a generous person 'for a reason'. Of course, the fact that you are generous, like any fact, may have an explanation, and in *that* sense we may speak of 'a reason why you are generous', (just as there may be a reason why you are nearsighted or right handed). Your generosity might be explained by the way you were raised, the sort of parents you had, or the like. But if generosity is a character trait, then it is not something like giving someone your old car or wanting to put him in your debt, where it makes sense to speak of your reason for doing or wanting these things. The shift to character traits in this way is, so to speak, a shift out of the first-person point of view, of the sort required when referring explicitly to 'the agent's reasons', to an essentially external or observer's point of view.[15]

So when we explain your wanting to help him out by citing the fact that you are a generous person, the explanation in terms of your reasons comes to an end at that point. The claim I am making then is that at least one clear way explanations of actions in terms of the agent's reasons can come to a satisfactory end is by referring, either explicitly or implicitly, to some character trait. This is a satisfactory end in the sense that we are not left with a question of exactly the same sort still unanswered, as we are if the answer is in terms of an attitude that is itself one you can hold for a reason.

In short, when we explain your giving him your old car by referring to the fact that you want to help him out, one of two things happens. Either you have a reason for wanting to help him out, a

---

[15] Typically at least. The issue of whether one can have such a trait intentionally will be taken up below.

reason we need to find to understand your action; or, in finding this particular attitude of yours, we have found out what *sort* of person you are, i.e. the sort who wants to help someone in this kind of circumstance. If we understand the answer in this second way, then the explanation comes to an end; no further explanation seems needed or appropriate, since we have found a feature of your character that itself explains the attitude. It is very much the same kind of thing that happens when we find that someone is doing something in order to avoid pain. It is not that one couldn't have a reason for wanting to avoid pain, since of course one could. (Pain can be very distracting, for instance.) It is simply that virtually all normal humans are the sorts of people (even the 'sorts of beings') who do indeed want this.[16]

It may be worth noting in passing that the account of the place of character traits in explanations of actions in terms of the agent's reasons that I am suggesting seems not to be subject to the objection on which Ryle's more 'minimalist' account of character traits seems to founder. As was mentioned above, Ryle often speaks as if character traits are *mere* dispositions, while at the same time he disallows any account of these traits in terms of their underlying features (Ryle 1949).[17] That seems to leave character traits as 'dormitive virtues' of the sort Moliere joked about. It would mean 'explaining' a bit of generous behavior by reference to the character trait of generosity and at the same time saying that generosity was nothing but the propensity to do generous things.

Since I have argued, more or less following Ryle, that character traits are not reducible to sets of desires and beliefs (which could then perhaps be understood to interact causally to produce actions), it may be useful to say explicitly why the account sketched here is not

---

[16] 'Ask a man *why he uses exercise*', Hume says; 'he will answer *because he desires to keep his health*. If you then enquire, *why he desires health*, he will reply, *because sickness is painful*. If you push your enquiries further and desire a reason *why he hates pain*, it is impossible he can ever give any. This is an ultimate end and is never referred to any other object' (Hume 1957, App. 1). One might think Hume is not quite right here, since of course one can have a reason for wanting to avoid pain; e.g., as mentioned above, it could be distracting, or it could keep one from getting to sleep. But in fact he speaks of 'hating pain', and in that I think he is right. It is a feature of humans, or normal ones anyway, that they 'hate pain'. We might not call this feature a 'character trait' but I think that this is only because, unlike generosity, say, or selfishness, hating pain seems virtually universal.

[17] Dennett points out that we could agree with Ryle about the meanings of character trait terms while still seeking an empirical theory to explain how these traits could work as they do (Dennett 1987, pp. 44–45).

subject to this same *virtus dormitiva* objection. The central point is that on the view we have been examining character traits are essentially features of reasons explanations of actions.[18] (They are thus essentially personal level facts.) To say that someone has a certain character trait is to say, roughly, that certain sorts of facts count for her as reasons (perhaps of a certain strength) to do certain sorts of things. That is why reference to a character trait can serve to stop the 'chain of reasons' by citing a feature of the agent which both explains why she took something as a reason for acting and is not itself something for which she can have a reason. No doubt there is a dispositional element in this, but it is at least not the sort of uninformative circle that Ryle's purely dispositional account of character traits seems to give us.

It is part of my argument here that character traits are not the sorts of things that agents have 'for reasons' in the way actions or some attitudes are. But couldn't someone be a generous person intentionally, so to speak? For instance, couldn't someone be persuaded to be generous by reading moral philosophy, say, and simply finding the reasons for being generous unrefutable? The answer certainly seems to be 'yes'. One could be persuaded to adopt what we might call a policy of generosity, of always or whenever possible doing the generous thing. And I think there is no doubt that someone who standardly followed such a policy, even with the occasional lapse, would be thought to 'be generous' or to 'be a generous person'.

To see what is happening here, it will help to contrast the kind of case we have been discussing, where a reasons explanation comes to an end in a reference to the agent's character, with the superficially similar but in fact very different case where the agent takes *the fact that* it would exemplify a certain character trait as a reason for performing some action. This is the case if for instance your reason for wanting to help out your neighbor's son was that helping him out would be the generous thing to do. In this sort of case, the 'chain of reasons' hasn't come to an end with your desire to help him out. You have a further reason for wanting this, namely that this would be the generous thing to do. But citing this fact as your reason still leaves us with the further question of why you want to do what is generous

---

[18] Or at least the ones I want to talk about are. If, say, clumsiness is a character trait, then it is not one of the ones I am referring to since it seems to apply only to things done unintentionally or accidentally and so not to things for which one could have reasons.

(why you have adopted this policy, why you think the fact that it would be the generous thing to do gives you a reason to do it).

The answer to that further question *might* be simply that you are a generous person in the way we have been discussing, since one way of exemplifying the character trait of generosity is consciously to try to be generous, that is, to have generosity as an explicit ideal. If that is what is happening, then, again, we have arrived at a reference to a character trait and no further 'reasons' question arises. But it is also possible that you have a still further reason for wanting to do what is generous, i.e. that it is not that you want to do this just because you are a generous person. A generous person is someone who *has* that particular character trait, not merely, and also not necessarily, someone who does things because the acts *exemplify* generosity.[19] As was said, you might want to do something that exemplifies generosity (and so want to help him out) because you have been persuaded to adopt this policy by your reading of moral philosophy. But equally, you could simply want others to think well of you; i.e., you might have adopted the *policy* of doing what is generous because you are a self-promoter, which is a very different sort of character trait from generosity.

Someone who takes as a reason for wanting to help someone out that it would be the generous thing to do (or the like) might do this because she is generous, but at the same time she *might* have, in Bernard Williams's phrase, 'one thought too many', since this is consistent with merely wanting to appear to be generous and so consistent with not actually being generous. But in any case, the point to notice is that in this sort of case, unlike the case where reference is made to the fact that the agent really is generous, the agent's reasons don't come to an end with a desire to help the other person out. We are still left with the question of what reason the agent has for wanting to do the generous thing. So in a case where this happens the explanation of the action in terms of the agent's reasons hasn't reached completion; the action has not yet really been explained. To see the issues involved here it will be better, I think, if we set this ('policy') sort of case aside for a moment. We can return to it below when we have gotten a bit clearer about the other sort of case we have focused on so far, where the 'chain of reasons' in fact runs out and the

---

[19] This is a feature of virtues that Williams thinks is widely true of virtues generally (Williams 1985, p. 10).

explanation shifts to a trait of character to explain the sort of person who uses these reasons.

If the discussion of this sort of case has been on the right track so far, then it has at least two interesting consequences. The first is that we have uncovered here a feature of reasons explanations of this kind, their dependence on references to traits of character of the agent who performed the action in question, that seems in no way reducible to, or explainable in, the terms required by the belief–desire strategy. There are many common cases of explanation of actions in terms of the agent's reasons where reference to the agent's character is an essential part of the explanation, even if this reference is only implicit. If, as I have argued, character traits cannot be 'reduced' to sets of desires and beliefs, then such attitudes will not be the only elements in explanations of actions in terms of the agents' reasons. Character traits, as a distinct kind of element, will be needed as well. This is not something that the move to the form of explanation advocated by defenders of the belief–desire strategy can accommodate.

Such a feature of reasons explanations creates another sort of difficulty for the belief–desire strategy as well, since, and this is the second consequence, descriptions of someone's character are very often *inherently* evaluative, as the generosity example should make clear. That is, character descriptions at least frequently involve what Williams calls 'thick moral concepts' (Williams 1985, chapter 8), meaning roughly that, while they are sometimes required for the accurate description of someone, they also contain an ineliminable moral or evaluative element. So if the argument above is correct, it follows that explanations of actions in terms of the agent's reasons at least sometimes must involve *evaluations* of a certain sort, for instance in at least some of those cases where to be complete the explanation must involve reference to some such character trait of the agent. Some character traits, such as impulsiveness, may perhaps carry no automatic evaluation, but many, such as generosity, certainly seem to.

Non-teleological, causal analyses of reasons explanations of the sort exemplified by the belief–desire strategy completely ignore this feature of these explanations, of course, as they must, since they hope to account for the explanatory force of reasons explanations causally, without any reference to such frequently evaluative concepts as character traits. But reference to traits of character is crucial to at least some explanations of action in terms of the agent's reasons. At the same time, it provides both the most obvious way in which the 'chain of reasons' comes to a natural end, and a clear place where, often at least, evaluation enters such explanations.

The considerations about character traits that we have just been surveying here go at least some way toward solving the puzzle about how reasons explanations of actions actually explain; the puzzle that I argued in Section 2.2 above was not really answered by the non-teleological belief–desire explanatory strategy with its claim that the agent's reasons 'cause' the action. As Thomas Nagel put it, the problem is that

[i]ntentional explanation, if there is such a thing, can explain either choice [to perform or not perform some action] in terms of the appropriate reasons, since either choice would be intelligible if it occurred. But for this very reason it cannot explain why the person . . . [performed the action] . . . for the reasons in favor . . . [instead of not performing it]. . . for the reasons against. (T. Nagel 1990, pp. 115–116)

If I am right in thinking that at least some reasons explanations of actions always involve at least an implicit reference to some character trait of the agent, then this looks like a start on a solution to this puzzle, in general at least, though specific cases may still present difficulties. The solution is to notice that merely referring to the agent's reason or reasons for doing what she did is to leave out an essential element of 'intentional explanations', as Nagel calls them. That element is the relevant character trait of the agent in question. The two parallel examples earlier in this section of my neighbor, who voted against that proposed tax increase, and me, who voted for it, contain all the same elements as Nagel's example of the person who takes the job for the reasons in favor rather than refuses it for the reasons against. The only difference is that, in place of Nagel's job seeker who makes one choice and not the other, I have imagined two similar people who nevertheless choose to vote differently. But the explanation in each case is the same (or of the same sort). Leaving complications aside for the moment, in each case the rejected alternative makes sense once we notice the *sort* of person involved. By the same token, not knowing the relevant character trait or traits leaves us with just the sort of incomplete explanation Nagel presents.

Nagel's example about choosing whether to take a job looks puzzling, as does for instance Davidson's discussion of the difficulty in accounting for the force of the 'because' in explanations where an agent acted for one reason and not another, partly at least because no details about the context of the action, the specific reasons, or the character of the agent are included. Once such details are filled in, even in the rather minimal way they were in the parallel voting cases, reference to a character trait of the agent can dissolve the puzzle. We can see this by adding a few such details (made up of course) to Nagel's job choosing example. Nagel gives us none of the agent's actual reasons, nor does he say anything about the agent's character. But suppose the reasons in favor of taking the job were that it involved lots of television exposure and had some prospects for advancement, while the reasons against were that it involved a complete change of profession and taking a significant salary cut. On the face of it, as Nagel says, learning that this person took the job for the reasons in favor leaves it very unclear why he didn't reject it for the reasons against. But if we also know, for instance, that he is quite vain, the puzzle seems to dissolve.

Of course, even in those cases reference to a character trait won't provide a *mechanical* explanation of how the reason led to the action at issue, of the sort the non-teleological desire–belief strategy wants (though we have already seen the problems with that strategy). But if character traits enter into reasons explanations in the way I am suggesting, it may be a mistake to think that the incompleteness of action explanations of the sort Nagel describes even can be, let alone must be, completed by reference to mechanical causation.

Even if the suggestion made here is accepted, though, plenty of issues remain. For instance, there is the question of what happens when the agent has several different character traits and all are relevant to the act in question. Being generous does not *exclude* also being a self-promoter, for example. And more generally, human beings standardly (perhaps even necessarily) have numerous character traits, some of which clash or conflict at least some of the time. Then too, people sometimes 'turn over new leaves' or act 'out of character'. Generous people do not always act generously and people who are not generous sometimes do. But though these and other problems will undoubtedly be very common and will raise questions of how explanation in such cases works, the existence of such cases doesn't (or at least needn't) call into question the sort of answer being suggested here for Nagel's puzzle. That puzzle, after all, did not depend on any such complications. It applies to even the simplest cases of 'intentional explanation' and if unsolved would stop *any* such explanation of action in its tracks. The complexities mentioned here (and no doubt there are many others) only show that the problem Nagel describes for intentional explanation is not the only one. These complexities remain even if the suggestion explored here for solving this puzzle, for at least some of the simplest cases, is accepted.

A deeper problem might seem to be suggested by the issue we set aside a few paragraphs above. If someone can be generous *for a reason*, by as I put it adopting a 'policy' of generosity, then how can appeal to a character trait such as generosity serve to halt the chain of reasons and provide a way of solving Nagel's puzzle? The answer I think is that, in a situation where this happens, the puzzle is not yet solved. But it seems a bit implausible to think that all, or even many, generous people are generous because they have adopted a policy of generosity for some reason. And of course, generosity is being used only as one example here. The suggestion that policies of exemplifying character traits are often (let alone always) adopted intentionally seems even less plausible if we think how many traits this would involve (being, e.g. trustworthy, loyal, helpful, friendly, courteous, kind, obedient, cheerful, thrifty, brave, fair, etc.), especially when we recall that it will also have to cover less attractive traits such as stinginess and vanity (as well as untrustworthiness, disloyalty, and so on).

So it seems plausible that in most cases character traits will *not* be exemplified as matters of intentional policy.[20] In those cases the suggestion here will apply straightforwardly. And for at least some of the other cases, where there is an intentional policy of exemplifying some trait, the reason the policy was adopted by the agent will itself be subject to the sort of suggestion about the role of character that we have been examining. If the fact that some action of mine would be a generous thing to do itself counted for me as a reason for doing it, then, to that point at least, we still face the puzzle Nagel describes of why I performed the act for the reasons in favor rather than rejected it for the reasons against. So, the suggestion is, we can solve this puzzle (or at least, given the other issues surveyed above, take a first step toward solving it) by finding a further (we might say 'real') character trait of mine that explains why I took this fact (that it would be generous) as a reason for performing this action.

Are there other sorts of cases, cases where the suggestion we have

---

[20] Not to mention the fact that at least some character traits would seem not to allow an intentional policy at all. Modesty and shyness seem to be examples.

been examining won't work because, so to speak, the agent's reasons 'go all the way down' and there is no room, or perhaps no need, for stepping outside the chain of reasons, in the way we have been discussing, to look at the character of the person who is doing the reasoning? Would this perhaps be the case of someone who looked with complete objectivity at all the relevant reasons, presumably many from the depths of moral philosophy, and then performed that action (or that kind of action) that objectively had the most reason on its side? For such a case to serve as an objection to the suggestion I am making, the agent could *only* have character traits that were intentionally adopted, so that *no* appeal to any of her character traits would stop the 'chain of reasons' in the way I have argued such appeals usually do. Is such a case possible? I am not sure.[21] If it is, though, then, in that case at least, the puzzle Nagel describes will remain unsolved.

Setting the possibility of such a case aside, however, the suggestion here seems to provide a way of starting to meet what Mele called 'Davidson's Challenge' to give an account of how reasons explanations explain, an account that does not appeal to a non-teleological, causal mechanism. It argues that at the very least it may be a mistake to hold that explanatory 'gap' in reasons explanations of the sort Nagel and Davidson cite can be completed only by reference to mechanical causation of the sort the non-teleological strategy proposes.

---

[21] For one thing, it would seem that such a person couldn't ever make any mistakes in reasoning (that is, couldn't be understood as ever making any mistakes) since there would be nothing about her to account for such mistakes, in the way that character traits such as impulsiveness do for the rest of us.

4

Explanations in Terms of the Agent's Reasoning

The point made in Chapter 3, that explanations of actions in terms of the agent's reasons are inherently evaluative, is in fact implicit in the account of practical reasoning that emerged earlier, even if we set aside the necessity of referring to the agent's character in the way just explained. It was argued above that practical reasoning necessarily involves an evaluative element. It was also claimed that this point is in no way undercut by the fact that it is often correct to describe the agent's reasons, from an observer's point of view so to speak, in terms of her pro attitudes toward something. I want now to explain these points in more detail. We will need eventually to look carefully at the issue of how the fact that practical reasoning must include evaluative elements shows that explanations of actions in terms of the agent's reasons are themselves inherently evaluative. But we can put that issue aside for the moment and look at the claim that practical reasoning must include an evaluative element. The most straightforward place to start is with the so-called 'practical syllogism', since it is often taken as a paradigm example of practical reasoning and, as usually described, seems to lack any evaluative element.

4.1 Problems with the Practical Syllogism

It is obvious that there are instances of genuine, explicit practical deliberation that result in actions. (People at least sometimes *do* actually *take* their mothers' advice and *think* before they act.) As we will see below, this a crucial fact for understanding explanations of actions in terms of agents' reasons. At the same time, probably as with any sort of reasoning, those engaged in actual practical deliberation will occasionally leave many or even sometimes all of the essential steps unstated, even 'to themselves'. Likewise, there are probably instances where the things to be considered are so few that, even if all the relevant factors of the situation were explicitly considered, not all the essential features of this sort of reasoning would emerge.

In any case though, and most importantly, it is essential to distinguish two very different kinds of questions. On one side there are *psychological* questions of at least two sorts. First, there is the question of what, so to speak, 'ran through the mind' of someone who was in the process of figuring out what to do, as would happen for instance if the agent explicitly deliberates about what to do. And, second, there is the different, if sometimes connected, question of what this person's reasons really were. It might not always be apparent even to the person herself, of course, what her reasons for doing what she did really were, at least without some serious self reflection. So knowing what ran through her mind, even if we allow that this tells us what she thought her reasons were, won't always tell us what they really were. But such psychological questions, interesting as they are, need to be sharply distinguished from, on the other side, the very different, *normative* question of what sorts of things really do provide good reasons for acting. That is, to put this another way, *someone's* reasons for doing something, i.e. what really did move her to do what she did, may or may not be *good* reasons for so acting, may or may not meet the relevant standard, whatever exactly it is. So we need to distinguish the psychological question of what someone's reasons really are for doing what she does from the normative question of what that standard is.[1]

It will help in this discussion to focus on specific examples; but at the same time for some reason in this context examining examples always seems to tempt one into psychology, perhaps because there is frequently some distance between the two psychological questions distinguished above (and it is so much fun to point that out). The things a person explicitly considers, what 'runs through her mind', could turn out to be only rationalizations; that is, they may or may not be what really moves her to do what she does, what her real reasons are. That is a psychological question. But it is the other, normative, question with which I want to begin. We will return to the psychological question, and the issue of how the two are connected, below.

---

[1] This is I think the distinction Michael Smith (1994) is aiming at in distinguishing what he calls 'motivating reasons' from what he calls 'normative reasons'. I have explained why I think the way he draws his distinction is problematic in Schueler (1996).

So here is one kind of example. Suppose that, standing on the side-walk waiting for the bus one afternoon, I suddenly see a car careen-ing out of control toward me and just manage to jump out of the way in the nick of time. In a case like this it would simply be false as a matter of psychological fact to say that I *reasoned* to the (practical) conclusion that I should jump out of the way, any more than that I reasoned to the (factual) conclusion that the car would hit me unless I moved. I didn't do any reasoning at all, 'theoretical' or 'practical', in all likelihood, if by that is meant explicitly considering premises and drawing conclusions in some sort of 'inner monologue'. I simply saw *that* the car was about to hit me (a factual conclusion drawn from what I more literally saw), realized at once what I obviously *should* do (a practical conclusion), and luckily was able to do it. We have already seen that the practical syllogism is defective as a general account of how practical reasoning either does or should go. At the same time, it might seem plausible in a case of this sort to say that at least a very close approximation to the correct reasoning for me to have used (that is, the considerations that made it the case that this was indeed what I *should* do) would more or less fit a practical syllogism of the following sort:

- I don't want to be seriously injured or killed in the next few seconds (that is, I want this not to happen, I want to avoid it).
- I can avoid being seriously injured or killed in the next few seconds if I immediately jump out of the way of this %&$# car.
- So, I should immediately jump out of the way of this car.

A case of this sort is exceptional, as I said, in that I didn't, do and in an obvious sense probably couldn't have done, any actual reason-ing. There just wasn't enough time. It is also exceptional in that there was apparently only one action—jumping out of the way—that had anything at all to be said for it. Clearly, there are cases of the sort already discussed that differ from this one, not merely in that the agent actually does engage in some reasoning, but also in that there is more than one course of action that had something to be said for it and more than one consideration to be weighed in deciding what to do. We will look more carefully at that sort of case in a moment.

It is important however to notice that, *even in this case*, where a practical syllogism of the sort just given certainly seems to fit if it fits anywhere, I *could have* decided not to jump out of the way, if for some reason that had seemed to me the thing to do (and I had been able to think fast enough, or perhaps had planned for it in advance). So even in this case the above practical syllogism does *not* in fact accurately represent the way I *should* have reasoned, if I had had the chance, simply because it provides no place to represent that alternative.

Presumably we are implicitly assuming, if we represent how I should have reasoned by the above practical syllogism, that there was nothing at all to be said in favor of not jumping. And, even though that is correct in this case as I have described it, it does not follow that the general form of practical reasoning can, so to speak, ignore the *possibility* that there is something to be said for not jumping even in a case of this sort. That very fact, that there is nothing at all to be said for not jumping out of the way, is relevant to my decision in this case, or at least to the question of how rational my decision was, and hence should be represented in the account of what the correct reasoning would be in this case. In other, perhaps very similar, cases there will actually be something to be said for not jumping (perhaps, for example, if I put others at greater risk if I jump).

So if we understand the question here to be not the psychological one of what reasoning I did in fact go through (answer: none), or even the related but 'deeper' psychological one of what actually moved me to jump (i.e. whether or not I realized it), what *my* reason for jumping really was (answer: I did not want to get killed or injured), but rather the *normative* one of what is the correct way to represent the reasoning I *should*, rationally, have gone through if I had had the chance (that is, what the correct reasoning would be here, what made it the case so to speak that I really had good reason to jump out of the way), we need to include a place for representing the possibility that there was something to be said for not jumping.

But once we notice this, we should also notice something else. It is not only that we are assuming (or asserting, since this is just a made up case) that there is nothing to be said for *not* jumping out of the way of that car. We are equally, and by the same token, assuming that my desire not to be run over by that car *is* a reason *for* jumping out of the way.

That may seem obvious, and I hope it is. But it is worth focusing on because not all conceptions of practical reasoning, and certainly not all versions of the traditional practical syllogism, have included this point. Robert Audi, for instance, is explaining a very widely accepted view when he says that what he calls the 'simplest basic schema for practical reasoning' goes as follows:

- Major premise—the motivational premise: I want to phi.
- Minor premise—the cognitive premise: my A-ing would contribute to realizing phi.
- Conclusion—the practical judgment: I should A (Audi 1989, p. 99).[2]

Clearly, the instance of the practical syllogism set out above to give the reasoning involved in my jumping out of the way of that car follows this pattern. And in particular, it does *not* include the thought that my desire is a reason, that is a good reason, to jump. The 'major premise' of that practical syllogism is (let's put it by saying) that I have a desire not to be seriously injured or killed in the next few seconds. The 'minor premise' describes a way of satisfying this desire (jumping out of the way). And the conclusion is that I should jump out of the way. That is, to put it a bit more dramatically, the practical syllogism set out just above, which so far as I can see follows Audi's schema exactly, just blithely moves from a fact about me—that I have a certain desire—and a fact about my situation—that I can satisfy that desire by performing a certain action—to a conclusion about what I *should* do, in short from 'is' to 'ought', as if no one had ever even *heard* of Hume. (Hume 1888, book 3, part 1, section 1)[3]

It moves from premises that record a couple of simple facts, i.e. that I have a certain desire and that there is a way of satisfying that desire, to a conclusion about what I *should* do, that is about what I have good, or good enough, reason to do. But surely that is can't be right. There are lots of desires (or wishes, urges, cravings, yens) that people have which give those who have them no good reason at all to try to satisfy. Whims are often like that. In fact, the term 'whim' seems to apply just to those urges or yens that are trivial or silly, usually not worth giving any weight to at all when deciding what to do. But in

[2] Audi also gives a reading of this sort of syllogism where the conclusion is about what I 'shall' do, rather than as here what I 'should' do; see Audi (1989 pp. 86–90 and 99).

[3] It is possible I think that the practical syllogism could be understood as referring not to 'wants' in any sense in the major premise, but to intentions (or to decisions or choices). So the question at issue would simply be how to carry out some intention that one had already decided on for whatever reason. Evaluative questions, and in fact all of what might be thought of as the *substance* of practical reasoning, would on this reading already have been answered or decided (well or badly). The only question remaining would be how to carry out what, as a result of this substantive reasoning, one now intended. Such a way of understanding the practical syllogism would avoid the sort of problem discussed here, since this would be to understand it as necessarily restricted to the last, instrumental, step in practical reasoning.

addition, there are all the various unhealthy or destructive cravings and urges and the like that all but the luckiest of us occasionally have and some have quite frequently. Most of these, I would say, give us *no reason at all* to act on them in the way Audi's 'basic schema' suggests. Suppose for instance that the 'phi' in Audi's schema (that is, what it is that you want) consists of smacking the person who just defeated you fair and square at squash (or, say, the crying baby who just will not go back to sleep) right in the face.[4]

What has led to confusion here, I think, is that at least most of the states that can fit Audi's 'major premise' (desires, cravings, urges, and so forth, i.e. what I have elsewhere labeled 'proper desires'[5]) are themselves inherently 'goal directed'. That is part of what they *are*. They not only *represent* some 'state of affairs', the way a suspicion or belief or conviction or doubt does: they represent that state of affairs *as a goal* for the person who has it. Desires (cravings, yens) are always and necessarily desires (cravings, yens) *for* something (or, more generally, desires that some state of affairs obtain). That is the feature of such states that the direction of fit argument was trying to explain or account for. Such states are, one might say, 'inherently purposive'. That means in part at least that it always makes sense to ask how to satisfy them, that is how to achieve the goal they represent or 'contain', in a way that does not make sense for other sorts of intentional states such as beliefs or suspicions.[6] (Not that there will always be an *answer* to such a question, of course. One can want impossible things, such as to be ten years younger, or can wish for things in the past, such as to have bought the latest 'hot' computer stock two years ago, when it was selling at 3⅛.)

But none of this makes the practical syllogism, as characterized by Audi's 'basic schema', correct as an account of practical reasoning, at least if we understand the 'I should' in the conclusion as meaning something to the effect that I have at least some good reason to act in

---

[4] These examples are versions of those in Watson (1975).

[5] See Schueler (1995a, ch. 1 and 2), and Sect. 2.1 above.

[6] This is however not what Sergio Tenenbaum, following Kant, calls a 'scholastic view' of wants or desires, that is one that 'is committed to a *conceptual* connection between motivation and evaluation' Tenenbaum 1999, p. 876; my emphasis). One could hold that desires are inherently goal directed, as I am claiming, without thinking that this need involve any sort of judgment about the value or apparent value of that goal. My cat, for instance, would seem to be a counter-example to such a scholastic view (as to so many others) since he certainly seems to have his share of proper desires without, so far as I can tell, making any genuinely evaluative judgments at all.

the way specified. My desire to not be killed or injured in the next few seconds, that 'mental state' of mine, represents my not being killed or injured in the next few seconds as a goal of mine. Perhaps it would be better to say that it *makes* my not being killed or injured in the next few seconds a goal, or at least potential or defesible goal, of mine (since I am not claiming that my desire not to be killed or injured merely represents me *as having* this goal, in the way my belief that I have this as a goal does, for instance). But the important point is this. The fact that I have this mental state, and hence this (potential) goal, doesn't by itself show that this goal is in any way worth pursuing (nor, though this is a different issue, that I think it is). How could it? The lack of any of a number of nutrients in your diet would produce in you a very strong craving to eat almost anything available including, in certain instances, soil.[7] Would you thereby come to have a *good reason* to eat soil? That is, would the fact that you have this craving make the goal of your eating soil worth pursuing?[8] Or consider the craving to smoke produced by nicotine addiction.

Thinking that my proper desire (or craving, or yen) for X gives me *all by itself* a reason to try to get X would be like thinking that my belief that p gives me, all by itself, a *reason* to hold that p. After all, the belief that p is a mental state which represents p as true, as being the case.[9] It differs in that way from, say, the suspicion that p, which represents p as possibly being the case, or the doubt that p, which represents p as probably not the case; etc. But it would clearly be a mistake to reason from the premise that I believe that p really is the case, i.e. that I am in a mental state correctly describable as 'belief that p', to the conclusion that I *should* therefore hold (or think, conclude) that p, at least if 'should' here means something to the effect that I have good reason to hold that p. Beliefs can be completely irrational and unfounded—when produced by hypnosis or drugs, for instance. So the mere fact that one has a belief that p, by itself, gives no reason at all for thinking that one *should* hold or think that p.

Kant's discussion of 'hypothetical imperatives', or at least one standard way of interpreting it, may be partly to blame here. It may

---

[7] Thanks to Gaynor Wild for this example.

[8] No doubt the goal of getting the nutrients you are lacking would be worth pursuing, but that is a different goal. The question here is just about the goal of eating soil, produced by (or identical with?) a craving for soil.

[9] Let's leave aside here issues about degrees of belief and consider only a full fledged, whole-hearted belief that p.

be that the thought that A's desire for X, together with the fact that doing Y is a (or the best or the only) way to achieve X, entails that 'A should do Y' simply comes from confusing the claim that A should do Y with the very different claim that doing Y is a way of A's satisfying her desire for X. The confusion starts when this latter claim gets (misleadingly) put by saying that if A wants X she should do Y. And that claim, together with 'A wants X', seems then to entail 'A should do Y' by *modus ponens*. But if 'If A wants X she should do Y' just means 'Doing Y is a way of A's satisfying her desire for X', then it is *not* of the form '$p > q$' and hence is not available for use in *modus ponens*. (Otherwise, together with 'A should not do Y', it would also entail 'A has no desire for X', by *modus tollens*, which obviously it does not.)

For me to have a desire, craving, yen, or the like is for me to be in a state which can be satisfied in a certain way. And of course, it is also true that for many such states their satisfaction will by itself be pleasurable. That is, for many such states, when the purpose or goal it specifies gets achieved, the person who is (or was) in the state will *feel* some satisfaction. (Though not always of course; my desire that those of my family and friends who outlive me remember me occasionally after I am gone, if it does get satisfied, will be so only after I am dead. Indeed, my desire not to be killed or seriously injured in the next few seconds is one I have had for as long as I can remember and, happily, has been satisfied every moment of my life so far, but alas without any particular pleasure or feeling of satisfaction being thereby produced, so far as I can tell.) But then if it is the prospect of enjoyment or satisfaction that gives one a reason for trying to achieve the goal specified in the desire (that is, 'satisfying' it in the other sense, achieving the goal it describes), we surely need to add that claim as a premise in our practical reasoning. It hardly follows *simply* from the fact that such states *can be* satisfied by something, even something pleasurable, that my having them gives me a good reason to actually satisfy them.

Human beings can come to have the sorts of intentional states covered in the major premise of Audi's basic schema in all sorts of ways, many of them completely unintentional on the part of the person who has that state. Walking by the bakery, smelling the freshly baked bread, might produce in one a craving for a slice of it, just as seeing that car careening toward me might produce in me a very strong desire to get out of its way. (Other, non-goal-directed, intentional states can also be acquired unintentionally of course—doubts are often like this, as for that matter are beliefs, such as my belief that

that car is about to hit me.) And being in such an inherently goal directed mental state, one might of course reason about how actually to satisfy it, that is to achieve the goal it specifies. If there is a way, or a best way, of achieving this goal, that will be described by what Audi calls the 'minor premise' of his 'basic schema'. But it is a mistake to think, from the fact that one has such a goal directed mental state and that there is a way or best way of satisfying it, that is of achieving the goal it specifies, that this shows (or somehow supports the conclusion) that one *should* act so as to satisfy it, at least if by 'should' we mean 'has a good reason' or 'has a good enough reason' to act. Those are different and much stronger claims.

Aficionados of the practical syllogism, I want to say, have noticed something *true* and important, namely that practical reasoning is purposive, that someone who does something because she thinks it is what she *should* do is thereby trying to achieve whatever goals or purposes are specified in her practical reasoning. But some have also held, which is false, that *only* inherently goal directed mental states such as yens or cravings (or more generally 'proper desires') can generate goals or purposes. (This is in fact the Humean Theory of Motivation in a nutshell.) So they have thought that practical reasoning must consist of reasoning about how to achieve the goals specified in such states. Of course we *can* reason about how to satisfy our cravings and yens. And we can act on the basis of this reasoning. The mistake is taking this as an account of practical reasoning (or practical rationality) generally.

So the practical syllogism described above about my jumping out of the way of that car, and more generally Audi's 'basic schema for practical reasoning' (which is itself, as I said, an example of a very standard way of understanding Aristotle's practical syllogism), are elliptical (and misleadingly so), but not only in leaving out explicit mention of other possible considerations: as they stand, they are in need of at least two further elements.

First, they need some way of representing the thought that my having the desire (craving, yen, urge), referred to in the 'major premise' gives me a reason (that is at least some good reason) to try to satisfy it. It seems obvious, as I said, that that won't always be true. For instance, it won't be true of desires where the goal is impossible to achieve, like my wish that I had bought that high flying computer stock when it was 3⅛. (Or think of the desire, discussed by E. Nesbit in one of her novels, (Nesbitt 1999) to be as beautiful as the day.) Nor will it be true of any of those cravings and urges that I would be better advised to try to extinguish than to satisfy.

It may be worth pointing out here that, just because we have been considering a case where, plausibly, it is my desire itself that gives me a reason to try to satisfy it, this provides no general reason to think that *only* my own desires, cravings, or yens give me reasons to do things (let alone that they always do). As in the earlier example, the importance (or worth, or value) of state subsidized day care might make it true that I have a reason to promote it in some way, say by voting for a tax increase to fund it. But in any case, whether it is true or not, adding such an element to this reasoning (that something gives me a reason to promote some goal) lets us non-fallaciously reason to an 'other things being equal' conclusion about what I should do.

Of course, other things are not always equal. So the second element we need to add here is a 'gap filling' premise of some sort, perhaps to the effect that other things are equal, or that there aren't any other things to be considered, or, more generally, that the consideration in question (in this example, my desire to not be killed or injured in the next few seconds) gives me more or better reason to act in the way proposed (jumping out of the way of that car) than anything else gives me not to. In its most general form—that is if it is going to fill the whole gap here—such a premise will have to take into account not only how much reason to act so as to satisfy it my desire gives me, but also anything else that is relevant.

There is for instance the issue of how likely it is that the means I am considering for satisfying this desire will actually work. We have been supposing in this example that the means I have chosen for satisfying my desire not to be killed, i.e. jumping out of the way, will work, and even that this is the only thing that will work, but, at least in other cases, the means selected might be much less sure (as, say, in the earlier voting example), and that will have to be taken into account. There also may be completely different considerations to weigh in, such as that my jumping out of the way of that car will endanger others around me or that, say, my family will collect on my insurance, and so be set financially for life, if I just stay put and let that car run me over. So it might seem that the other sort of element needed here, the one that will allow me to reason non-fallaciously to the conclusion about what I should do, is a completely general premise to the effect that, all things considered, there is more to be said for doing this, i.e. jumping out of the way, than for anything else open to me (including just not jumping).

But I think this cannot be right. Certainly when we add that premise, the conclusion that I should jump follows, that is, is entailed. But that hardly shows that this is the premise we need, because, after all, what the conclusion here *says* is in essence that, all things considered, I should jump out of the way. *Of course* this conclusion will be entailed by a set of premises that includes one to the effect that, all things considered, this is what I have most reason to do. The conclusion would then just be nothing but a restatement of this very premise. The question would at once arise, though, as to what could make one think that this *premise* was itself true; and then, since it is really just a restatement of the conclusion that we are interested in, we would be back where we started, asking how to support this conclusion. And even if we could somehow manage to state this 'gap filling' premise without making it just a restatement of the conclusion, it still seems inherently unknowable. What it has to say is something to the effect that nothing else, that is none of the things I have not yet considered, tips the balance of reasons in the opposite direction from the one it seems now to go toward, based on the things I actually have considered. And how in the world could I possibly know that?

What this shows, I think, or at least strongly suggests, is that if it is ever the case that we really have good reason to do anything, it must be that our reasons can *support* the thought that some action is what we have most reason to do without *entailing* it.[10] The conclusion of a piece of practical reasoning, the judgment on which one acts, is an 'all things considered' claim about what one has most reason to do, understanding this to include the thought that this includes having enough reason to do it.[11] Such a conclusion always goes beyond whatever things one actually considers, or ever could consider, in deciding what to do.[12] No matter how strong are the reasons for acting that one

[10] I am simply assuming here that the antecedent of this sentence is true, that we do at least sometimes have good reasons to do certain things. Denying this would indicate a skepticism, or rather I suppose nihilism, about practical rationality itself.

[11] It is at least not obvious that this will always be so. Why couldn't it happen that, whatever it is that I have most reason to do, I still have only very little reason to do—perhaps in fact not enough to actually justify doing it?

[12] This is what Davidson sees as giving rise to the problem of weakness of will: see Davidson (1980a, essay 2). Much the same general account of practical rationality is advocated by Bernard Williams (1985, ch. 7).

actually considers, it is hard to see how there could be any way in principle of ruling out the possibility that something else, of which one was perhaps utterly unaware, might tip the balance the other way entirely. Even in the case of jumping out of the way of that careening car, for instance, it could be that, unknown to me, one of its front tires is about to blow out, causing it to swerve away from where I stand but exactly in the direction in which I am about to jump. So if I only knew that, and so knew to stay put, I would be fine.

In this respect, practical reasoning is just like so called 'theoretical' reasoning (reasoning intended to support factual beliefs) on at least one very common way of understanding it. Most—indeed, perhaps all—of one's beliefs about the world, no matter how well *supported* by evidence, still go far beyond the actual evidence one has for them. So even though the evidence one has really is evidence, really supporting one's belief,[13] and even if one's reasoning is so to speak the best anyone could possibly do, given the limitations of human life spans, brain capacity, and so on, there could still be things of which one is unaware, of which one perhaps couldn't even possibly be aware, that undercut it completely. It is always possible that between one's evidence and conclusion 'the course of nature has changed' (in the Humean phrase).

But though practical and theoretical reasoning are alike in this way, there is also a way in which at least the standard examples of them seem to differ. Practical reasoning is about what I (or someone) should do, all things considered; that is, it is about what I have the best reason or the most reason to do. The *object*, so to speak, of practical reasoning is always an action one is considering (or perhaps a course of action—anyway something one can do, something thought to be in one's power[14]). That is what one is reasoning about. It is what one has reasons for or against doing. The *conclusion* of a piece of practical reasoning, however, seems to be a proposition to the effect that this is what I should do, all things considered, what I have most reason to do. But theoretical reasoning, standardly, is not thought of as being about what one *should* believe; that is, it is not usually represented as trying to arrive at a conclusion of the form 'I should believe

[13] I am also just assuming here without any argument that the 'problem of induction' shows only that we need a clear explanation of how this can be so, not that it is not so.

[14] Or at least that is the usual case, reasoning about what one should do. But it also seems possible to reason about what someone *else* should do, that is where the person doing the reasoning is not the same as the proposed agent of the action.

that p, all things considered.' It is supposed to be about 'p' itself, so to speak. So why this difference?

Suppose I am trying to figure out what is wrong with my car. It has begun stalling, say, and has even less power than usual. To me (though certainly I am no mechanic) there would seem to be only a few distinct possibilities: 'bad gas' (maybe of the wrong octane or with some sort of adulteration) at a recent fill-up, fouled spark plugs, a clogged air filter, or maybe the engine timing is off. Those are the only possibilities I can think of. But I have gotten gas at the same station for years without any problems, and the spark plugs were changed when the car was tuned up a few weeks ago, at the same time the timing was adjusted. On the other hand, I drove on some very dusty roads recently and the stalling started right afterwards. So, it seems I should conclude that I've got a clogged air filter.

Now what is the actual *conclusion* of this bit of reasoning; that is, what actual sentence or proposition is being claimed to be supported by it? 'I have a clogged air filter' or 'I should conclude that I have a clogged air filter'? The answer, I think, is that there really are two distinct questions here. If the question is 'Given my evidence, what proposition is most likely to be true?' then the answer is 'I have a clogged air filter' (and not, e.g. 'My timing is off'). But if the question is 'What have I got most reason to conclude, given this evidence?' the answer is 'I should conclude that I have a clogged air filter'. The reasons given in the above paragraph are reasons *for believing* (or concluding) that I have a clogged air filter. The facts I considered— that my spark plugs were changed recently or that my gas station is reliable, etc.—in the context of trying to figure out why my car is stalling serve to rule out the other possible causes. So these facts constitute evidence that I have a clogged air filter; that is the claim they support. Hence, together they constitute *reason to think* (or believe, or conclude) that I have a clogged air filter: that is what I should conclude, given this evidence.

So we need to make a distinction here. The proposition whose truth value I am interested in is 'I have a clogged air filter' (or perhaps, 'My car is stalling because I have a clogged air filter'). That is what I am reasoning *about*. But at the same time, in reasoning, that is in using my rational faculties (such as they are), I am trying to decide whether to *do* something, namely to conclude something or to form the opinion that something (that I have a clogged air filter). My reasons for concluding that I have a clogged air filter are reasons *for concluding* this. Likewise, if they are good reasons, they are good reasons for concluding this. They are not good reasons *for its being the case* that I have a clogged air filter (whatever that could mean).[15] The reason *that* I have a clogged air filter (if I really do) is (let's suppose) that I drove on those dusty roads and some of that dust got into my air filter. The other facts I considered—that my spark plugs were changed recently or that my gas station is reliable, etc.—have nothing at all to do with my air filter, clogged or otherwise. But in the context of trying to figure out why my car is stalling, where they serve to rule out the other possible causes (that occurred to me), together they constitute reason *for me to think* (or believe, or conclude) that I have a clogged air filter.

Believing, concluding, opining, and the like are things I can do, in a broad sense of 'do'.[16] Hence they are things I can have good or bad reasons to do, just as I can have good or bad reasons for jumping out of the way of that car, which is something else I can do. When I reason about such things as whether I have a clogged air filter, I am trying to decide whether I should believe that I have a clogged air filter. The reasons I have are reasons for or against *forming that belief*. And when

[15] The phrase 'the reason I have a clogged air filter' refers to whatever *explains* my having a clogged air filter. It exactly overlaps the use of 'because' in 'I have a clogged air filter because . . .' This context simply does not *allow* a question as to whether this is a good reason or not. The phrase 'the reason' here simply refers to whatever is being claimed to be the explanatory factor. It is thus quite different from 'My reason for doing X or believing p', where the question of whether *my* reason is a *good* reason is quite in order. (See Schueler 1995a, ch. 2, for a fuller explanation of the different uses of the term 'reason'.)

[16] Of course so are growing hair and digesting donuts. These are things I can do too, in a still broader sense of 'do'. The difference I think is that at least some believing and concluding, etc., is like performing actions, and unlike digesting food, in that we can be and are held responsible for it. We can have reasons for at least some of what we believe or conclude, which can be good reasons or not, and so on. Clearly this is a large (and widely discussed) issue. But at a minimum I think we need to distinguish at least two sorts of belief. One sort seems 'outside our control', and it is at least plausible to think my cat can have such a belief just as well as I can. My belief that there is a red ball rolling across the floor in front of me, when simply a perceptual belief, would be of this sort. The other sort we might call 'explicit' or 'considered' (or 'potentially considered'). These are beliefs which we hold for reasons, which can be good or bad reasons, and these it seems implausible that my cat can possibly have. My belief that the earth is over four billion years old would be an example. There is some sense in which such beliefs are under our direct control in a way in which 'perceptual beliefs', and growing hair for instance, are not. Someone who decides that she has to conclude that her spouse is cheating on her does, thereby, conclude that; someone who decides to grow hair still has a long wait, and perhaps a trip to the pharmacy, ahead of him. And it is not clear that it is even possible for someone to decide not to believe that there is a red ball on the floor in front of her, in spite of what she sees (at least without some pretty intense reading of Descartes).

I do form that belief, I do it *for those reasons* (at least sometimes). Why then does it sound odd (to the extent it does) to say that theoretical reasoning is about whether I *should* believe that p, rather than that it is about whether p is true? I think it is just because it is the content of my belief, p, that I am interested in.

At the same time, all this seems to me to suggest that it is a mistake to think that there is any sharp opposition between practical and theoretical reason. Indeed, I have been implicitly claiming that there is a way in which it makes sense to think of the latter as simply a part of the former. If that is right, it makes sense of the parallel noted above between the two and at the same time suggests a way of dealing with the deficiencies of the practical syllogism that we have been examining. The parallel was between the fact that the premises of pieces of theoretical reasoning seem never actually to entail the conclusions they support (at least in the interesting cases) and the fact that the sort of 'weighing' principle, needed to insure that the reasons considered as supporting the performing of some action actually entail the conclusion that this is what one should do, doesn't seem available. If, as I am suggesting, there is a way in which we can think of theoretical reason as part of practical reason, then there is in fact no 'parallel' here between two problems, but rather two manifestations of the same problem. It is the problem of how there can be reasons for doing things, reasons that is that support, but do not entail, the claim that one should do these things. In theoretical reason it is the problem of how a set of facts can be evidence for some claim, how they can give one reason to think this claim is true, without actually entailing this claim. In practical reason it is the problem of how some set of facts can give one reason to do something without eliminating the possibility that there may actually be better reason not to do it. I will return below to how this suggests dealing with the deficiencies of the practical syllogism.

First though it is important to notice that, though believing things and performing actions are both things I can do and so both things I can have good or bad reasons for doing, there is still a significant difference between theoretical and (the rest of) practical reason. Beliefs, which are the states being justified by theoretical reasoning (and so are what I will mostly focus on here), have 'built into them' certain sorts of standards of success in a way that other states, such as cravings/wishes and actions, do not. Beliefs are not, like imaginings, *merely* representations of certain states of affairs (even very 'forceful

and lively' representations, in Hume's phrase):, they are representations of these states of affairs *as obtaining*, that is as being true. So no
matter how terrible (or even non-existent) are my reasons for holding some belief, that is no matter how 'irrational' it is in that sense, it
can still be completely successful, as a belief, by being true. Similarly,
no matter how good are my reasons for holding some belief, that
belief can still be a total failure, as a belief, if it is false.

For lots of other mental states, such as desires (and certainly for
actions), neither of these things is true. If I have good (or even, let's say,
the best possible) reasons for wanting something, or for doing something, then it follows that this want or action is as rationally justified as
such things can get. There is no further, so to speak, independent standard at which they can turn out to have failed. Desires can of course be
satisfied, or not. But that is quite a different thing. Whether a desire of
mine is satisfied or not says nothing at all about how reasonable or
sensible it was for me to have that desire. I can have very good reason
indeed for wanting to jump, if that is the only way I can get out of the
way of that car, whether or not I succeed in doing so. And obviously,
giving in and satisfying an utterly irrational desire, like a yen to drink a
saucer of mud, makes that desire not a bit more rational.

Rawls distinguishes between what he calls perfect (and also imperfect) procedural justice, on the one side, and pure procedural justice
on the other (Rawls 1970, p. 85). Card games such as poker exemplify
the latter. If the rules of the game are strictly followed, that is if no
one cheats or the like, then the configuration of stacks of chips in
front of the players at the end of the game is just (or fair), period. In
such a case there simply is no other standard for justice than that the
rules really were followed. In other sorts of situations however there
is such an independent standard. And if there is, then it may or may
not be the case that there is a procedure that insures it will be met.
For a criminal trial there would seem to be no such procedure. All the
rules can be carefully followed, and so the trial can be 'just' in that
sense, even though the result is the conviction of someone who is in
fact innocent or the acquittal of someone who is in fact guilty. So
there is another sense of 'justice', in which justice in such a case will
not have been done, even if the correct procedures were followed
carefully and to the letter.[17]

---

[17] So this is an example of imperfect procedural justice. Rawls's example of *perfect*
procedural justice, where there is an independent standard of justice *and* some procedure

Beliefs, and many other 'cognitive' states such as suspicions, doubts, and so on, have a similar 'independent' standard for their success—independent that is of any of the procedures for rationally justifying them, namely whether they are true. Theoretical rationality, like the rules of evidence and other procedures of criminal trials, has to try as far as possible to assure that we meet this independent standard. But the standard so to speak always outruns the procedures devised to meet it, or at least is liable to. The procedures of theoretical reason, in the end, are themselves judged against the standard of whether the states they certify as rationally justified are in fact true. But these procedures of rational justification are 'imperfect' in Rawls's sense, because even if rigorously followed they still do not insure success.[18] In this, however, these procedures diverge from the procedures of practical rationality. This is not because the procedures of practical reasoning insure that the outcome meets some independent standard. It is because there simply is no such independent standard for actions (nor, for that matter, for desires, yens, hopes, or wishes) analogous to truth for beliefs.

In both theoretical and practical reason, 'being a reason', I want to say, is the reflection of some value, a value derived from the purposive activity in which the agent is engaged. To think that some consideration is a reason (that is, a good reason) for doing something is to think that this consideration shows that *there is something to be said in favor* of doing that thing in the context of the purposive activity in question. The difference between theoretical and practical reason is that in the case of theoretical reason the value is already presupposed by the enterprise itself, which is to produce true beliefs. Practical reason in general is about what one should do. One thing one can do

---

that insures it is met, is dividing a cake among different people. The procedure he suggests is that the person who cuts the cake gets the last piece.

[18] So I am disagreeing here with C. S. Peirce, as I understand him. In 'How to Make our Ideas Clear', he says: 'The opinion which is fated to be ultimately agreed to by all who investigate, is what we mean by the truth, and the object represented in this opinion is the real' (Peirce 1956, p. 268). Peirce has a footnote to the word 'fated': 'Fate means merely that which is sure to come true, and can nohow [sic] be avoided. . . . We are all fated to die.' This view of the connection between opinion and truth would seem to require that science, and theoretical reasoning generally, involve what Rawls calls 'pure' procedures, since even 'perfect' procedures are not ones we are 'fated' to apply unerringly. This view seems implausible as a way of understanding 'truth'. As a way of understand in 'the good', however, it is perhaps more plausible. Denying that practical rationality involves 'pure' procedures would seem to commit one to the view that there is a standard of the good that is independent of what humans have reason to do or avoid.

is form beliefs. Theoretical reason is therefore, as I have suggested, plausibly regarded as a part of practical reason. It is the part concerned with what one should believe.

Beliefs are states that represent their contents as being true. So to engage in what philosophers call 'theoretical reasoning' is to engage in an enterprise that presupposes the worth or value of the truth (i.e. of having mental states that are representations of how things really are). When we say that the fact that I just had the spark plugs changed in my car gives me a good reason (in conjunction with the other considerations mentioned above) to think that my air filter is clogged, we are saying this in the context of the enterprise of trying to produce in ourselves mental representations (beliefs) that are true. There are other things one can do, such as imagining things or wishing for things, for which one can have good or bad reasons but where there is no presupposition in the enterprise that the representation in question be true. What counts as a good reason for wishing for something, or imagining something, will thus be quite different from what counts as a good reason for believing something.

The difference between theoretical and practical reasoning is not, therefore, that while practical reasoning is purposive (reasoning about how to satisfy some desires, or more generally about what actions to perform), theoretical reasoning is not. No, both are purposive. The difference is that for theoretical reasoning the purpose is achieving mental representations that are true (that is beliefs). That goal is presupposed by the enterprise itself. But in both cases, calling something a reason for doing something, whether this 'something' is forming a belief or performing an action, is saying that the thing in question (the thing said to be 'a reason') makes it the case that *there is something to be said* for doing whatever is being considered. This also lets us see why, when we are trying to figure out what we should do, the fact that the considerations brought in favor of performing some action (or forming some opinion) don't ever *entail* that we should do this, doesn't preclude these considerations from *supporting* the thought that we should, just as reasons for believing something can support the thought that we should believe it without entailing that we should. We are in such cases judging, even if only implicitly, that the considerations in question are reasons for (or against) doing whatever we are considering.

What does all this tell us about how to repair the practical syllogism? I want to say that the practical syllogism described by Audi's 'basic schema', if it were adequately to describe the *standard* for practical reasoning, would need to be supplemented by at least two further elements. First, we need to add the crucial idea that the consideration or considerations mentioned (such as my desire not to be killed or injured in the next few seconds, combined with the thought that I can satisfy this desire by jumping out of the way of that car) are being held to *constitute reasons* for the agent to perform (or perhaps not perform) some action. We have seen that proper desires by themselves may or may not serve as such reasons, and that other things, such as subsidized day care being a good thing, can as well. So a practical syllogism of the Audi sort will simply not be good reasoning if the desire (or other fact) that it mentions in the major premise does not in fact give one any reason to act in the way specified.

Second, we need somehow to make room for the 'weighing' or evaluating of the considerations for and against performing the action in question, in something like the way my neighbor and I weighed up the reasons for and against voting for that tax increase. That is, we need to add something to the effect that, given the considerations surveyed and the actions available, there is or seems to be *more* reason to perform the action in question than to do anything else. Both these elements are inherently evaluative. They are needed to capture the thought that something *rationally supports* my performing some action.

The problem though is that, once we add these elements, it is very difficult to see that what we would have is anything that looks at all like a 'form' of practical reasoning, of the sort that had the practical syllogism as an example (even if, as I have been arguing, it is a defective one). The idea that some reasoning can be or even must be understood in terms of its *form* is most plausible when, as in formal logic, it makes sense to think that such a feature can be used to understand an important element of correct reasoning, such as entailment. But as I have argued, in practical reasoning, and the sort of theoretical reason that seems to be part of it (sometimes called 'inductive' reasoning), it seems just to be a mistake to think that the considerations that constitute even very good reasons for doing (or believing) something actually *entail* that one should do (or believe) it. That seems to me to suggest that it may also be a mistake to think that, in order for the sorts of elements I am arguing are required in practical reasoning really to be required, they must somehow be encoded in a correct 'form' of practical or theoretical reasoning.

It would probably be a mistake to think, for instance, that we could repair the practical syllogism simply by adding the elements that I am suggesting are needed in the form of extra *premises*, e.g. the premise that my desire not to be killed in the next few seconds gives me a reason to try to avoid its happening. That would be like thinking that the reasoning above, about whether my car's air filter is clogged, would be somehow weaker or even defective without a premise to the effect that these facts give me reason to think the air filter is clogged. They do indeed give me reason to think this, but the idea that we need to record this *as an extra premise* cannot be right. The thought that such an extra premise strengthens this reasoning makes it hard to see why a further premise, to the effect that this first new premise gives me yet more reason to think the air filter clogged, wouldn't strengthen it even further. And down that path lies Lewis Carroll's Tortoise.[19]

What this suggests, I think, is that what is required for correct practical reasoning is not that the agent employ any extra *premises* about what gives her reason to act, but simply that she in fact accord the appropriate facts the correct weight in her reasoning. Some facts (or whatever they are) give her reason to act in a certain way. She will reason correctly if she sees this, that is sees *on the basis of these facts* that this is what she should do, what she has most reason to do. And seeing this will of necessity involve weighing the reason giving force of these facts correctly. Having said this, though, I will for simplicity of exposition still speak below of the need for an extra evaluative *premise* comparing the reason giving 'weights' of the other considerations involved in practical deliberation. That premise should be understood not as an extra reason providing element,[20] but as a description of what is required for the reasoning to be correct, which is the evaluative comparison of the reason giving weight of the various things being considered.

I have been arguing that, even in what appears to be the most straightforward case of acting unreflectively on a desire (my jumping out of the way of a speeding car), these extra elements are required if we want to describe how the agent *should* reason, that is *what makes it rational* for him to act as he does. It is not clear that it follows though that there must be some correct form (e.g. with specific sorts

---

[19] I have discussed this problem in Schueler (1995*b*).
[20] Which would be what would have the Tortoise sharpening his pencil.

of premises or the like) into which this reasoning must be put. We will examine below the question that this raises of just what sort of 'requirement' this is. Before turning to that issue, however, I think it will be useful to look at a rather different sort of example.

4.2 Practical Reasoning and Explanations of Actions

In the example we have been examining there was only one real consideration, my desire not to be killed or injured, and it was not on its face an evaluation. Also, of course, there was no actual *reasoning* done. In the earlier example of voting for the tax increase, however, the reasoning was explicit. And it involved an explicit evaluation (that state subsidized day care was a good thing) as well as an explicit weighing up of one consideration against another, both features I am arguing are required for practical reason generally. So it will be instructive to look a bit further at how that example works.

There is also another point. Surely, in at least *some* cases of the weighing up of possible actions and different considerations, the agent who is trying to figure out what to do reasons *correctly* and acts on the basis of her reasoning. In any such case, the agent explicitly surveys the alternative actions that seem possible given her circumstances as she understands them, considers what seem to her to be reasons for and against each one, evaluates the relative weight or importance of each of these considerations, decides what she should do all things considered, and, as a result, does it. At each step she might of course go wrong. But that means I think that she might also not go wrong, that she might have an accurate view of her circumstances, correctly see what actions are open to her, and so on. That is, she might be correct in figuring out what action she has most reason to perform and then in fact perform that action just for this reason.

This point can be put more strongly. Even if we poor humans typically (or even always) foul it up when we are reasoning about what to do, it has to be at least *possible* for us not to foul it up, in order to make sense of the thought that there is any difference between reasoning well and reasoning badly. If there wasn't at least the possibility of reasoning correctly about what to do and then as a result actually doing it, it is hard to see what the point could be in engaging in such reasoning in the first place, let alone what sense could be made of the difference between reasoning well and reasoning badly. (If there is no possibility of acting on what is claimed to be correct practical reasoning, what possible force could there be, for instance, to criticizing someone for not acting on such reasoning?) And by the same token, *holding* that it is not even possible for us to act on the basis of correct practical reasoning is not a position that allows any view at all about how we *should* reason. It is rather a way of rejecting the very idea of practical reasoning. So if we are going to accept the idea that there is such a thing as practical reasoning, and with it the idea of correct and incorrect practical reasoning, it is important to think about the sort of case where in fact such reasoning is completely successful.

To this end, let us try out the thought that the voting case already introduced fits these conditions. To make it slightly less artificial, we may suppose that I am in the voting booth, finger poised pensively in front of the 'yes' and 'no' buttons, and trying to think out which to push. My reasoning (you will recall) was this:

1. Subsidized day care is a good thing, [I say to myself].
2. This proposed tax increase is necessary if there is to be subsidized day care in my community.
3. At the same time, it will cost me some money, which I would like to use elsewhere, if this tax increase is passed.
4. Still, it is more important that my community have subsidized day care than that I keep for my own use the few dollars it will cost me each year.
5. So, I should vote for this tax increase.

On the basis of this reasoning, I push the 'yes' button.

Two of the steps in this reasoning, premises 1 and 4, are explicitly evaluative, and of course the conclusion is a normative one, about what I should do. I want to claim, or as I said 'try out the thought', that in this situation the reasoning described here gives (or anyway could give) *the whole story* about my reasons for voting as I did, i.e. that I voted just on the basis of the things I explicitly considered. If that is so, these considerations will simply *constitute* my reasons for my action in this case. Of course, even if this is right it will be true that I wanted us to have (that is, had a pro attitude toward our having) subsidized day care. Indeed, as I hope is clear by this point, in the relevant sense of 'want' and of 'pro attitude', this follows from the description of how I voted and why (see also T. Nagel 1970, p. 29). The fact that my view that subsidized day care is a good thing convinced me to vote for this tax increase *is what makes it the case* that I have a pro attitude toward subsidized day care. This is the same conclusion already argued for above: that the agent's understanding of her own reasons is logically prior to what I have been calling the observer's view in terms of what she wants or has a pro attitude toward.

And I hope it is now clear as well that it would be a mistake to argue that, since, having reasoned like this and acted on this reasoning, I clearly want subsidized day care, so this pro attitude toward subsidized day care must appear in the *content* of my reasoning, that is must have been one of my reasons. No, someone who votes for this tax increase because *she wants us to have* subsidized day care has voted on different grounds than I have. I voted for the tax increase not because *I wanted* us to have subsidized day care, but because I thought subsidized day care a good thing. So, in this case at least, given the assumptions we have made here, reference to my evaluative belief (premise 1 above) in the explanation of my action is not eliminable without misrepresenting what my reason really was.

A case like this is worth keeping in mind if for no other reason than because it is easy to forget that people sometimes act on the basis of their deliberation and that, sometimes at least, this deliberation does not (or not only) involve reference to desires of the agent but does refer to explicit evaluations. The supposed counter claim, that I must have *wanted* to promote subsidized day care (that is, the 'zigzag' argument advocated by Blackburn[21]), is in fact no counter at all since, though true, it gets the explanatory story exactly backward (see also T. Nagel 1970). The *entire* argument for the claim that I wanted subsidized day care, in this case, is that I voted as I did and that my reasons for so voting are as just described.

There is a line of thought however that can cover this up and lead to confusing such a pro attitude, discoverable from the observer's point of view, with a proper desire. Though, as I argued above, 'theoretical' reasoning is always in support of the reasonableness of believing or concluding something, still, when one is engaged in such reasoning, one concludes 'p' and not 'I believe (or conclude) that p'. Likewise, though it might be said that one uses ones beliefs in this sort of reasoning, it is the thought 'My plugs were recently changed', not the thought 'I believe that my plugs were recently changed' that one uses in trying to figure out whether the air filter is clogged. My

---

[21] See Blackburn (1998, p. 91) and the discussion in Sect. 2.1 above.

belief that my plugs were recently changed 'shows up' (to me, the person doing the reasoning) in my theoretical reasoning as the *content* of my beliefs, that is not in the form 'I believe that my plugs . . .' but rather in the form 'My plugs . . .'. Now, if we ask the analogous question in practical reasoning about wants and desires, i.e. how they 'show up' in this reasoning, what is the answer?

One apparently tempting line of thought is this. Clearly, my desire that we have subsidized day care can't 'show up' in my reasoning simply as 'We have subsidized day care', which on the face of it would seem to be the 'content' of this desire, since that is just how a *belief* that we have subsidized day care would show up. So, one might think, my desire that we have subsidized day care will have to show up as something like 'Our having subsidized day care would be a good thing.' That will be the thought that someone who *wants* us to have subsidized day care will have when she reasons about, say, how to vote on that tax proposal, just as someone who believes that his plugs have recently been changed will have the thought 'My plugs have recently been changed' when he is trying to figure out why his car keeps stalling. But if 'Our having subsidized day care would be a good thing' is the way a desire that we have subsidized day care appears in practical reason (that is, if this is the thought that 'runs through the mind' of the person doing the reasoning), it is hard to see any real difference between the reasoning I attributed to myself above and the reasoning of someone who explicitly and consciously reasons only on the basis of her own desires, cravings, and the like.

But even if we set aside the fact that there clearly *is* a difference between these two (about which more in a moment), we have already seen several reasons why this way of representing how desires appear to those who have them can't be right. For one thing, someone who *believes* that our having subsidized day care would be good, on the basis say of reasoning from things she knows about working mothers plus perhaps some principles of political morality, will herself have the thought 'Our having subsidized day care would be good' as the conclusion of her reasoning. And this would be, or anyway certainly would look like, 'theoretical' reasoning. Her conclusion that subsidized day care would be good might, depending on the circumstances, have no connection at all to any action she is considering. In short it would be a belief.

And if she can have that thought as the conclusion of such reasoning, that is come to *believe* it on these grounds, it is hard to see why she couldn't also use it as a premise in her practical reasoning (later, perhaps, in a completely different context, when it is relevant to some action she is considering). So using this same thought as the way of representing the content of someone's *desire* that we have subsidized day care simply conflates desires with evaluative beliefs. That is an easy mistake to make, since people tend to want what they think good and vice versa; but still it is a mistake. After all, as was mentioned earlier, it is quite possible to *want* subsidized day care to be a good thing. So on this proposal someone with *that* desire would have to be characterized as having the thought that subsidized day care being a good thing would be a good thing, whatever that could mean.

Beyond this sort of problem, however, it seems obviously possible to want something *without* thinking it good (and vice versa, alas).[22] But the proposal that we characterize the contents of a desire for X as 'X would be good' makes this impossible. So, following this suggestion, someone who had a craving to smoke but had no opinion as to whether smoking was good or bad would be not just badly informed, but logically impossible, which seems absurd.[23]

Both these points show, I think, that there are serious difficulties with this idea, but neither really gets to the heart of the confusion here, which is the thought that desires somehow get *used in* practical (or any other) reasoning *at all*. That is, the real confusion here is thinking there is a problem in the first place. Of course, someone who wants something might well also think that having it is a good thing (but also might not, as I said). But it is just a mistake to think that desires are somehow *used in* any reasoning, any more than are hopes, fears, wishes, or cravings. For that matter, beliefs are not *used in* reasoning either, whether theoretical or practical. The sorts of things that *give one reason* to act are facts or, perhaps, 'states of affairs'. It was

[22] So I am denying the 'Scholastic view', as Sergio Tenenbaum (1999) calls it, that there is a conceptual connection between wanting something and thinking it good.

[23] Sergio Tenenbaum has suggested that to have a desire for something is not (as the view being attacked here would have it) to *believe* it good, but rather for it to *appear* good to one (Tenenbaum 1999). This would escape the objection here, since something could appear good to me without my having any belief that it really is good, just as the curved lines in the Müller–Lyer illusion continue to appear to be different lengths even after we understand the trick and so have no further inclination actually to believe they are different lengths. Accepting this suggestion about desire would explicitly identify the 'purposiveness' of states such as cravings and the like with 'appearing good', and so would rule out as a matter of logic (or metaphysics) the possibility of having a craving or desire for something that appeared bad or appeared neither good nor bad.

the fact that that a speeding car was about to hit me that gave me a reason to jump to the side. But one *reasons with* propositions (or sentences, if you like), the *contents* of beliefs, doubts, suspicions, hunches, and so forth, the things that can *describe or refer* to facts or states of affairs. Some of these propositions might well be those that one believes to be true (and some might not, if for instance one is considering a possible reductio or the like where a premise is considered only 'for the sake of the argument'). The content of the desire that we have subsidized day care is just the same as the content of the belief that we have subsidized day care (and of the doubt that we do, the fear that we do, etc.). Desires (like beliefs, hopes, doubts) do not 'show up' in practical (or any other) reasoning except in those cases where they are *described* or *referred to* in the propositions in question. Even in Audi's 'basic schema' for the practical syllogism above, the 'major premise' ('I want phi') is not claimed to *be* a desire; it is a *description* of a desire.[24]

The confusion here comes I think from the idea already mentioned as one of the problems behind the practical syllogism: the idea that only proper desires (and the like) can generate purposes, that is can 'motivate'. This is in fact the very conclusion for which the direction of fit argument was arguing, that is that Davidson's principle 'BD' should be understood as referring to proper desires, in short that BD should be understood as the Humean Theory of Motivation. And the solution, I claim, is to see that BD should be understood in the way I have been advocating, which involves seeing that 'wants' are required for motivation *only* in the sense that it follows from the fact that someone acted for some reason that she 'wanted' whatever was mentioned in that reason. On the other, defective, view, someone engaged in practical deliberation must 'at bottom' have *and be moved by* a 'proper' desire to achieve something or other if she is to be moved to act at all. So the person who apparently acts *on the basis of* her practical reasoning won't—in fact can't—*merely* describe or refer to her desires, but must somehow, in her reasoning, also *have* the

---

[24] Audi (1989, pp. 95–6 also says that this premise 'expresses' my desire, but it is not clear that he hangs much on this. It is not true, at least, that the sentence 'I want X' is the *expression* of my desire for X. My *utterance* of this sentence *might* express my desire for X (or think, say, of a 2-year-old saying this). By the same token, though, and for the same reason, this utterance might simply 'express' my belief that I want X (a belief I could presumably have even if I did not in fact want X). And in the context of practical reasoning, there is no reason to think it does anything more than this.

desires she is (sometimes) describing or referring to.[25] Likewise, on this view, some desire must be there to move her even when she doesn't explicitly refer to it, for instance when her premises refer not to what she wants but to what she thinks good or bad.

Once we see this confusion, we can also see that the idea that there must be a proper desire present to explain every intentional action is in fact simply *incompatible* with the thought that people sometimes really do act *on the basis* of their deliberation. My deliberations don't even always purport to contain references to my proper desires, and even when they do it need not be the case that I actually have the desires I am attempting to refer to. And even when I do in fact have the proper desire I refer to in my deliberation, it still plays no role in producing my action if I really do act *on the basis* of my deliberation. So the idea that there must be a proper desire present to explain every intentional action is just incompatible with the assumption we have been making here: that at least in some cases the agent's reasons for doing whatever she did are *correct* and fully spelled out in the deliberation on the basis of which she acts, that is that she sometimes reasons correctly and acts on the basis of that reasoning.

Even in a case such as the one discussed above of my jumping out of the way of that careening car, where the main reason providing element was my desire not to be killed or injured in the next few seconds, the reasoning we decided I would have had to use in order to reason correctly about what to do involved only the *thought* that I had this desire, not the desire itself (plus, we decided, the thought that this constituted a reason for me to act on this desire). So if I *had* actually deliberated in that case and then acted *on the basis* of that deliberation, then even though I had the desire not to be killed, it would have been my reasoning *about* this desire, and not the desire itself, that 'moved' me to jump. So, for all that was said above, my reasoning in that case (had I done any) could have gone exactly the same way, and led to my jumping, even if all the premises turned out to be false, including the one that said I wanted not to be killed or injured in the next few seconds. Though it is hard to imagine in a case of that sort that I could be wrong about what I want, in general one

---

[25] This is what I think leads Audi to say that that the first premise 'expresses' a desire. It couldn't express a desire unless there really were a desire there to express. Of course I am using the terms 'describe' and 'refer to' here in the sense in which I can describe or refer to things that don't actually exist.

can be led to act, just as one can be led to believe, by reasoning from false premises as well as from true ones, even from false premises about what one wants.

Of course, in the example of my jumping out of the way of that car, especially as I have described it, where I do no reasoning at all and simply react, it is very plausible to think that it is really my desire itself, and not any belief I have about it, that leads me to jump. The cat who happens to be standing next to me on the curb, and who also jumps out of the way when he sees the car careening towards us, presumably also jumps because he wants to stay alive, and yet it hardly seems that he can do any practical reasoning, or even have beliefs about his own desires for that matter. We will consider below what exactly is going on in this sort of case, where no reasoning takes place or even perhaps could take place. For the moment, however, let us continue to focus on the cases that involve explicit practical reasoning.

The view that it is *always* a proper desire itself that figures in the explanation of intentional action, and not (or not merely) my reasoning about my desires, would raise the question, in the cases where I actually do deliberate, of what the connection could be, in the explanation of my action, between this proper desire and my reasoning. To see this let's change this example slightly and suppose that, in the case of my jumping out of the way of that careening car, I actually did reason in the way we decided would be correct and that I then acted *on the basis* of that reasoning. (I had a bit more time, perhaps, and weighed up the alternatives.) One question that raises is this: what, in this case as we are now describing it, is the role in the explanation of my action of (my belief in) the premise that *describes* my desire not to be killed or injured in the next few seconds?

If it is my *actual* desire to avoid death or injury, rather than my *belief* that I have this desire, that explains my action, it looks like it simply cannot be true that I acted *on the basis* of my deliberation. My reasoning includes that premise as an essential element; in fact, it would not be good reasoning without it. Yet if it was my desire not to be killed that did the explanatory work (e.g. if it somehow simply and directly caused my action in some sort of 'mechanical' way), it looks like we will have to say that I would have jumped even if I had (falsely) believed I did *not* want to live, or had no opinion one way or the other about whether I wanted to. And in that case, it becomes very hard to see what the *rest* of my reasoning (i.e. about how to avoid that car) was doing. This reasoning makes sense only in the context of my *belief* that I wanted to avoid being killed. So, again, it seems that if it really was my desire *itself* that explains my action: it cannot be true that I acted 'on the basis' of my reasoning. The desire would have directly 'triggered' my jump, no matter what *reasoning* I did.

The only way I can see of trying to hold that the reasoning described in the car case (or indeed any of the cases we have been looking at) *and* an underlying, proper desire can *both* figure in an explanation of my action (that is, that these two claims are compatible) is by holding that the desire needed is not the desire not to be killed or injured in the next few seconds, but rather some sort of 'underlying' desire, such as a desire to do what it is most rational for me to do, or, as J. David Velleman has suggested, a desire to be in conscious control of my actions.[26] Since Velleman (1996) has worked out his suggestion in some detail, it is worth considering here. Analogous to the two parallel cases of jumping out of the way of that car—(1) simply as a 'reaction' without any sort of deliberation, and (2) doing so on the basis of practical deliberation—Velleman considers, first, a case where you reach out purely as a reflex to catch a falling water glass someone has accidentally brushed off a table, and second, a similar case where the glass is tossed to you after a warning and you catch it 'as a fully intentional action' (Velleman 1996, p. 715).

There is a difference, Velleman says, between the first case, in which 'you extend your hand without any guiding knowledge of what you're doing', as a reflex so to speak, and the case when your action 'is performed in, and out of, a knowledge of what you're doing', i.e. when you have a bit of time to think before you act and can 'exercise conscious control over this activity'. That is, he holds that we should distinguish between the case where the desire to catch the glass moves me directly, with no intervening reflection, so that the first premise of the associated practical reasoning ('I want to save that glass') would be an *expression* of my desire, and the case where I reflect on what I want and in which the first premise records my *recognition* of my desire (1996, p. 724).

This second sort of case, Velleman says, lets us see that the 'influence of reasons' on action is not the same as the 'motivation' of the

<hr />

[26] Velleman (1996). Michael Smith and Phillip Pettit (1990) have suggested that the issue here can be dealt with if we distinguish 'background' and 'foreground' desires. I have explained why I think this does not help in Schueler (1995a, chapter 5).

desire and associated belief referred to in the traditional Humean Theory of Motivation (or what he calls the 'internalist' account[27]). But, rather than completely abandoning this account, he suggests a way of understanding how reasons influence actions in this sort of case that incorporates the central internalist or Humean Theory claim. Velleman suggests that the relevant sort of inclination is inside agency itself, that is that in order to be an agent at all one must have a certain sort of aim. The aim required for agency, he suggests, 'is simply the aim of being in conscious control of one's behavior', that is 'autonomy' (1996, p. 719). This is an aim that one must have in order to be an agent at all (at least in what he calls the central, 'full blooded' sense).

I want to consider whether the second sort of explanatory schema distinguished in the two versions of the glass catching example (i.e. where deliberation is involved) is in fact explained by Velleman's suggestion. If it is, then it will not be true, as I claimed above, that the idea that there must be a proper desire present to explain every intentional action is in fact simply *incompatible* with the thought that people sometimes really do act *on the basis* of their deliberation, since Velleman thinks such a desire is included in the explanation of how this sort of case works. Velleman's idea is that, while the Humean Theory of Motivation is right that this depends on a prior desire (or 'inclination') in the agent, this is 'not an inclination that distinguishes some agents from others, but rather an inclination that distinguishes agents from non-agents' (Velleman 1996, p. 705).

When we look at Velleman's Humean suggestion about the second, deliberative case, though, the *content* of the 'aim' supposed to be required for agency seems problematic. According to him, in order to be an agent at all, one must have the aim of being in conscious control of one's behavior. And he thinks that this aim is accomplished when (in essence) one reflects on what one has reason to do and then consciously acts on that reflection.[28] When that happens, as he puts it, one's 'movement thus becomes autonomous precisely by manifesting [one's] inclination toward autonomy; and in becoming

---

[27] Velleman uses the term 'internalist' to refer jointly to the claims that (1) there is an 'antecedent inclination', that is a proper desire, which (2) motivates the action, and (3) justifies it (meaning, I take it, makes it at least minimally rational). For the most part it is only the first two that concern us here.

[28] He also sketches an account of how this might work, the details of which would lead us off the track here.

autonomous, it becomes a full-blooded action' (p. 723). The problem is that this aim, i.e. the aim of being in conscious control of one's behavior, has as its content not any goal or state specific to this particular action, such as saving that glass or getting out of the way of that car, but simply the goal of consciously controlling one's behavior. So it would seem that, if it works to explain anything at all, it will only explain one's 'consciously controlling' what one does, not one's actually doing it. Plus, of course, if it is to work as the Humean Theory says proper desires are supposed to work (e.g. in the reflex case) it will also require a *belief* that, by deliberating in the way Velleman describes, one can acquire conscious control of one's behavior. That is crucial to how the Humean Theory pictures explanations as working.

But even if we suppose that all agents have this belief (though why should we—not everyone has read Velleman's essay), there is a complete loss of relevance here. The content of the 'aim' that Velleman is claiming is required for agency has nothing at all to do with saving that glass, or indeed with any other specific action. So how exactly does adding this aim to all genuine acts (or all genuine agents) serve to explain what they actually *do*, rather than their 'consciously controlling' what they do? If it is supposed to explain actions in the same way that the Humean Theory of Motivation says my desire to save that glass explained my reflexively reaching out to catch it in the first kind of case then it doesn't look like it can. Its content doesn't 'connect' so to speak with any particular action at all.

So there is a serious puzzle here. If in the first, reflex, case my desire (to save the glass or to dodge that car), when combined with the relevant belief, directly explains my action, what does adding this other desire (to be in control of my actions) do in explaining the second case, where I reflect? If the first desire did not go away, there is no work for the second desire to do. And if it did go away, then the second desire doesn't seem to have the right sort of content to connect with my belief (that I can catch the glass by reaching out, or save my life by jumping) so as to produce the action.

Velleman says two rather different things on this topic. He says that my inclination toward being in conscious control of my behavior 'reinforces' whatever other motives I have for acting as I do (1996, pp. 722–3), as if this inclination were just another, distinct desire with the same object, which of course it is not. So I don't think this will help at all. But he also says that my aim of being in conscious control of my behavior shows the true 'influence of reason' in a way that my wanting to save the glass does not. 'What exerts the influence of reason in this example is the *recognition* that you want to save the glass', he says (my emphasis). 'And this recognition *doesn't influence you by engaging your desire to save the glass*. . . . The recognition that you want to save the glass engages. . . . your inclination toward autonomy—toward behaving in, and out of, a knowledge of what you're doing' (p. 725; again, my emphasis).

This second answer seems much better to me, but it also gives up a big part of the point at issue. It no longer clearly defends the Humean Theory. What Velleman is saying here is that in the second, deliberative case, my *actual* desire to save the glass has become irrelevant to the explanation of my reaching out to grab it insofar as the 'influence of reasons' is concerned. What explains my reaching out, according to this second answer, is, first, my desire for (or 'inclination toward') being in conscious control of my behavior, a desire or aim I share with all genuine agents, and, second, my *recognition* that I want to save that glass. But of course I could have that *recognition*, or at least the part of it that is up to me, the *belief* that I want to save that glass, even if I didn't in fact want to save it.[29] That is, on this view the explanation of my reaching out to catch that glass, when it involves not just a reflex action but 'full blooded' agency, where I am in conscious control of my action, simply doesn't involve my *actual*, proper desire to save the glass *at all*. The explanation could be just the same even if there were no such desire (i.e. as long as I believed there was). That is why Velleman can suggest that, 'if desire-based reasons derive their influence from something other than the desires on which they are based, then perhaps the same influence is available to considerations that aren't based on desires at all' (1996, p. 726).

None of this, however, answers the questions posed a few paragraphs above. Velleman's account of the influence of reasons, that is how reasons explain action, in the sort of case where I can think about what I am doing and act on that basis, involves two elements. First, all agents, as a condition of being agents, want to be in

---

[29] Of course it is difficult to see how one could be wrong in one's belief about such a desire, though for other cases it seems quite possible. In any case, Velleman seems committed to the coherence of this possibility, since he makes a distinction between understanding 'I want to save that glass' as an 'expression' of my desire and understanding it as a 'recognition' of my desire, a distinction that is empty without at least the logical possibility of my 'recognition' sometimes being mistaken.

conscious control of their behavior (they have this 'antecedent aim'). Second, in this case, I believe (or recognize) that I want to save that glass. How exactly *these* two elements are supposed to combine so as to explain my reaching out to catch the glass is still in need of explanation.

According to the Humean Theory, which Velleman thinks applies to the reflex case, my desire to save the glass combined with my belief that by reaching out I could save it, to produce my action of reaching out. Velleman seems to hope that finding a desire (or 'aim') to be in conscious control of one's behavior in *all* genuine action will be enough to explain the 'influence of reasons'. But to fit this aim into a Humean Theory account, at least two more elements are required. First, in order to get 'reasons' into it, he will have to say something to the effect that I (or all agents?) think I have reason to try to satisfy the proper desires I have (e.g. to catch that glass). And second, in order to connect with the aim of being in conscious control of my behavior, he will have to say something to the effect that I (or all agents) think that I will be in conscious control of my behavior if I (intentionally?) do what I (think I have?) reason to do. This will result in an explanation that starts from my desire (aim) to be in conscious control of my behavior and my *recognition* of my desire to save that glass. It then explains my reaching out to catch the glass by citing my belief that my desire to save the glass gives me reason to save it and my belief that I will be in conscious control of my behavior by doing what I have reason to do. Without these two additional beliefs, my aim of being in conscious control of my behavior simply won't connect with my belief that I want to save that glass.

One small oddity of this account is that it seems to entail that *all* ('full blooded') actions are performed in order to be in conscious control of one's behavior: that is the aim they are trying to achieve. But there are bigger problems too. For one thing, as was mentioned above, the extra beliefs we need to ascribe to agents to make Velleman's schema work (e.g. the belief that I can be in conscious control of my action by doing what will achieve my first-order desires) seem both implausible in themselves and in any case not at all generally believed. This by itself would seem to undercut completely the project of basing the 'influence of reasons' on the supposed fact that genuine agents aim at being in conscious control of their behavior. If I don't believe I can achieve some goal by doing some specific thing, then we can't explain my doing that thing by citing my desire for that goal.

It is important to see here that according to Velleman it is my aim of being in conscious control that moves me to (full blooded) action. My desire to save the glass is now given *no* motivating role at all. According to Velleman's account, I might merely *believe* I want to save that glass, and that would be enough for my desire to be in conscious control to move me to reach out to save it. So what would happen if I merely *believed* I wanted to be in conscious control of my actions but did not really have this desire? Intuitively, I want to say, this would be no different from in any other case where I falsely believe I have some desire and act on this false belief. But for Velleman's account to work, he will have to hold that, unless I *actually have* that 'antecedent aim' of being in conscious control of my behavior, no action will result; otherwise the whole idea of saving the essence of the Humean Theory by inserting this underlying desire to be in conscious control will have done nothing.

But this means that Velleman's suggestion of an underlying desire to be in conscious control of one's behavior simply misfires as a way of meeting the central charge I am making here. Holding that such an underlying desire is essential to the explanation of intentional action would still mean giving up the thought that people at least sometimes reason *correctly* and act *on the basis* of that reasoning. The point is perhaps somewhat easier to see if we imagine the content of this underlying desire to be something like 'being rational' or 'doing what one has most reason to do', but the difficulty is the same.

Even if the occasional philosopher added to her practical reasoning a 'zero premise' to the effect that she wanted to do what was rational (or, if Velleman is right, that she wanted to be in conscious control of her behavior), she would still not act on the basis of her *reasoning* from this new premise: she would act from this desire *itself*. So the gap between this desire and her actual practical reasoning would still be there. This supposed underlying desire to do what is rational, or to be in conscious control, could not itself be *her reason* for doing what she did. If it could be, she could ask (as with any reason of hers) whether or not it was a good reason for her to do whatever she did, with the possibility that she judged that it wasn't. And so the possibility of her deciding not to act on it.

This last point can be put another way. Suppose we accept the view that, even in cases of explicit practical deliberation, where the agent acts on the basis of her reasoning, there must always be an 'underlying' proper desire to do what is rational (or to do what she has the best reason to do, or to be in conscious control). The problem with this thought is that there would be nothing to prevent an agent from becoming *aware* of this desire (perhaps by reading and becoming convinced by the writings of the philosophers who advocate this kind of position) and then taking it into account in her practical reasoning. That would mean adding to the considerations she was weighing up a *further* premise to the effect that she 'wants to do what is rational, or what is required for her to be in conscious control of her behavior' as determined by the other factors she was considering. Perhaps Velleman is thinking that adding such a premise to her practical reasoning could have no 'substantive' effect, like adding a rule in a game that said that players had to follow the rules. But this is not so.

A proper desire to do what is rational or to be in conscious control of one's behavior, if it really *is* just another proper desire, like the desire to have another beer or to spend Christmas in the Southern Hemisphere, can be evaluated as to its reason giving 'weight'. And there would be nothing to prevent someone from deciding, rightly or wrongly, that it was the kind of desire that one should resist or try to overcome, rather than satisfy, that is to weigh it *against* doing whatever the other considerations being evaluated argued for doing. It seems possible that in some cases this might even be decisive, convincing the agent (again, rightly or wrongly) that she should *do* what the other considerations she was considering argued on balance *against* doing, or vice versa. Suppose she then acts on the basis of this reasoning; that is, she does what she regards herself as having less reason to do, as a way of trying to overcome her desire to do what is rational, or to be in conscious control. This may not be wise of course, but if we are really speaking of just another proper desire here, then it very difficult to see why it wouldn't be possible, and if it really is possible; how could an underlying-desire view of the sort Velleman gives explain *this* action?

What this shows, I think, is that an 'underlying desire' view of this sort, whatever one says the content of the desire is, could not allow that such an action (i.e. with this sort of explanation) really is possible. That is, it could not allow that an agent might discover, and then weigh in her deliberations, the supposed underlying proper desire. To allow this would be simply to abandon the idea that it is this underlying desire that is doing the explanatory work here. But at the same time, this means that this supposed underlying desire is not a proper desire at all.

4.3 Practical Reasoning and Evaluations

The broader issue here is really what sort of explanation we have when, in explaining someone's action we cite her reasons for doing whatever she did. This is an issue I will take up explicitly below. Before doing that, however, it is important to see that genuine evaluations, that is evaluative beliefs and not merely expressions of cravings or other proper desires, must always figure into practical reasoning. We have, I claim, one example of this in the case of my reasoning about whether to vote for that tax increase, where there is both an explicit evaluation of the goal—subsidized day care—and of the relative weights, as reasons, of the considerations I thought relevant to my decision.

One example (or, really, one set of examples) of course doesn't show that *all* practical reasoning *must* involve evaluations on the part of the agent (which is what I am claiming); indeed, the example briefly mentioned above of the person who really does vote *only* on the grounds of what she herself *wants*, which seems perfectly possible, might suggest that this is not so. I have already argued above, in the context of the example of jumping out of the way of that car, that if the reasoning is to be correct a weighing of the importance of the relevant considerations is always involved, and that each consideration itself must be taken as constituting a reason. Each of these features of practical reasoning is evaluative, and I argued that neither can be dropped. But perhaps we can see this more clearly by looking at what happens in the voting case when we try doing without them.

So consider my (other) neighbor, who reasons about what to do *only* on the grounds of her own desires and other proper attitudes such as hopes, fears, and so on; that is, her own desires, wishes, hopes, and the like are the *only* items she ever considers when deciding what to do.[30] This certainly seems possible, if perhaps not very admirable. For the sake of clarity, let us suppose that she finds herself in the voting booth, just as I did, finger poised just as pensively between the 'yes' and 'no' buttons. She reasons as follows:

> 1d. I have a yearning that we have subsidized day care [she says to herself].

[30] My first neighbor, considered above, is different because she accepts the claim that subsidized day care is a good thing; that is, she reasons at least partly on the basis of an evaluation that does not depend on her own proper desires.

2. This proposed tax increase is necessary if there is to be subsidized day care in my community.
3. At the same time, it will cost me some money, which I would like to use (i.e. which I have a yen to use) elsewhere, if this tax increase is passed.
4d. Still, it is more important that my desire that my community have subsidized day care be satisfied than that my desire to keep for my own use the few dollars it will cost me each year be satisfied.
5. So, I should vote for this tax increase.

It is, I would say, rather implausible that anyone would actually reason in this way, since people who want us to have things like subsidized day care typically want this *for some reason*, such as that they think it a good thing. But that will not be the case here, otherwise we would seem to be back to the very reasoning I used (i.e. with premise 1 rather than 1d).[31] So let's just ignore the implausibility of this reasoning for the moment. (Alternatively, we could use a more plausible case, for instance where someone really might weigh up two or more of her own desires, say her strong desire to avoid lung cancer against her craving to smoke.)

Even someone who reasons only on the basis of her own desires, as I have characterized my other neighbor as reasoning, however, still needs a fourth premise similar to number 4 in my original reasoning, that is a premise that evaluates the *importance*, i.e. the reason giving power, of the various considerations described in the other premises. This is what 4d does for my other neighbor. And such a premise is clearly evaluative; in fact, it includes both the extra points that I argued earlier were needed to make the practical syllogism we looked at above non-fallacious. This premise says in essence that the two considerations at issue *constitute* reasons for and against voting for that tax increase, and that one is weightier, i.e. is a *better* reason, than the other. So if my other neighbor reasons as just described, her reasoning still makes essential use of an evaluative premise that contains these two considerations.

We can see that such an evaluative premise (or anyway something that includes both these points) is needed if we try to substitute for it one that looks superficially similar perhaps but in reality involves

---

[31] The description of my reasoning is given in Sect. 3.2 (and repeated in Sect. 4.2) above.

only some factual claim about the desires in question. Suppose for instance that someone claims that my other neighbor, when deciding how to vote, uses not 4d but

4s. Still, my desire that my community have subsidized day care is *stronger* than my desire to keep for my own use the few dollars it will cost me each year.

The problem with this premise is that it is utterly irrelevant to the conclusion, which speaks of what my other neighbor *should* do. Premise 4s merely describes a fact about my other neighbor's desires. It is thus no more relevant to the question of what she should do than, say,

4i. Still, my desire that my community have subsidized day care is more *intense* than my desire to keep for my own use the few dollars it will cost me each year

or than

4f. Still, my desire that my community have subsidized day care is more *frequent* than my desire to keep for my own use the few dollars it will cost me each year.

or even than

4p. Still, my desire that my community have subsidized day care is more *pleasant* (or, heck, *painful*) than my desire to keep for my own use the few dollars it will cost me each year.

Facts about the strength, or intensity, or frequency (or duration, etc.) of one's desires are not relevant *at all* to what one *should* do unless we suppose that such facts support some claim about the *importance* or value of satisfying these desires, i.e. about their status *as reasons* for acting so as to satisfy them, which is what premise 4d is about.[32] That is, in order for claims about the strength or intensity or the like of one's desires to be relevant to the conclusion about what one should do, we will need to add another premise, to the effect that it is important (or good, valuable, etc.) to act on one's strongest (or most intense or most frequent or most pleasant) desires. In other words, we will need to add a premise that *evaluates* these desires as to

---

[32] Compare Scanlon (1998), especially sect. 1.

their reason providing status, tells us how reasonable or important or good it is to act on them, on the basis of the feature in question.[33]

Leaving aside the question of how plausible such an extra premise would be (not very I would say), the point here is that without such a premise the reasoning my other neighbor uses doesn't even *look* rationally acceptable, any more than when we tried reading 'importance' in premise 4 above as 'importance to me', or when we tried to use the practical syllogism above to reason from the mere existence of my desire to avoid being killed or injured to the conclusion that I should jump out of the way of that car (skipping, that is, blithely from 'is' to 'ought'). In this case too, without adding some genuinely evaluative premise to her reasoning to the effect that the considerations in question constitute reasons for acting, my other neighbor would also commit the fallacy of *ignoratio elenchi*.

As we have seen, practical reasoning is always intended to support a *normative* conclusion about what the reasoner *should* do, all things considered, that is, what the reasoner has most reason to do, all things considered. A list of facts, even if they happen to be about the likes, desires, urges, or inclinations of the agent doing the reasoning, cannot rationally support such a conclusion, any more than can a list that contains only a single desire, even if it happens to be the desire not to be killed or injured in the next few seconds. Some premise about the importance, worth, or good of acting on these things, that is about their *status as generators of reasons*, will always be needed. I have already argued that such premises, or rather the holding of them, will at least sometimes be a reflection of some feature of the character of the agent doing the reasoning. The point here however is that all practical reasoning, in order to have any shot at all at rational acceptability, needs such evaluative premises. If we assume that people sometimes act on the basis of their practical deliberation, it follows that we can explain their actions (in these cases at least) only if we understand how they *actually* deliberated, and that necessarily includes understanding their evaluations.

[33] Rational choice theorists, welfare economists, and some moral philosophers seem sometimes to think that we can solve the problems here by referring to 'preferences' rather than wants or desires. (Neither 'desire' nor 'want' occurs in the index to David Gauthier's *Morals by Agreement* (Gauthier 1986), and not just because they are so heavily used. 'Preference' in its various contexts receives dozens of citations.) How exactly this magical feat is supposed to be accomplished, I have never understood. (Of course one might *sidestep* at least some of these problems by explicitly using the term 'preference' in such a way as to do so, a perfectly legitimate move if one simply wants to discuss different issues.)

Of course sometimes people reason badly. So it might be objected here that, even if practical deliberation, in order to be *correct*,[34] requires at least one evaluative premise, people don't always reason correctly. Plus of course there is a difference between claiming that an *agent*, in order to reason correctly about what to do, must use some evaluative premise and come to some normative conclusion, and saying that an *explanation* of this agent's action must involve an evaluative claim somehow. It was the latter claim that was made when we were discussing the necessity of bringing into action explanations a reference to the agent's character, but it seems to be the former claim that is being urged here. Answering these two objections will let us see more clearly the account I want to give of explanations of actions in terms of the agent's reasons. I will take up the first one in the next section of this chapter, the second one in the following chapter.

There is another possible objection, though, that we should consider first. I have been urging that practical reasoning is always intended to support a *normative* conclusion about what the reasoner *should* do, all things considered, that is, what the reasoner has most reason to do, all things considered. It is not an objection to this claim that people, even when they actually do reason about what to do, frequently don't use these terms. ('This is what I should do, or have most reason to do, all things considered.') It is easy to think of cases where they do not. ('Let's see, how will I spend my evening? I could read. Go to the movies. Watch TV. Heck, I'm just going to watch TV.') But the point here is that, if we are going to use this bit of reasoning as a basis for understanding what this person did (spent her evening

---

[34] 'Valid' would of course be the wrong word here, as I hope is clear from the earlier discussion. A bit of reasoning is, strictly speaking, valid only if it is not possible for the premises to be true and the conclusion false, i.e. only if the premises actually entail the conclusion. This is never the case in practical reasoning, however, as I have tried to explain. Indeed, as I have argued above, it is a misconception of practical reasoning to think that validity, in this strict sense, is the standard. Some piece of practical reasoning is good reasoning when the considerations listed in the premises really do give the agent good reason to do what is described in the 'should' conclusion, which is always about what the agent has reason (or enough reason) to do. That means there is always the possibility that some other considerations, not yet noticed perhaps, cancel or outweigh the considerations listed as premises. And that in turn means that, even when the considerations listed really do support, even overwhelmingly support, the conclusion that this is what the agent has the strongest reason to do, they still do not entail that conclusion. So as I am using the term 'correct', correct practical reasoning is practical reasoning in which the considerations described in the premises really do give the agent good (or good enough) reason to act in the way described in the conclusion.

watching TV) in terms of *her reasons* for doing it, we have to regard her as thinking that there is something more to be said in favor of watching TV than the other alternatives she lists. Of course in a case like this that 'something more' may just mean that watching TV was more relaxing or less effort or whatever than the other things she might do. And perhaps it sounds rather officious to put this by speaking of 'what she has most reason to do, all things considered' or falsely moral if we speak of 'what she *should* do, all things considered'. So perhaps it would be better to speak of 'what there is more to be said in favor of doing'. But really these are just stylistic considerations. The phrases are intended to be interchangeable.

So, with this caveat in mind, I will continue to put this point by saying that, if we are to understand someone *as engaged in practical reasoning*, we must at a minimum understand her as reasoning to such a conclusion, one about what she *should* do, all things considered.[35] This will be so even if we think that her reasoning is fallacious in some way. Unless the conclusion is about what the agent should do, then, whatever it was, it wasn't a case of *practical* reasoning. So all practical reasoning, of necessity, involves at least this normative thought on the part of the reasoner.

It also seems very plausible (to me) to say that, in order to understand something *as an intentional action*, we must understand the agent as having done it *for a reason*; that is, this is a defining or essential feature of actions. As Anscombe puts it, intentional actions 'are the actions to which a certain sense of the question "Why?" is given application; the sense is of course that in which the answer, if positive, gives a reason for acting' (Anscombe 1963, p. 9).This is a distinct claim, of course, and one that would take us off the track to defend

---

[35] It is very important to distinguish what Phillipa Foot has labeled 'type one' and 'type two' 'ought' or 'should' judgments, that is, roughly speaking, judgments that some consideration provides some reason to perform some action from judgments that sum up all such considerations and say that some action is what one has most reason to do, so far as one can tell (Foot 1983). If John Searle (1964) is right in holding that 'I promised that I will do X' entails 'I ought to do X', then this must be an example of the former sort; that is, the 'ought' here must be understood as saying that one has *some* reason to do X. After all, I might also have promised (mistakenly, or even perhaps intentionally) not to do X. That would by the same argument mean that it was true that I ought not do X. So those two claims must be consistent, and that means they must be understood as saying only that a promise gives me a reason, that is *some* reason, to act so as to fulfill it. Such a claim leaves it open that I might have a reason, perhaps even a better reason, to act differently. I still have to figure out, in such a situation, what I really should do, that is what I should do all things considered, what I have most reason to do.

here. If it is true, though, it follows that, in order to understand some-thing as an intentional action, we must understand the agent as acting on a view about what she should do, that is on a view that can stand as the conclusion of a piece of practical reasoning. Whether this is true of all actions, however, it clearly will be true of those actions that are in fact done for a reason—surely at least a very important subset of intentional actions if not all of them. But if actions done for a reason are only a subset of all intentional actions, it is that subset that is being examined here.

Consider again my other neighbor, the one whom we have been imagining to think that only her own desires, yens, urges, cravings, and other such states—her proper desires—give her reason to act. I argued above that, in order to understand her as engaged in practical reasoning, we had to understand her as accepting premise 4d, the evaluative premise that weighed up the relative *importance* as reasons (in her view) of the desires of hers that she thought relevant to decid-ing how to vote. My claim is not that 4d itself is required, but that *some* premise of that sort is, i.e. that some evaluative premise is needed in order for her to assign weight as reasons to the desires she thinks relevant to her action. Otherwise her 'practical reasoning' would just consist of a list of factual descriptions of her mental states, along perhaps with descriptions of their intensity or duration, followed by a 'conclusion' about what she should do, a conclusion that was utterly irrelevant to the preceding list; that is, it would be (yet another case of) an *ignoratio elenchi*. Without some evaluative premise, her conclusion about what she should do all things consid-ered won't even be relevant to the facts she lists. Hence these facts would give no hint as to why she thought there was something to be said for doing what she did.

4.4 The Principle of Charity

But so what?, someone might say. Some people just reason really really badly, even sometimes drawing 'conclusions' flatly and totally unsup-ported by their premises. (Read some of the letters people write to the newspapers, for Pete's sake.) But though that is true of course, exam-ining such cases will help us see why *explanations* of actions must themselves involve a normative element. The first question to ask here is how much sense we actually can make of someone's action if we do *not* attribute to her some evaluative premise in her reasoning.

So suppose that, when I ask my other neighbor why she voted for that tax increase, this is just the kind of answer she gives, one that seems to involve no evaluation whatsoever. That is, suppose that she says she wants us to have subsidized day care (and knows the tax increase is required for that) and she of course also wants to use the money she would otherwise have to pay in taxes for herself (i.e. premises 1d, 2, and 3 above), but she wants subsidized day care more intensely (premise 4i). So, she says, she decided she should vote for the tax increase.

How should we understand such a speech (which would be roughly analogous to my just giving the 'practical syllogism' in Section 4.1 above in response to a question about why I had jumped out of the way of that car)? The most natural way, I think, would be either to take her use of the term 'wanted intensely' as a sort of short-hand for 'thought to be of more importance or worth', or else to ascribe to her the implicit, unstated view that more intensely felt desires are the ones that ought to be acted on or are more worth following (in short, are the ones that give her most reason to act). The second of these views is perhaps in itself not very plausible, but in the context described ascribing either one of these views to her seems much more plausible than the third alternative, that is, is much more plausible than holding that she came to a conclusion about how she *should* vote on the basis of 'reasoning' utterly irrelevant to the issue.

In other words, what we need and use (and I claim must use) here is some version of the so-called 'principle of charity', which says that we should understand people in such a way as to make them as rational as possible (consistent with the evidence we have, of course).[36] It is worth reflecting on why this is so. It is the key, I think, to answering the question raised above about why we are *required* to include the extra, evaluative premises in practical reasoning, and therefore understanding why explanations of actions in these terms always have a normative element. The first of the two interpretations just suggested would, as I said, in essence turn my other neighbor's reasoning into the reasoning I described myself as using to decide how to vote (Section 3.2 above). It would interpret my other neighbor as holding

---

[36] The Principle of Charity can't, I think, be understood merely as saying that we should interpret people so as to make *some* rational sense of them, if only because the constraint then goes too slack, so to speak. There will almost always be numerous, conflicting, or even inconsistent interpretations of any action, each of which will make *some* sense of it.

it to be more important or valuable that we have subsidized day care than that she have those few extra dollars the tax increase will cost her. Her conclusion that she should vote for the tax increase then seems perfectly reasonable, since (other things being equal at least) it is reasonable to do what one can to achieve ends one regards as more important in preference to ends one regards as less important when a choice has to be made.

Suppose, however, that for some reason this interpretation is ruled out, perhaps because we somehow know on other grounds that my other neighbor is *not* speaking of the importance or value of these things, but really is referring only to her own, proper desires and their different intensities, just as she seems to be. It is still much more plausible to understand her as implicitly accepting the view that it is more important (or in some way better) to satisfy more intense desires than less intense ones, than it is to understand her as holding no such evaluative view at all. And this will be true even for those who, like me, find this particular evaluative claim to be quite implausible. This is because, without *some* such evaluative premise that allows us to understand the considerations she lists as, in her view, constituting reasons for her to vote as she does, it is no longer clear what justifies understanding her conclusion (which is supposed to be that she *should* vote for this tax increase) as a genuinely normative one, and hence is no longer clear that we have actually been given *her reason* for voting as she did.

The question is why she voted for that tax increase, that is what *her reasons* were for voting for it. So we need to understand her response to this question as somehow describing her reasons. This means that we need to understand her response as *somehow*, at least in her own mind, supporting the thought that she *should* do it, that is as giving considerations *she took to be* reasons for doing it. If we rule out ascribing to her the implicit belief that the more intense the desire, the more important it is to try to satisfy it (or some other evaluative thought along this line), it is hard to understand what she says as doing this. The things she lists, her two desires and a comparison of their intensities, have somehow to be seen *by her* as giving her *at least* some reason (even better, enough reason) to vote as she does, in order for them to be cited as her reason for this vote. The desires by themselves, even when we include their intensities, frequencies, durations, etc., simply do not do this. So it looks as if, unless we ascribe *some* evaluative thought to her, we haven't gotten anywhere in trying to figure out what her reason was. There will be as yet no justification for ascribing to her the thought that this is what she *should* do.

One might ask why we couldn't understand her as taking what I have called an observer's point of view toward her own action when she lists the intensities of her two conflicting desires and cites the greater intensity of her desire for subsidized day care as being what led her to vote as she did. But, though one can of course take such a point of view toward one's own actions or reasoning, it doesn't seem possible to do so *while* (or rather, *in*) *trying to figure out what to do.* Recall that we are imagining my other neighbor as hovering, so to speak, at the point of decision. Her finger is poised between the 'yes' and 'no' buttons on the voting machine. She is deliberating about which one to push. It is not a matter, for her, then, in that situation, of figuring out what *led* (or is leading or will lead) her into one decision or the other. It is a matter of figuring out which decision *to make*, which way to vote. If she simply takes the observer's point of view, describing to herself what desires she has and their strengths and the like, it is hard to see how she will ever actually *do* anything. She will be like the determinist in the joke who, when asked by the waiter in the restaurant what he wants to eat, replies that as a determinist he can't make a decision, since he doesn't believe there are such things as 'decisions', and so like everyone else will just have to wait and see what he orders.[37]

So, I want to say, though we can of course take the observer's point of view toward her, and she can take it towards herself, thinking of *her* as taking the observer's point of view in this way would not in fact do us any good in answering the question of why she voted as she did, at least if we understand that as a question about what *her reasons* were for voting this way. It would just be a way of imagining her as joining us in trying to figure out why she voted as she did. She can certainly take the observer's point of view on her own desires, perhaps even use them to predict what she is likely to do. But for her to note that she has these desires, and that they have certain intensities or the like, will be relevant to her in trying to *figure out* what to do only if she takes these facts, even if only implicitly, as somehow providing her with some reason to vote one way or the other, that is only if she takes it as important, or valuable, or worthwhile, to satisfy more rather than less intense desires.

---

[37] This example is John Searle's.

Suppose however that someone refuses to accept this and just 'digs in her heels' here. That is, suppose someone still wants to hold that no such implicit evaluation is needed, that my other neighbor simply *decides* to push the 'yes' button *because* she realizes that her desire for subsidized day care is more intense than her desire for the few extra dollars she will have if there is no tax increase. That is, the claim would be that this is the whole story here so to speak, and no attribution to my other neighbor of any evaluative thought about how much *reason* to act these desires give her is needed. I don't think it is really possible to understand such a case, i.e. one described in this way.

The question is whether we are allowed here to think of her as taking the intensity of her desires as *grounds* or *reasons* for pushing the 'yes' button. If she does, then of course this is an evaluative thought. But if the idea here is that she does *not* think of the intensity of her desires as grounds for pushing the button, but simply notes these intensities and then, a bit later, decides to push 'yes' (or just pushes it), there is a puzzle about why (or indeed *whether*) she 'decided' here. What is supposed to be the connection between her noting that she has these desires and her subsequent pushing of that button (or her 'decision' to push it)? What, that is, justifies the claim that she pushes that button, or decides to, *because* she noted that she had these desires?

She may have lots of other thoughts in the time just prior to her pushing of the button. She remembers she has a dental appointment perhaps, or wishes she had worn lighter clothing since the day is so warm. If we are not allowed to attribute to her the evaluative thought that the intensity of her desires provides her with reason to act to satisfy them, then it is not clear why her thoughts about the intensities of her desires are supposed to be any more connected to her pushing that button than are her thoughts about her coming dental appointment or her clothes (or, of course, any other thoughts she has just prior to pushing that button). Of course, any such thought might mechanically 'trigger' her pushing the 'yes' button, just as suddenly remembering her dental appointment might cause her to feel faint, but that would hardly make it *her reason* for pushing that button. In fact, it would seem to undercut the idea that her pushing the button was an intentional action at all.[38] In short, withdrawing the attribution to her of the

---

[38] It would not, in the jargon, produce her action 'in the right way'.

thought that the intensity of her desire (or something anyway) *gives her some reason* to push that button leaves it completely mysterious what is meant by the claim that she intentionally acted 'because' she saw that this particular desire was the more intense one, short at least of some sort of mechanical cause. But if we say that her thought that this desire was the more intense one was what *triggered* her hand movement, we seem to remove this movement from the realm of being an intentional action.

The problem here could be rather covered up by the fact that the claim we are considering is easily confused with the *very different* claim that my other neighbor pushed the 'yes' button because she had a more intense desire for subsidized day care than for the few extra dollars she would have were there no tax increase (not, that is, because she *realized or believed* that she did). This is a description from what I have been calling the observer's point of view. The question is whether we can understand her actions if we regard *her* as taking the observer's point of view. There is a huge difference between saying that she decided to vote as she did because she *realized* (that is, came correctly to believe) one of her desires was more intense than another, which is the claim we are considering, and saying she voted as she did because one of her desires *was* more intense than another (i.e. whatever she did or did not believe about these desires or anything else). The latter claim is just the observer's description, which follows from the fact that she acted as she did. It is true *whatever* it was that led or moved her to vote as she did. It would be true even if she had been moved (as I was claiming I was) by the thought that subsidized day care is a good thing, and not (as we are here supposing) by her own yearning for subsidized day care. So this is not even relevant to the issue here.

The claim we are considering is that my other neighbor *reasoned*, on the basis of what she (correctly) took to be the intensity of her desires, to a conclusion about what she should do, without however thinking that it was in any way important or valuable to act on more rather than less intense desires, that is without having any thought that the intensity of her desires *gave her a reason* to do anything. This seems to me to make (or at least to come very close to making) my other neighbor's action unintelligible. It would be like claiming that someone simply 'reasoned' from the fact that today is Thursday, or that the sky is blue, to the conclusion that she should vote for this tax increase (or that Hawaii is an island). 'Let's see,' she thinks. 'Today is

Thursday and the sky is blue. So I should vote for this tax increase.'
(Or: . . . 'So Hawaii is an island.') It seems possible that such thoughts
might run through someone's mind. The question is whether it is
possible to understand them as giving what can legitimately be called
'her reasons' for voting as she does (or for holding this opinion).

While there seems to be nothing logically incoherent or contra-
dictory about such descriptions, without *some* further explanation of
what my other neighbor could possibly have had in mind, we are left
at a loss. It is still deeply unclear what *her reason* for voting as she did
really is, indeed whether she had a reason at all. In short, if we drop
the attribution of some evaluative premise (along the lines of 4d in
this example) to the practical reasoning of the agent performing the
action, we are thereby dropping, or are certainly in serious danger of
dropping, the thought that this person acted for a reason at all, and
hence the thought that the agent 'intentionally acted' at all.

This is at, or at least very close to, the heart of the matter here. It is
not that an agent must explicitly subscribe to some evaluative premise,
aloud or even silently to herself. Nor is it even that she must be willing to agree to some such premise if asked. It is rather that, in trying
to understand what she did as an intentional action, we must *ascribe*
to her some evaluative thought along the lines of premise 4 or 4d if we
are to understand her as acting for a reason, that is if we are to understand what she did as an intentional action at all. If we are to understand her as *deciding* how to vote, we must understand her *as seeing
herself* as acting for a reason, that is as having a reason to vote 'yes'
rather than 'no'. That is, we must understand her as voting on what
seems to her some grounds or basis, if we are to understand her as *deciding* to vote as she does. And for that we need to see her as having an
evaluative belief about the importance or 'weight' or reason generat-
ing capacity of the things she considers that bear on her decision.

If we drop the ascription to her of some evaluative belief, along the
lines of premise 4 or 4d, we call into question our ascription to her of
the normative conclusion that she should vote for that tax increase,
that she had reason (or even enough reason) to do so. This is to call
into question whether she understood herself as having a reason to
vote as she did, hence to call into question whether she understood
herself as acting for a reason.

Much of the point here can be summed up by saying that, in order
to understand the agent's reason for acting as she did, we must understand her reasons *as conceived by her*. The 'first person' point of view,

or rather the point of view of the person deliberating, is not elim-inable. It is obvious that this frequently involves more or less explicit evaluations of the various alternatives. But I am arguing that, since practical reasoning necessarily involves a normative conclusion about what the agent should do (in the sense of what she has the strongest reason to do, what has the most to be said for it), understanding an agent as acting for a reason necessarily involves attributing to her that normative judgment, and hence some evaluations on the basis of which this judgment is made. Understanding someone as acting for a reason, that is, necessarily involves seeing what see herself thought argued in favor of doing what she did.

It is of course always possible, as I said, to take a third person or external perspective on the agent's reasons, even if one is oneself the agent in question. In the case of my reasoning about whether to vote for that tax increase, this would mean describing my belief that subsi-dized day care is a good thing (the belief, that is, on which I based my conclusion that I should vote for that tax increase) as my having a pro attitude toward subsidized day care. But, I claim, it is not possible for me to take this perspective while deliberating about how to vote. Or rather, as I said, it is not possible for me to take this perspective *in* deliberating about how to vote. I can of course, *during the course of* my deliberations, that is while deliberating, describe my evaluative belief as a pro attitude toward subsidized day care, either to others who ask or simply to myself. But to do this is not to deliberate. It is more like observing myself in deliberation. If I *base* my deliberation on the thought *that I have* a pro attitude toward subsidized day care (such as a belief that it is a good thing), it becomes a different delib-eration, a different piece of reasoning. This would be to regard *the fact that I have this pro attitude* as itself providing me with reason to vote for the tax increase (rather in the way my other neighbor took the fact that she had a yearning for subsidized day care as providing her with a reason to vote as she did).

Cases of explicit practical deliberation, with evaluative premises and a normative conclusion about what the agent should do (of the sort we started with above), are thus paradigmatic for understanding what it is to act for a reason. Cases where some or all of the essential steps are not set out, even cases like jumping out of the way of that car, where there is and even could be no reasoning at all, still require that we *attribute* these steps (or rather, beliefs) to the agent *on pain of not understanding her action as having been done for a reason.* That is *what it is* to understand her action as having been done for a reason. So the point is not that people can never reason badly, even very badly, or that they cannot act on the basis of very bad practical reasoning. The point is that, if we attribute practical reasoning that is *this* bad to someone (that is, with no evaluative premise at all), we have failed to understand it as reasoning at all and so have failed to understand what she is *doing*. If we for some reason end up deciding that my other neighbor's 'reasoning' really is just as described above (Section 4.4), that is with no evaluative judgment *at all* on her part to support her conclusion that she should vote for that tax increase, then it is still a complete mystery what her reason for voting as she did really is, because it is still not at all clear that she voted as she did *for a reason*. To ascribe to her the thought that she *should* vote for the tax increase (that she had at least good enough reason to do so), which was the conclusion of this supposed reasoning, without ascribing to her any evaluation of the sort contained in premise 4 or 4d, is to try to understand her as voting for the tax increase *for a reason*, that is as *taking something* as a reason to vote as she does, without understanding her as thinking that anything actually is a reason for her to vote as she does. It is not at all clear that this is intelligible. (This is not to deny of course that we might conclude that someone acted for a reason but that we can't *figure out* what that reason really is. The case we have been considering is rather one where (the claim is) that there is nothing more to figure out, that we have the whole story before us.)

None of this should be surprising. The agent's reasons for performing some action, what she had in mind in doing what she did, give or contain the purpose or point of the action. To understand what she did, pushing the 'yes' button and thereby voting for the tax increase, *as an intentional action* that she performed *for some reason* is to think of it as *having* some purpose or point. To understand her as reasoning about what to do, therefore, is to understand her as weighing up, that is evaluating, the relative worth or importance, in her judgment, of the possible purposes that would be furthered by the alternative actions open to her. If we drop the thought that she makes, or at least accepts, such an evaluation, if only implicitly, we therefore cast doubt on the idea that she thinks there was any reason for her to do what she did, and so, really, we cast doubt on whether she acted for a reason at all.

The Inherently Normative Nature of Action Explanations

Intentional actions are inherently purposive. To understand someone as acting is therefore always to understand her as having a purpose or point in doing what she did, that is, to understand her as doing what she did for a reason. The practical reasoning the agent used in deciding what to do, when it occurs, is thus crucial to understanding what she did, because it sets out what *she* conceived of as giving her reason to do what she did; that is, it sets out *her reasons* for acting as she did. I have been arguing however that, even when such practical reasoning doesn't explicitly occur, or when some steps are left out, we are still required to attribute the relevant evaluative beliefs and normative conclusion to the agent in question, on pain of not understanding her as acting for a reason, and hence (I would say) perhaps not 'acting', or at least not intentionally acting, at all.

5.1 Normative Explanations I: The Deliberative Model

This view can be brought into sharper focus if we contrast it with the other, superficially similar, account of how actions are explained, which lies behind many of the views I have been attacking above and which constitutes a central element of what I called above the non-teleological belief–desire explanatory strategy. I suggested earlier, in discussing the inadequacies of the practical syllogism as an account of practical rationality, that thinking that something like Audi's 'basic schema' for practical reason was correct involved the mistake of thinking that what Audi calls the 'motivational premise' ('I want phi') simply referred to a proper desire, a craving or yen or urge or the like.[1] The assumption behind such a view is presumably that only by

---

[1] See Sect. 3.2 above.

means of such mental states, or proper desires, can purposes be generated; that is, only such states can 'motivate', as it is sometimes put. This is the Humean Theory of Motivation reading of Davidson's principle BD advocated by defenders of the direction of fit argument.[2]

The account for which I have been arguing, in contrast, involves holding that practical rationality itself is a generator of purposes. So the structure of any explanation of an intentional action will have to be such as to take account of this. On this view, trying to figure out what one has most reason to do and then acting on that judgment doesn't require, as a precondition, that one have some proper desire that would provide the purpose, aim, or goal of one's action. Rather, on this view, one can simply act *on the basis* of such practical deliberation, even though this deliberation involves nothing but 'judgments', some of which, of course, are evaluative ones.

These two accounts are not just different but, as I argued above, are in fact incompatible; that is, explaining an action in terms of the agent's reasons in the way I have been defending *precludes* explaining it in terms of any proper desires, whether referred to in her reasoning or not. It doesn't follow from this alone, however, that there are no actions explained in terms of proper desires. So it makes sense to consider a case where such an explanation does seem in order.

It certainly seems reasonable to describe at least some of the behavior of intelligent animals as explainable in terms of their proper desires. This is the way, for instance, Jerry Fodor characterizes the intelligence of his cat. According to Fodor, there is a striking difference in behavior between, on the one side, such things as 'rocks, trees, worms, and spiral nebulae' and, on the other side, intelligent animals such as his cat. His account of this difference is that his cat—'unlike rocks, worms, nebulae, and the rest—has, and acts out of, beliefs and desires'. The behavior of rocks and the like 'are different from [his cat's] because they are, in this respect, differently caused' (Fodor 1987, preface).[3] This seems plausible. Thurber, one of my cats, seems to

---

[2] What Bernard Williams calls that agent's 'subjective motivational set', if it is thought of as containing only elements outside our rational control, would then refer to 'proper desires' in my sense (see Williams 1980). Christine Korsgaard has argued persuasively, however, that in fact Williams's way of explaining the elements of this set would not rule out anything that actually moved an agent, including the driest and most abstract reasoning (see Korsgaard 1988).

[3] Of course, Fodor thinks that in this respect at least cats are no different from people, a view I have been at pains to dispute.

have it as one of his main aims in life to find and make use of comfortable sleeping places. (Thurber does not lead what would be called a strenuous life.) Among his favorite such spots are people's laps. So very frequently, while I am sitting and reading, I will notice him looking up at me from the floor, clearly ready to jump onto my lap unless I actively discourage him. If I say anything at all by way of encouragement he at once jumps up onto my lap and curls into a serious napping position for the duration.

In such a case it seems hard to deny that Thurber jumped because he wanted to curl up on my lap and thought that by jumping in that way he could do so.[4] But it is important to notice that if this is correct we are explaining his action (or at least his 'behavior'[5]) here not in terms of any *reasoning* he does *about* what he wants and how to get it, hence not in terms of the content of such reasoning, but just in terms of his desire *itself*. It is one thing to hold that cats and at least some other non-human animals have and act on beliefs and desires, another thing entirely to claim that they reason, or even form beliefs, *about* their own desires. So, even though ordinary speech might allow us to say of Thurber that 'his reason' for jumping was that he wanted to sit on my lap, that will be deeply misleading if it causes us to assimilate this sort of case to those I have been discussing where the explanation is in terms of the actual or implicit practical deliberation of the agent.

In those cases, to speak of the agent's reason is to speak of those considerations *on the basis of which* the agent decided (or can be regarded as having decided) to do whatever she did. As I said above, speaking of the agent's reason or reasons in this sort of case is not to say that the agent 'believes something to be valuable', or 'believes it to constitute a reason' for doing whatever she did, or the like, if that is taken to mean being willing to assert this or to agree to it if questioned.

---

[4] Fodor would say this, of course, but so would any adherent's of Dennett's 'intentional stance' explanations so far as I can tell. (More on this below.) On the other hand, Davidson's views (in 'Thought and Talk' for instance—Davidson 1975) seem to preclude non-language users from having genuinely contentful mental states, such as beliefs. (More on this below as well.) Likewise, any view that understands desire as conceptually connected to evaluation, such as Tenenbaum's view that to have a desire for something is for that thing to appear good to you (Tenenbaum 1999), seems to rule out non human animals from having genuine desires.

[5] This would be to use the term 'behavior' in a non-intentional sense, where no genuine purposiveness is implied, as when we speak of the 'behavior' of some protein molecules when the PH of the medium in which they are contained is raised or lowered.

Thurber won't do that either, not being a language user. Rather, speaking of an agent's reason or reasons in this sort of case is to say that the agent does, or would, *use* this consideration in deciding what to do, that is accord it some weight in her practical deliberation.

It is certainly true that these considerations might well be her own proper desires (or hopes, yens, etc.). That is how, in the earlier discussion of voting on that proposed tax increase, I pictured my neighbor—the one who decided to vote against the tax on the ground that she wanted to use the extra money for herself. And it is how I pictured my other neighbor, who voted for the tax increase on the ground that her yearning that we have subsidized day care was more important than was her desire to use the extra money for herself. At the same time though, the considerations on which agents act need not be, and often are not, their own proper desires. They could just as well be something else that the agent thinks important, valuable, worthwhile, or the like. That was how I pictured my own vote for that tax increase, which I claimed was done on the ground that subsidized day care is a good thing. (Not, though, on the ground that I *believed* subsidized day care a good thing, which would be a very different, and weirdly self-centered, ground on which to base some action.)

It should be clear that one important difference between these two sorts of account, the other based directly on proper desires such as Thurber's desire to sit on my lap and the one based on practical deliberation, is that on the latter the explanatory mechanism essentially involves reference to the *content* of the agent's practical deliberation, what she *saw as* reason giving considerations, but *not* (or anyway not 'directly') the states of affairs themselves, that is the things *to which* she is referring in her reasoning, even in those cases where these are the agent's own proper desires. This is an absolutely crucial difference which gets obscured if we miss the ambiguity of simply thinking of 'someone's reason for doing X' as 'her desire for Y'. Not seeing this difference could then lead to missing a second, equally important, difference between these two sorts of explanation, i.e. the one set out at length above. An explanation in terms of the agent's deliberation, but not one based directly on proper desires themselves, essentially involves attributing evaluative judgments to the agent in question.

It may also be worth pointing out here that these two different sorts of explanation carry with them quite different ways in which the agent can be mistaken or in error. Explanations directly in terms of the proper desires of the agent, of the sort used to explain

Thurber's jump onto my lap, make use of states that have representational content. So these states might fail accurately to represent. Thurber might I suppose want something, say a bird sitting on a branch of a cherry tree, that doesn't exist (if for instance it is really a decoy put there to frighten real birds away from the cherries).[6]

Explanations in terms of how the agent deliberates of course allow for this sort of error, since they also make use of the agent's representational states. Suppose I am weighing my yen to drink the beer in the fridge against my judgment that I really should work for another hour or two. If there really is no beer in the fridge, then that particular proper desire of mine is defective in much the same way Thurber's desire for that bird was. But there are at least two other possible kinds of error open to agents subject to deliberative explanations. It is also possible that, whether or not there really is a beer in the fridge, I don't really have a yen to drink it. Maybe what I think is a yen to drink the beer in the fridge is really just thirst, which would be satisfied by almost any liquid. Or maybe what I really want is just to get up and walk around a bit. This sort of error, about the nature or content or perhaps even existence of the proper desires on the basis of which I am reasoning, is possible only in deliberative explanations. And of course, even if there is a beer in the fridge and I really do have a yen to drink it, I may weigh or evaluate this yen incorrectly in my deliberation. That sort of error on my part is also of a kind that is logically possible only when my action is thought of as subject to a deliberative explanation.

Since it is implausible to attribute to cats either judgments about their own mental states or genuinely evaluative judgments (as opposed to merely stronger and weaker desires), it is implausible to think we can explain Thurber's jumping onto my lap by using the deliberative model. At the same time, it seems perfectly reasonable to attribute to him the desire to curl up on my lap, and equally plausible to think that that desire must figure essentially in the explanation of his jumping. (Certainly in ordinary speech, talk of what a cat wants, for instance, is perfectly in order.) So there clearly *is* a form of explanation of action (or at least of behavior) that appeals in the way just described to the agent's desire itself, rather than to her judgment about this desire, at least as long as the 'agent' in question is a cat.

---

[6] Hume discusses this as one of the ways in which desires can be in error (Hume 1988, bk 2, pt. 3, sect. 3).

Is there any *human* action (or behavior) to which such a form of explanation applies? The clearest cases to which the deliberative model applies are some of the voting examples we have considered, where the agent really does engage in practical deliberation and then acts on the basis of this. Such cases are, as I said, paradigmatic examples of this sort of explanation. So it might be thought that the model that appeals directly to the agent's desires will apply to those cases where no explicit deliberation takes place. But clearly, it can't simply apply to all such cases since, as we have seen with the earlier example of my jumping out of the way of the careening car, there are cases where, even though there wasn't and indeed in a sense couldn't have been any actual deliberation, the deliberative model apparently still applies. And beyond that, I have in any case been at pains to argue that what the agent's reason for performing some action was is not necessarily determined by 'what went through her mind' by way of practical deliberation before she acted. That is the paradigm case all right, but that is all.[7]

I will call 'direct desire explanations of actions' explanations of the sort that I claimed above apply to Thurber's jump onto my lap, that is explanations where the central explanatory factor is the agent's desire *itself*, not her evaluation of or deliberation about this desire or some other reason giving consideration. To find examples of human actions where such explanations work, I think, we will need (at least) to find cases that lack the two features I have been focusing on so far, namely the normative element of genuine reasons explanations, and the reference to the agent's character. Here is one such possible case. Suppose I want to explain why an acquaintance who is addicted to nicotine smoked a cigarette on a particular occasion. By way of contrast, let's also suppose that I know that, in addition to being addicted to nicotine, she wants to impress someone with her worldliness and thinks that smoking a cigarette (in these circumstances) would at least push that project along a bit.

There would seem to be two quite different sorts of explanation possible here, the very two different sorts we have been comparing. If

---

[7] As I hope the discussion here will make clear, I now think that many of the examples of 'direct desire' explanations given in Schueler (1995a), e.g. impulsively and unreflectively eating a cookie out of the cookie jar, are not in fact examples of this sort of explanation at all. The fact that one does not actually reflect on or deliberate about what to do is not enough to make the explanation a 'direct desire' explanation. Many cases in which deliberative explanations are called for are also like this.

we cite as her reason for smoking that cigarette that my acquaintance wants to impress this person, we seem to (or at least can) bring in all the features of such explanations that we have been examining. She would then, for example, be regarded as thinking that there is something valuable or important about impressing this person (or about satisfying her desire to impress him, if that is how her reasoning goes). If she knows of the damage smoking does to her lungs, etc., then we must suppose that she weighs this reason not to smoke as having less importance than impressing this person (and perhaps satisfying her craving); and so on, in the end perhaps citing some character trait or traits involved in being the kind of person who reasons in this way.

But suppose we merely cite her craving to smoke, which I am supposing is a manifestation of some physiological facts about her which constitute her addiction to nicotine. We do not, that is, cite her *belief* that she has this craving. We cite the craving itself. On the face of it, the form of this explanation is then very different. We don't have to ascribe to her any belief about the *importance* or worth of satisfying this craving for instance. Even if she has such a belief, it plays no role in *this* explanation of her smoking. If it did, then we would be back to explaining my acquaintance's smoking not in terms of her craving to smoke but in terms of what she thought gave her *reason* to smoke (and hence in terms of her belief that she has this craving, not of the craving itself).

Indeed, if it is the craving itself that explains her smoking, she need not even (be supposed to) have any belief *that* she has this craving. Presumably most people are in fact aware of their own cravings, at least most of the time. But whether or not that is so, if it really is the craving *itself* that explains her action, any belief she has *about* whether she has this craving need not come into it. At this point though we encounter a possible source of confusion.

In the usual accounts of explanations of actions where reference is made to the agent's proper desire, such as a craving to smoke, it is held that the agent also needs, along with her desire to smoke, a belief about how to satisfy this desire. And that seems right. If Thurber had not believed that by jumping he could reach my lap (if I had not been sitting down, for instance, or had appeared to him to be seated too far from where he was), presumably he would not have jumped. At the same time, we cannot suppose here, even implicitly, that any *reasoning* is done by my acquaintance (or by Thurber), on pain of shifting back to explaining her smoking as an outcome of deliberation, not of the craving to smoke itself. So the sense in which she believes that, say, she can smoke by putting a cigarette in her mouth and lighting it will have to be the same sense in which Thurber sees that by jumping he can make it to my lap.

This is a point at which direct desire explanations get confused with deliberative ones, I think, because it is easy to slip from the thought that if she hadn't (in *some* sense) been aware of how to smoke the cigarette she wouldn't have done it, to the thought that she had a 'full blown' belief to this effect (and then to the thought that she at least implicitly reasoned about it and so to the deliberative model of explanation). But of course there are—indeed probably must be— states of awareness for both humans and other animals that fall well short of the sort of 'belief' paradigmatically exemplified in explicit reasoning. Most of our awareness of our immediate surroundings would seem to be of this sort, as well as our awareness of how to do things of the sort we can do 'without thinking', such as speak, open doors, scratch our heads and ride bicycles—things that we know how to do and have perhaps done innumerable times before but which we could usually not describe or explain. (These are presumably the sorts of things Ryle was referring to with the phrase 'knowing how', which he opposed to 'knowing that': Ryle 1949, chapter 2). It would seem that there must be such states if we are to explain animal behav- ior, such as Thurber's jumping onto my lap, in the way I have described, that is as involving a desire and belief but without any reasoning or evaluation, even implicitly.

So let us try out the idea that this is how it works in this cigarette smoking case. My acquaintance's desire to smoke somehow combines with her awareness of how to do so in such a way as to result in her smoking, that is, in just the way Thurber's desire to sit on my lap somehow combines with his awareness of how to get there results in his jumping onto my lap. Is this enough to show that what I called a direct desire explanation works for this action, i.e. my acquaintance smoking that cigarette? It might seem that the answer has to be yes, but in fact I think we still don't know enough about this case to say that. What is missing, I want to say, is an answer to the further ques- tion of whether it was *possible* for my acquaintance to deliberate about whether to do what she did. In the case of Thurber's jump onto my lap, the answer would seem to be that it was not, since presum- ably cats cannot deliberate.

For my acquaintance, however, the question seems open. No doubt there is a whole range of possibilities here, but let's look just at two relatively clear ones. It could be simply that my acquaintance *in fact* did not deliberate. Her action was 'automatic' or 'habitual', as we sometimes say, as when one unthinkingly pops the last cookie into one's mouth or turns one's car down the street one has lived on for years. The cigarette was available (someone was handing them around perhaps). She was completely absorbed in something else, say explaining some intricate philosophical point to someone. 'Without thinking', she took the cigarette and started smoking it, something she has done many times before.

If this is the whole story, then I think we will want to treat this case like the case of my jumping out of the way of that careening car. Even though in fact my acquaintance does not deliberate, we will want to attribute to her the thought *that* she has a craving to smoke, that it is more important to satisfy this craving (and perhaps impress others) than to do this tiny bit to head off lung disease, and so on. That is, we will treat her as acting for a reason in just the way we have been examining. I don't mean here to preclude the possibility that we will decide that her 'will was weak'. That is a description of her character, based on the thought that she evaluated things badly even by her own lights. In a situation such as this one, though, it would seem more accurate to say that she behaved impulsively or unthinkingly. Had she stopped to think, she might have realized that there was more to be said against smoking that cigarette than in favor. But the point is that in a case such as this one the mere fact that she *could have* deliberated and acted on the basis of that deliberation seems enough to earn her some criticism for acting on the weaker reason (satisfying a craving) rather than a stronger one (avoiding lung disease). So even though she did not in fact deliberate, we are still explaining her action in terms of the deliberative model.

This comes out if we contrast this smoking example with the case of my jumping out of the way of that careening car. Much of the discussion of that case above was about how I should have reasoned in that situation, if I had been able to do so, i.e. what the correct reasoning would have been. And of course, we were assuming that there was nothing to be said for any other course of action than jumping out of the way. But suppose we change the example and assume, first, that there was a strong reason (in the estimation of the agent, namely me) for not jumping, say because doing so would endanger the child I was carrying on my shoulders. And second, assume that things happened so fast that the act of jumping out of the way really was the direct and immediate result of seeing that car bearing down on me, rather like the 'startle' reaction one has when say a firecracker goes off behind one.

The elements of these two cases are now much the same, with one striking difference. It seems plausible to say that in each case the agent acted as a direct result of some strong desire. No deliberation was involved. And in each it is arguable that there was a stronger reason for not doing what was done. The difference is that, in the case of my jumping out of the way of that car (as now described), the fact that my terror of the car triggered my movement directly blocks any criticism I would otherwise be subject to for not acting on the stronger reason (avoiding endangering the child I was carrying). Not so for my cigarette smoking acquaintance, whose character it seems plausible to criticize as 'unthinking', or even perhaps 'imprudent', for smoking that cigarette even though she knew she had good reason not to. Likewise, if we suppose that I could have deliberated before jumping out of the way of that car, say because I had a few seconds to watch events unfold, but that in fact I still did not do so and was moved only by my fear (i.e. I didn't take the opportunity I had to try to figure out what it would be best to do), that by itself seems to reinstate the deliberative model and says something very unhappy about the *sort* of person I am.[8]

Similar considerations apply to the cigarette smoking case. Suppose that it is not merely that my acquaintance does not in fact deliberate, but that for some reason deliberation, and acting on the basis of that deliberation, would not be *possible*, in some strong sense, in this case. The craving to smoke was so strong that deliberation wouldn't have mattered, perhaps (if that makes sense); or this desire was somehow 'hidden' so that she could not become aware of the fact that she wanted to smoke. (A craving to smoke may not be the most plausible case for this, but think of the desires that psychoanalysis at least claims to discover—the 'death wish' for instance.) If such a situation is possible, the sort of explanation in terms of the agent's reasons that I have been describing cannot apply. Perhaps that doesn't automatically mean that her smoking that cigarette wasn't 'an

---

[8] Though not of course the same sort of thing that would be said if I did indeed deliberate and simply decided to save myself, even if it meant risking the child I was carrying.

action'. It was certainly something she did voluntarily,[9] as a result of being in an inherently purposive mental state, i.e. craving to smoke. But it does make it problematic to say that she acted 'for a reason', just as it would be problematic to say that Thurber jumped onto my lap 'for a reason'.[10]

If the 'deliberative' model of explanation in terms of the agent's reasons is blocked, then it becomes very problematic whether we can make any sense of the question of what *her reason* was for acting on this craving to smoke *rather than* on her desire to avoid lung disease, for instance, or (even more problematically) her belief that it is wrong to expose others to health risks without their permission. This is because nothing in such a direct desire explanation licenses us to attribute to her any normative or evaluative judgments about the importance or worth of any considerations that might speak for or against smoking that cigarette. So it is hard to see that any sense can be made of attributing to her the thought that one of her desires was more important. The direct desire model allows speaking of the 'strength' of desires here, but that is all, and the best it can do for her *belief* that it is wrong to subject others to second hand smoke would seem to be to treat it too as a desire with a certain 'strength' (and we have seen above how problematic that is). Nor will such a direct desire explanation allow us to make any claims about her character, at least to the extent that such claims are grounded on and required by explanations of her actions in terms of the normative or evaluative judgments contained, at least implicitly, in her practical deliberations.[11]

---

[9] Though perhaps not intentionally, since in one sense she did not do it 'for a reason'.

[10] There is obviously an issue here about just what sort of 'impossibility' is at issue. In the car jumping case described earlier, I argued that there was a straightforward sense in which I couldn't have reasoned about whether to jump or not; there was simply not enough time to do so. Still, I argued, in the relevant sense I acted for a reason when I jumped, and (so) what I am here calling the deliberative model of explanation applies. If that is right, then the impossibility (or whatever exactly it is) that blocks the deliberative model will have to be different. Simply not deliberating, or even not having enough time to deliberate, will not be enough. Intuitively, I think, the two suggestions here—that the desire in question is 'overpowering' or that it is completely hidden from the agent—do seem enough. But this still leaves many cases unaccounted for.

[11] Of course there are also 'character traits', or at least features of someone's personality, that do not depend in this way on deliberation, such as Thurber's preference for a lap over a chair as a place to sleep. If the view here being advocated is correct, then presumably such features will not by themselves license any genuinely normative claims about the person, or cat, in question.

Most importantly, perhaps, blocking the deliberative model of explanation in favor of the direct desire model makes very problematic what could be meant by then asking whether the desire to smoke on the basis of which we explain her smoking was 'a good reason' for smoking. Such a question clearly makes sense in the context of actual or possible practical deliberation, that is in the context of the possibility of evaluating the different weights or values *as reasons* of the considerations that seem to the agent to argue for or against doing something. In blocking the deliberative model of explanation, such a context is also blocked. So it becomes very unclear what sense we are supposed to attach to this sort of question. In the case of Thurber jumping onto my lap because he wanted a warm place to curl up, there seems to be no sense in asking (or inclination to ask) whether this was a *good* reason for him to do this. That is presumably because cats cannot deliberate and hence the only model of explanation possible here is the direct desire model.

In short, it very much looks as if to use such a direct desire explanation is to remove my acquaintance (in the case of her smoking that cigarette) from the status of 'rational agent, at least in the sense of being capable of evaluating considerations that seem to her to speak for or against some action and acting on the basis of such deliberation (just as I was removed from that status, in the re-described car example, when I suddenly saw that car coming at me and, *purely* as a reaction, jumped out of the way). Thurber, presumably, being a cat, never had that status. But my acquaintance did, and does usually. So the burden of proof' will be carried by the argument that removes her from that status. That is I think at least partly why we need the thought that in some strong sense she *could* not have acted on the basis of deliberation before we feel comfortable using a direct desire explanation in a case like this.

If this argument is correct, then what it means is that purposive explanations of actions, that is explanations of actions in terms of the agent's reasons, to the extent that they regard agents as *genuine rational agents*, are always implicitly normative in at least the minimal sense that they necessarily attribute to the agent a normative view (about what she should do) based on evaluative premises. Such explanations will use the deliberative model. They will not be 'direct' desire explanations. And this will be true not only when the agent reasons well, but also when she reasons badly. In fact, it will be true in the many cases when she doesn't reason at all. For an action to have a purpose or point on this model is for the agent to think (even if falsely or on bad grounds) that there is something about the action that makes it worth doing, that is that gives her a reason to do it.

We have been looking at two strikingly different ways in which desires can figure in the explanations of actions. They may do so 'directly', as they do when my cat jumps onto my lap because he wants a nice place to sleep; or they may be among the things about which I reflect when trying to decide what I have most reason to do, what I should do. According to Davidson, in order to be a genuine believer, one must also have the concept of what a belief is, since it is essential to beliefs that they can be false. 'Can a creature have a belief if it does not have the concept of belief?' he asks. 'It seems to me it cannot, and for this reason. Someone cannot have a belief unless he understands the possibility of being mistaken, and this requires grasping the contrast between truth and error—true belief and false belief' (Davidson 1975, p. 22).[12] So on this view someone, or some 'creature', who merely had some 'belief-like states', that is representational states, which she did not realize could be false, would not therefore have genuine beliefs. (Perhaps such states are the best that can be ascribed to Thurber and other non-human animals.) Only creatures with enough reflective ability to see that their representational states might also *mis*represent, on this sort of view, are capable of genuine beliefs.

One might make an analogous point about desires. I argued above that proper desires are inherently goal directed states. But perhaps, following Davidson here, we should say that no one can have a *genuine* desire without having the concept of desire, in the sense of understanding that desires are *merely* goal directed states, that is in the sense of understanding the possibility that the thing desired may not in fact be worth having. No doubt to some extent at least this is a terminological point about how to use the terms 'belief' and 'desire'. As was mentioned above, ordinary speech apparently allows saying that cats and some other non-human animals have beliefs and desires. But at the same time, however we decide this terminological issue, there is an important distinction here. The ability to *reflect* on one's beliefs and desires, to consider that one's beliefs might be false and that one's desires might not be worth satisfying, is an essential

---

[12] Davidson goes on to argue that the distinction between true and false beliefs can arise only in the context of interpretation, and so is available only to a user of language.

feature of rationality and hence of rational agency. I have been arguing that, therefore, explanations of the actions of such rational agents
requires understanding them as evaluating the considerations that
seem to them to argue for or against performing the actions that
seem to them possible.

If this is right, one of the two questions posed at the beginning of
Chapter 4 is answered. All explanations of actions in terms of the
agent's reasons, to the extent that they understand the agent as a
genuine rational agent, presuppose the deliberative model, and hence
must as a minimum ascribe to the agent the normative thought that
she has reason to perform this action, i.e. that she *should* do it. But in
fact, I want to argue, the other question is answered here as well.

5.2 Normative Explanations II: The Agent's Perspective

The other question was why attributing evaluative and normative
beliefs to some agent in order to explain her actions should be
thought to require *those doing the explaining* to make any evaluations.
Ascribing to some agent an evaluative or normative belief, that is
holding that this agent has such a belief, is not after all itself an evaluative or normative belief. The answer to this second question comes
from the role played in the above argument by the principle of charity.

To focus the discussion on a specific case, recall, yet again, my
other neighbor— the one who voted for that tax increase and lists, in
response to the question of why she did it, nothing but the various
desires she has and the intensity with which she feels each of them. I
have claimed, first, that we have to understand her as somehow
reasoning to the conclusion, or at least holding the view, that this is
how she *should* vote and, second, that this way of understanding her
requires that we also understand her as at least implicitly *evaluating*
her more intense desires as more worth satisfying (or the like).
Assuming, possibly rashly, that the second point was established
above, let us concentrate on the claim that we have to understand her
as somehow holding that this is how she *should* vote, that is holding
that there is more to be said for voting this way than not. This is the
central claim and one that perhaps seems on its face open to question. The issue is what the force of this 'have to' really is.

One way to attack this issue is to try to imagine dropping this
claim. That is, we might try to imagine *not* attributing to my other

neighbor the belief that she should vote for this tax increase, while still leaving in place all the other beliefs we have been attributing to her. And in particular of course we want to leave in place the thought that she did indeed vote for that tax increase intentionally. The question is whether we can make sense of such a situation. So let's consider the possibility that the only things we are justified in ascribing to her as beliefs are the premises labeled 1d, 2, 3, and 4i above (and in particular of course *not* any conclusion about what she should do, or has most reason to do):

    1d. I have a yearning that we have subsidized day care [she says to herself].

    2. This proposed tax increase is necessary if there is to be subsidized day care in my community.

    3. At the same time, it will cost me some money, which I would like to use (i.e. which I have a yen to use) elsewhere, if this tax increase is passed.

    4i. Still, my desire that my community have subsidized day care is more *intense* than my desire to keep for my own use the few dollars it will cost me each year.

Since the point here is to block the idea that she thinks she *should* vote for the tax increase, we can't understand her as engaging in any actual practical reasoning using these sentences. To regard her as engaging in practical reasoning would be, I am claiming, to ascribe to her the implicit conclusion that she should vote for the tax increase. So it would just beg the question here to assume that she could engage in such reasoning without such a conclusion. We might perhaps regard her as doing a sort of third person or detached survey of her own mental states, though that by itself doesn't provide any connection between these beliefs and her vote for that tax increase. If someone *else* had noted that she had this particular pair of desires with these relative intensities, that person might use this information to predict how my other neighbor would vote. So I suppose we might try thinking of her as making such a prediction about herself.

Of course, since we are imagining her to hold these beliefs at the time she pushes the 'yes' button, it is rather implausible to think that she would be predicting an action she was then essentially in the process of performing. In any case though it is hard to see what could be the *point* of imagining her to be *predicting* her vote if we are blocked from ascribing to her the thought that these things bear on how she *should* vote. That is the crucial problem. Merely imagining her to be taking an external or third person point of view here (even if we decide she is for some reason predicting the action she will perform a few milliseconds hence) doesn't seem to be of any help in explaining her action. It still seems impossible, given the assumption we are making, to see any *explanatory connection* between what she *thinks*, given by 1d, 2, 3, and 4i, and what she *does* when she pushes the 'yes' button.

Of course it is crucial here that we are ascribing to her the *beliefs* whose content is given by 1d, 2, 3, and 4i. We are not taking any stand about the *actual desires* described by those sentences (e.g. the yearning for subsidized day care referred to in 1d, the yen, referred to in 3, to use for her own purposes the money that would go for that tax increase, etc.). This is because to explain her action in terms of these actual desires would be to shift to a 'direct desire' explanation of the same sort used to explain my cat jumping onto my lap, and so would remove from this explanation her thought that her desires *give her reason* to act as she does (reasons that can be good ones or not); and so on. So we would be (by this move) explaining her action solely by reference to her proper desires, exactly the way we explained Thurber's jump onto my lap.

Thinking of her as acting for a reason, therefore, means in part at least thinking that *she herself* thinks there is something to be said in favor of doing what she does. That is why, when we considered above (Section 4.3) dropping the ascription to her of any positive evaluation that could support a 'should' judgment, it became very difficult to understand what she could be thinking. We were in the position of ascribing to her the thought *that* there is something to be said in favor of voting for this tax increase, but at the same time not ascribing to her anything she herself thinks actually favors this vote; in fact, we were considering the view that there just is no such thing. Here however things are even worse, since now we are dropping the ascription to her even of the thought that *there is something to be said* for voting for this tax increase. Without that thought, however, it is hard to understand her as thinking she *has a reason* to vote for the tax increase, and hence hard to see her as acting for a reason at all. So how do we explain her pushing that 'yes' button?

Various *alternative* stories are possible here of course. Perhaps she pushed the 'yes' button because she wanted to swat a bug that was walking across that particular button. But alternatives of this sort really, and obviously, change the subject. They understand her action of pushing the 'yes' button to be something other than a way of intentionally voting for the tax increase. So they explain her reasons for doing that other thing, not for voting for the tax increase. If we disallow such alternatives however, and just insist that she intentionally voted for that tax increase by pushing the 'yes' button, then dropping the ascription to her of the belief that she *should* vote for the tax increase seems to make the situation (or our description of it) unintelligible, unless we reduce our claim to the one involved in what I have called the 'direct desire' form of explanation. But as we have seen, that sort of explanation also removes her from the status of 'rational agent'.

Why should this be? The 'short answer' is that the principle of charity demands that we interpret my other neighbor's behavior so as to make her as rational as possible. And dropping the ascription to her of the thought that she should vote for the tax increase doesn't do that; in fact, it makes it hard to see her as a rational agent at all, since it makes it hard to see her as acting for a reason (assuming we rule out alternatives of the sort just discussed, which change the subject). I think that this is correct as far as it goes, but it raises the further question of why we should accept the principle of charity.

It is worth pointing out though that to accept this answer in terms of the principle of charity is to accept an answer to the second question posed above, the question of why *the person doing the explaining* has to use normative or evaluative concepts in her explanation of the action in question. The principle of charity is a normative principle in both its form and its content. It tells us what we *should* do in order to understand someone's action, and the content of its advice is that we should understand people as (treat people as) rational beings, that is as beings who reason about how to act and then act in accordance with this reasoning. If all practical rationality were instrumental, based only on satisfying one's proper desires, the principle of charity would apply only to the means by which agents tried to achieve their ends. We have seen, however, that this is not so.

Hence the principle of charity must be understood as applying to the rationality of the purposes or goals that agents have in acting as they do, as well as the means they use to achieve them. That is, it must be understood as applying to the evaluations on which agents base their actions. At the same time, accepting the principle of charity is a requirement for understanding actions in terms of the agent's reasons. That is why it seems impossible to make sense of the case we have just been considering, where we are trying to understand the thought that my other neighbor *intentionally* voted for that tax increase while at the same time trying not to ascribe to her the normative thought that this is what she should do.[13]

In short, in arguing that the principle of charity is required of those doing the explaining if actions are to be intelligible to them (i.e. in the full blown sense in which actions can be performed only by rational agents), we are arguing for the claim that action explanations must themselves use certain normative concepts, the ones involved in 'rationality'. But 'rationality' here must be understood as applying not merely to the means used to achieve one's goals, but to the goals themselves. That is entailed by the claim that practical reasoning requires genuinely evaluative principles.

That this is so is, I think, beyond doubt. Cases like the ones we have been considering throughout this book show this. There is an obvious sense in which we simply fail to understand what someone is doing when, as in the last case above, we hold that someone performed an intentional action without ascribing to her the thought that there was something to be said for her doing it, that is, (in this case) while not regarding her as positively evaluating the satisfaction of her own desires in such a way as to furnish a ground for her action. In such an explanation we are reduced to understanding her in the same way we understand cats and other non-human animals, where direct desire explanations are the best we can do. Exactly *why* this should be so, however, is perhaps not so clear.

To make a start on answering this question, it will help to stand back a little from the details of the argument we have been pursuing and do a bit of stocktaking. The intuitions behind what I have called the non-teleological belief–desire explanatory strategy (where the relevant desire and beliefs are regarded as the efficient causes of which the action is the effect) are two very plausible 'naturalistic' ones. First, human beings are after all parts of nature, organisms with an evolutionary history like that of any other organism and a biological makeup that, even if much more complex in some ways, is still in

---

[13] Of course, one way of describing weakness of will is to say that someone intentionally does something she believes she should not do. I can't solve that puzzle here. But it is important to notice that, even in a case of weakness of will, the agent still acts for a reason in the sense of thinking that there is something to be said in favor of acting as she does. In the case we are considering here, even that is not supposed to be so.

no way different in kind from other similar organisms. So, second, human behavior (in the broadest sense) must be explainable at some level in exactly the same evolutionary and biological (hence causal) terms as that of any other organism.

Neither of these two claims seems to me at all doubtful. The further conclusion needed, however, if these points are to support the non-teleological belief–desire strategy, is that, since human behavior must be governed by the same causal mechanisms as that of any other organism, ordinary reasons explanations of actions must themselves work via causal interactions of beliefs and desires. (And these presumably will then be somehow reducible to, or 'grounded in', or 'supervenient on', causal interactions of brain states, or of some other evolutionarily selected mechanisms or the like.) But this simply does not follow. The most that follows is that reasons explanations must be *consistent with* the two 'naturalistic' claims just mentioned, a much weaker requirement. It could turn out, for instance, that the conceptual apparatus used in biology, chemistry, and so on is just of the wrong conceptual type to deal with human actions. The 'explanatory mechanisms' of the different forms of explanation might simply not correlate.[14]

If, as I have been arguing, reasons explanations are inherently teleological and include as an essential feature their use of normative concepts such as rationality, then the gap between reasons explanations

[14] Consider this example. Suppose we have a field of sheep, many hundreds, some male and some female, but mixed together completely randomly. We decide to count them, and to that end we herd them one by one through a small chute into another field, counting each and stamping it with its assigned number as it goes by. Once all the sheep are through the chute, each will have been assigned and labeled with a number. So now each sheep will have two perfectly determinate properties. Each will be of one sex or the other, and each will have either an odd or an even number assigned to it. And for each of these properties (sex and number) there will be a determinate explanation of how the sheep in question came to have that property (the usual genetic story for its sex, and the counting story just given for its assigned number). But there might be no systematic relation at all between these two explanations. Of course, assuming a finite number of sheep, there would have to be some formula that described the relation between the sex and the assigned number of each animal. But even that formula would do nothing but describe the sheep already covered. It would give no underlying relation between the two properties (i.e. it would be in no way 'law-like'). Suppose it turned out that there were, say, another few dozen sheep hiding in the far corner of the second field which had been assigned numbers but which we had not noticed while we were writing our descriptive formula and which were therefore not yet covered by the formula we had written. In that case the formula would provide no grounds at all for saying whether, for instance, the next odd numbered sheep would be male. So there would be no sense in which we could explain one kind of property in terms of the other. (This example is adapted from Davidson 1980*a*, essay 11.)

and non-teleological explanations that make no essential use of normative concepts (including of course biological, or chemical, or neurological explanations of brain state interactions) seems unbridgeable. Whatever exactly it means to say that two explanations involve concepts of different 'conceptual types', explanations that stick to mechanical/physical interactions and teleological explanations that use normative concepts would seem to be paradigm examples of it. At the same time, this essential use of normative concepts in reasons explanations should help us see how these explanations work and why they seem to differ so sharply from the explanatory model envisioned by defenders of the non-teleological belief–desire strategy.

In general, it seems true enough that one wants the concepts and distinctions used in any explanatory schema to match or be smoothly explainable by the things or stuff being explained (as revealed that is by the next 'lower' or more sophisticated level of explanation). The concepts employed in any explanatory schema should be seen to 'carve nature at its joints' when we get a closer look at what 'nature' is through a new and more sophisticated theory. In chemistry, for instance, it was a nice outcome when a relatively old set of concepts such as 'acid' and 'base' turned out to match a systematic set of differences revealed by the newer analysis in terms of molecular structure (which could then be used to extend these terms to substances to which they had not been applied before, such as DNA).

So it is very understandable for advocates of the non-teleological belief–desire explanatory strategy to attempt to ground reasons explanations of actions in the explanatory schema provided by the sophisticated sciences obviously applicable to human beings. One wants to find the concepts one uses, or rather the features of reality that ground or justify these concepts, in reality itself. When that doesn't happen, as for instance with a concept like 'witch', or 'humor' (of the body), the explanatory schema that makes use of the suspect concept itself becomes suspect.

This is, as I said, true 'in general'. But there are some concepts and distinctions where it couldn't possibly be true on pain of incoherence. If we couldn't find anything in molecular chemistry to match, and so explain, the acid–base distinction, then at the very least a serious question arises as to whether that distinction is confused or illegitimate. But suppose someone sets out to find the features of reality that in a similar way match or explain the true–false distinction. It would have to be some features of mental states such as beliefs, or perhaps of sentences or propositions (i.e. the contents of these mental states), since these are the things that can be true or false. Of course, no such feature will be found.[15] But that is not because the true–false distinction is somehow illegitimate. It is because this distinction is presupposed by the idea of 'reality' itself. Without too much exaggeration, one might say that the idea of 'reality' is simply the idea of what is described by true sentences rather than false ones. In order to make sense of the enterprise, that is the purposive activity, of 'investigating reality', therefore, one must presuppose the distinction between what is real and what is not real; that is, one must presuppose the true–false distinction. So it would be a confusion, though maybe a natural one, to try to find what features of reality match or ground this distinction—to look 'inside' reality for a distinction presupposed by the idea of 'reality' itself.[16] Another way to put all this, I think, is to say that 'truth' is the norm inherently involved in the enterprise of 'investigating reality'. It is the norm, that is, essential to beliefs. The investigation of reality is a purposive, goal directed activity, and hence presupposes a distinction between success and failure at achieving the goal. And this particular purposive activity, the investigation of reality, is successful just to the extent that one manages to sort out what *is* 'reality' from what is not, that is to sort out true beliefs, or propositions, from false ones.

Something like this same relationship, I think, holds between the normative concepts that we find in reasons explanations of actions and the concept of an intentional action itself. This is easiest to see if we focus on the first person case. When I do something intentionally, I conceive of myself as also being able not to do it if I choose, and I conceive of my action as having a purpose or point; that is, I conceive of myself as having a reason for doing what I do. These thoughts are not detachable from the action itself. In order for me to perform some action intentionally, such as voting for that tax increase, I must

[15] For sentences or propositions this is straightforward. There can't be a syntactic definition of a semantic concept such as 'true'.

[16] An analogous issue faces empiricist epistemologists who want to reject skepticism. If one looks for the distinction between genuinely informative experiences and such things as dreams and hallucinations *inside* experience itself, some 'earmark' of experiences that separates the informative ones from the rest, the enterprise is hopeless. One might have dreamt or hallucinated the earmark in any particular case. The informative–illusory distinction, for experiences, is not itself a distinction that could be discovered through experience. For a convincing argument for this see J. Nagel (2000).

as a minimum *understand myself as doing this very thing*, e.g. voting for that tax increase. Otherwise my act would be unintentional—if for instance I pushed the button to vote for the tax increase thinking that I was buying a soft drink. Or it might not be an 'action' in the required sense at all—if for instance I just leaned against the voting machine while trying to figure out what to do and my elbow happened to hit the 'yes' button. But understanding myself as doing this, I am suggesting, entails conceiving of myself as doing it for some reason, a reason I can evaluate and decide not to act on if I choose.

Another way to say this is that the normative concept of my having a reason for what I am doing is part of the idea of my doing it intentionally. That is, in order to be *doing* something intentionally I must *understand* myself as doing that very thing and as doing it for some reason, the 'reason giving' nature of which is subject to my evaluation. Of course this is just the other side (the 'inside') of the point made above, that to understand someone as performing an action is to understand her as acting for a reason. Someone who acts for a reason must at a minimum take some consideration, at least one, as *providing* some reason for her to act as she does. But this is not to say that she herself needs to *conceptualize* this consideration as providing her with a reason. She need not 'say to herself' that this consideration provides her with a reason, for instance. *That* she takes it as providing her with a reason is shown by the fact that she considers it in deciding what to do. She might weigh it against other considerations, for instance, and then act on the basis of this consideration and not those others.

Of course, in addition to weighing up this consideration and (let's suppose) acting on the basis of it, she might formulate the explicit thought that this consideration gives her a reason to act in this way. But formulating the explicit thought, and even perhaps sincerely agreeing to it, say, verbally, is neither necessary nor sufficient for it to be true of her that she regards this consideration as a reason to do what she does. What is essential is that she actually give this consideration some weight in her deliberation (in the paradigm case, where she actually does deliberate), or that she would do so in the appropriate circumstances. And she can do this without ever formulating to herself the explicit thought that this consideration provides her with reason to act in this way.

What all this suggests, I think, is that the notion of acting for a reason, and the connected idea that one's reasons can always be better

or worse ones, stands to the notion of an intentional action in something like the same way the distinction between true and false stands
to the notion of 'investigating reality'. It makes no real sense to look
for the true–false distinction 'inside' reality, that is by looking at the
features reality has, because the distinction is presupposed by the
activity of investigating reality in the first place. Similarly, it makes no
sense to look for the essential features of the idea of an agent's reason
for acting inside the physical mechanisms of actions themselves,
because the idea of the agent regarding something as *giving her reason
to act*, and so the distinction between better and worse reasons for
performing actions, is already presupposed by the idea of intentional
actions.

One way of making sense of this would be to hold that, when I
explain someone's action in terms of her reasons for performing it,
what I am doing is understanding her on the model of myself, that is
of my own deliberations and actions. I am understanding her as
weighing various considerations and acting on the basis of the one or
ones that seem weightiest to her in essentially the same way I myself
do when I act for a reason. That is how I understand my own actions.
If this is right, there is nothing in it that entails that I have to regard
her as taking as reasons the things I *would regard* as reasons, or as
assigning the weights, that is the importance, to these things that I
myself think they deserve. (Even in my own deliberations, the things
I regard as reasons are always problematic, always such that I might
decide I was mistaken about them.) But I regard her as going through
the same *sort* of process I go through when I act for reasons, on pain
of assigning different meanings to the phrase 'acting for a reason' in
the first and third person cases. So, though when I act on the basis of
my own practical deliberation I do not at the same time explain my
action to myself, my explanations of the actions of others in terms of
their reasons have as their essential explanatory element that I regard
them as doing as I do when I act. That is the central, and essential,
explanatory mechanism of such explanations. If this is correct, then
clearly it makes sense of the idea that the first person case is prior.

On this view, there is a 'non-theoretical' element at the heart of
reasons explanations, namely the way I understand my own case
when I act for a reason. That is the model for how I understand
others. It might help to make clear how this suggestion works if we
examine briefly a problem that Daniel Dennett encounters in
explaining his own account of how reasons explanations of actions

work (Dennett 1987, especially the first few esays). According to Dennett, reasons explanations are what he calls 'intentional stance explanations'. This means that, rather than presupposing the truth of some physical theory, as 'physical stance' explanations do, or some sort of purposive design of the thing to be explained, as 'design stance' explanations do, reasons explanations operate by ascribing beliefs, desires, and (most importantly) rationality to the 'system' being explained. But, Dennett says, ascribing beliefs and desires to the system in question does not commit one to the claim that there are any specific internal states of this system corresponding to these mental states. Rather, beliefs and desires function in such explanations as 'abstracta', that is as hypothetical entities analogous to 'center of mass', which may not correspond to any actual states or features of the system being explained.

All this seems to me a good way of describing reasons explanations, so far as it goes. Since it follows from Dennett's account that the terms 'belief' and 'desire' do not describe (even 'functionally') internal states of the system in question, it would seem that intentional stance explanations as Dennett describes them cannot get their explanatory force from the physical laws that of course also describe the behavior of this same system. So, in spite of his use of the terms 'belief' and 'desire', and of the prominent role that beliefs and desires play in his account, Dennett is *not* engaged in what I have been calling 'the non-teleological belief–desire explanatory strategy'. That strategy depends essentially on accounting for the explanatory force of reasons explanations of actions by appealing to the causal interactions of the mental states (or their physical realizers) to which terms such as 'belief' and 'desire' refer. In Dennett's terminology, supporters of the non-teleological belief–desire strategy view reasons explanations as something like physical stance explanations (though they would have to be well disguised examples of them).

The explanatory force of the paradigm examples of physical and design stance explanations on Dennett's account are pretty clear. They depend on the relevant physical laws in the former case and on these laws plus some sort of intentional design in the latter. Denying that reasons explanations work like either of these leaves Dennett with the question of how exactly intentional stance explanations themselves really do work. And on that question, what he says seems harder to understand, even perhaps a bit misleading. According to Dennett,

We approach each other as *intentional systems*, that is, as entities whose behavior can be predicted by the method of attributing beliefs, desires, and rational acumen according to the following rough and ready principles:
(1) A system's beliefs are those it *ought to have*, given its perceptual capacities, its epistemic needs, and its biography. . . .
(2) A system's desires are those it *ought to have*, given its biological needs and the most practicable means of satisfying them. . . .
(3) A system's behavior will consist of those acts that *it would be rational* for an agent with those beliefs and desires to perform. (Dennett 1987, p. 49)

This seems misleading because it *seems* to commit Dennett (needlessly, I would say) to the error pointed out above of understanding the fact that someone takes some goal as her reason, and so wants (that is has a pro attitude toward) that goal, as the thought that it is part of the *content* of her reason that she wants this goal. That is, it seems to commit him to the view that all practical reasoning is about how to get what one already wants, as if there were no difference between simply wanting something and thinking it important or worthwhile or whatever. But so far as I can tell, there is nothing in Dennett's central idea of intentional stance explanations that requires this instrumental account of practical rationality.

Beyond this, many of the things Dennett says by way of explaining how the intentional stance works make it sound as if it is merely a matter of noticing objective features of reality which are different from the ones described by (say) physics. This is what he says in response to an objection he attributes to Robert Nozick, to the effect that super intelligent beings (from Mars of course), who have an exhaustive, so to speak Laplacean, knowledge of their physical environment but who don't use the intentional stance, wouldn't need concepts such as 'belief' and 'desire' and 'rationality' to predict exactly the same human behavior that Dennett says gets predicted from the intentional stance. In response, Dennett says that these Martians 'would be missing something perfectly objective: the *patterns* in human behavior that are describable from the intentional stance, and only from that stance, and that support generalizations and predictions. (Dennett 1987, p. 25).[17]

---

[17] Dennett is making much the same point I think in his discussion of the game 'Life', where the underlying rule of the game allows construction of very complex patterns that persist for long stretches of the game. As in this game, he says, 'the patterns the Martians miss are really, objectively there to be noticed or overlooked' (p. 37).

This makes it sound as if these poor Martians, though 'super intelligent', suffer from some strange brain dysfunction which keeps them from noticing or describing some patterns right in front of their eyes (or their weird green sensors). They would be like a dyslexic who could describe in precise geometric detail the shapes on the page before her but could not see that they were letters (or words or sentences). So on this view the intentional stance would be simply a sort of pattern recognizing ability we humans have and those Martians lack.

That invites the retort that under the surface so-called 'intentional stance explanations' are really just using shorthand summaries of very complex physical patterns, i.e. that they aren't really at all different from physical stance explanations in the end. So it would seem that what those Martians should do is just get off their high horses and put their 'super intelligence' to work on constructing some pattern recognition programs for their computers analogous to the text recognition programs used by the blind or dyslexic to speak the words scanned off a printed page. The Martians could then detect the same patterns in human affairs that the 'intentional stance' lets us detect; but there would not be anything in these patterns that was not describable (much more laboriously) in straight physical terms.

What is needed to forestall such a retort I think is something Dennett doesn't really provide: an explanation of how the explanatory mechanism employed in intentional stance explanations differs from the ones employed in physical and design stance explanations. A strong hint of how this will have to go is given by something else Dennett says about these Martians, something that seems utterly mysterious on the 'pattern recognition' view just described: namely that, when they are trying to understand *themselves*, the intentional stance is *unavoidable*.

This unavoidability [he says], is itself interest relative; it is perfectly possible to adopt a physical stance, for instance, with regard to an intelligent being, oneself included, but not to the exclusion of maintaining at the same time an intentional stance with regard to oneself at a minimum, and one's fellows if one intends, for instance, to learn what they know . . . (Dennett 1987, p. 27)

The suggestion I made above about the centrality of the first person case would, I think, explain this 'unavoidability'. It is the same unavoidability involved in regarding oneself as a rational agent. In brief, the suggestion is that reasons explanations make essential use of the normative notion of rationality by picturing the action to be explained as springing from the same sort of process the person doing the explaining herself engages in when she acts for some reason. To put this another way, regarding another person whose actions one wants to explain *as a rational being*, which is what the principle of charity requires, means regarding her actions as the results of the same sort of deliberative process as one's own actions. It also means regarding her actions and the considerations on which they are based as subject to the same sort of rational criticism as one's own actions. That normative element—that reasons for doing something may be better or worse ones—applies to her actions as well as one's own and in the same way.

There is nothing, as I said, in regarding the person whose action I am explaining as acting for a reason, that requires that I regard her reasons as ones I would accept as good reasons. But it does require that I regard her actions and reasons as being *open to the same standards of rational criticism* as mine. That is part of what it is to regard her as a rational agent, and hence part of what it is to explain her actions in terms of her reasons. To think of oneself as evaluating the various considerations that seem relevant and then deciding to act on the basis of this deliberation is to think of oneself as the person responsible for performing this action, since one could have chosen not to do it, and it is to think of the action itself as open to rational criticism, something that reasons can be brought in favor of and against. To think of someone else as acting for reasons is to think of that person in the same way.

Practical deliberation is the process of trying to figure out what one has most reason to do and is thus *essentially* evaluative. Such deliberation is possible because actions are (indeed, are paradigms of) the sorts of things that are under one's control and also the sorts of things that reasons can be brought for and against. To conceive of oneself as acting is to conceive of oneself as the agent responsible for this process. And to explain someone else's action in terms of her reasons is to conceive of her as the agent responsible for this same sort of process. In both cases the evaluative, critical element is essential. To act for a reason always carries with it the possibility that the reason for which one acted might not be a good one, or at least not good enough. And the question of whether or not it is good enough is one that necessarily extends beyond the question of whether or not it really is one's reason for doing what one did. Just as it is essential to beliefs that they can be false and to desires that they may be desires for things not worth having, so it is essential to one's reasons for acting that they may not be good reasons.

It was argued above that reasons explanations of actions, since they depend on the principle of charity in ascribing rationality to the person whose action is being explained, always involve an evaluative element. But this 'critical' feature of rationality that we have been discussing in the last few paragraphs involves a separate point. Ascribing rationality to someone is not merely another way of evaluating her, in the way ascribing generosity or honesty would be for instance. Rationality, one might say, is not just another character trait, but also the ground or condition for character traits of the sort we have been discussing, and indeed of the possibility of intentional action itself. Ascribing rationality to someone *is* evaluating her, of course, and doing so in terms of a character trait; but it is a character trait that entails thinking of her actions and the reasons she has for them as subject to the same sorts of evaluations as one's own.

Ordinary reasons explanations of actions are thus normative in two distinct senses. They ascribe rationality to the person whose actions are being explained. At the same time, in virtue of so doing, they open this action, and the reasons for which it was performed, to critical or rational evaluation which is of exactly the same sort that one's own practical deliberation focuses on one's own actions and possible actions.

Bibliography

Anscombe, G. (1963). *Intention*. Ithaca: Cornell University Press.

Antony, L. (1989). 'Anomalous Monism and the Problem of Explanatory Force'. *Philosophical Review*, 97, 2 (April): 153–187.

Audi, R. (1989). *Practical Reasoning*. London: Routledge.

—— (1993). *Action, Intention and Reason*. Ithaca, NY: Cornell University Press.

—— (ed.) (1995). *The Cambridge Dictionary of Philosophy*. Cambridge: Cambridge University Press.

Austin, J. L. (1962). *How to Do Things with Words*. Oxford: Oxford University Press.

Blackburn, S. (1998). *Ruling Passions*. Oxford: Oxford University Press.

Bolton, N. (ed.) (1979). *Philosophical Problems in Psychology*. London: Methuen.

Brand, M. (1984). *Intending and Acting*. Cambridge, Mass.: MIT Press.

Bratman, M. (1999). *Faces of Intention*. Cambridge: Cambridge University Press.

Brichcin, M. (1993). 'Intentional Guidance of Human Actions'. *Journal of Russian and East European Psychology*, 31, 5 (Sept.–Oct.): 79–99.

Butler, K. (1992). 'The Physiology of Desire'. *Journal of Mind and Behavior*, 13, 1 (Winter): 69–88.

Chang, R. (ed.) (1998). *Incommensurability, Incomparability and Practical Reason*. Cambridge, Mass.: Harvard University Press.

Cleveland, T. (1997). *Trying without Willing*. Aldershot, Hants: Ashgate .

Collins, A. (1997): 'The Psychological Reality of Reasons'. *Ratio*, (n. s.) 10 (September): 108–123.

Cullity, G. and Gaut, B. (eds.) (1997). *Ethics and Practical Reason*. Oxford: Oxford University Press.

Cummins, R. (1975). 'Functional Analysis'. Journal of Philosophy, 72: 741–764.

—— (1983). *The Nature of Psychological Explanation*. Cambridge, Mass.: MIT Press.

Dancy, J. (1993). *Moral Reasons*. Oxford: Blackwell Publishers.

—— (2000). *Practical Reality*. Oxford: Oxford University Press.

Darwall, S. (1993). *Impartial Reason*. Ithaca, NY: Cornell University Press.

—— Gibbard, A. and Railton, P. (eds.) (2000). *Moral Discourse and Practice*. Oxford: Oxford University Press.

Davidson, D. (1995). 'Actions, Reasons and Causes'. *Journal of Philosophy* 60; reprinted in Davidson (1980a), pp. 685–700.

Davidson, D. (1975). 'Thought and Talk'. In S. Guttenplan (ed.), *Mind and Language*. Oxford: Oxford University Press; reprinted in Davidson (1980b).

—— (1980a). *Essays on Actions and Events*. Oxford: Oxford University Press.

—— (1980b). *Inquiries into Truth and Interpretation*. Oxford: Oxford University Press.

—— (2001). *Subjective, Intersubjective, Objective*. Oxford: Oxford University Press.

Dawkins, R. (1995). 'God's Utility Function'. *Scientific American*, 273, 5 (November): pp. 80–85.

Dennett, D. (1987). *The Intentional Stance*. Cambridge, Mass.: MIT Press.

Dretske, F. (1988). *Explaining Behavior*. Cambridge, Mass.: MIT Press.

Ehring, D. (1986).'Teleology and Impossible Goals'. *Philosophy and Phenomenological Research*, 47, 1 (September): 127–131.

Fodor, J. (1987). *Psychosemantics*. Cambridge, Mass.: MIT Press.

—— and LaPore, E. (1992). *Holism: A Shopper's Guide*. Oxford: Blackwell.

Follesdal, D. (1982). 'The Status of Rationality Assumptions in Interpretation and in the Explanation of Action', *Dialectica*, 36, 4: 301–316.

Foot, P. (1983). 'Moral Realism and Moral Dilemma'. *Journal of Philosophy*, 80, 7 (July): 379–398.

—— (2001). *Natural Goodness*. Oxford: Oxford University Press.

Frankfurt, H. (1971). 'Freedom of the Will and the Concept of a Person', *Journal of Philosophy*, 68, 1 (January): 5–20.

Gauthier, D. (1986). *Morals by Agreement*. Oxford: Oxford University Press.

Ginet, C. (1989). 'Reasons Explanations of Action: An Incompatibilist Account'. *Philosophical Perspectives*, 3: 17–46.

Godfrey-Smith, P. (1998). *Complexity and the Function of Mind in Nature*. Cambridge: Cambridge University Press.

Goldman, A. (1970) *A Theory of Human Action*. Princeton: Princeton University Press.

Gordon, R. (1986). 'Folk Psychology as Simulation'. *Mind and Language*, 1, 2 (Summer), 158–171.

Grice, H. P (1991). *The Conception of Value*. Oxford: Oxford University Press.

—— (2001). *Aspects of Reason*. Oxford: Oxford University Press.

Hampton, J. (1998). *The Authority of Reason*. Cambridge: Cambridge University Press.

Harrison, R. (ed.) (1980). *Rational Action*. Cambridge: Cambridge University Press.

Haugeland, J. (1998). *Having Thought*. Cambridge, Mass.: Harvard University Press.

Heil, J. and Mele, A. (eds.) (1993). *Mental Causation*. Oxford: Oxford University Press.

Herman, B. (1993).*The Practice of Moral Judgment*. Cambridge, Mass.: Harvard University Press.

Hitchcock, C. (2001). 'The Intransitivity of Causation Revealed in Equations and Graphs'. *Journal of Philosophy*, 98, 6 (June): 273–299.

Hornsby, J. (1997). *Simple Mindedness*. Cambridge, Mass.: Harvard University Press.

Howard, G. (1988). 'Science, Values, and Teleological Explanations of Human Action'. *Counseling and Values*, 32, 2 (January): 93–103.

Hume, D. (1957). *An Enquiry Concerning the Principles of Morals*. New York: Liberal Arts Press.

—— (1888). *A Treatise of Human Nature*, ed. L. A. Selby-Bigge Oxford: Oxford University Press.

Hurley, S. (1989). *Natural Reasons*. Oxford: Oxford University Press.

Kant, I. (1964). *Groundwork of the Metaphysic of Morals*, trans. H. J. Paton. New York: Harper & Row.

Kim, J. (1993*a*). 'The Non-reductivist's Troubles With Mental Causation'. In Heil and Mele (1993).

Kim, J. (1993*b*). *Supervenience and Mind*. Cambridge: Cambridge University Press.

Kim, J. (1996). *The Philosophy of Mind*. Boulder, Colo.: Westview Press.

Korsgaard, C. (1988). 'Skepticism about Practical Reason'. *Journal of Philosophy*, 2, 1 (February): 5–25; reprinted in Korsgaard (1996a).

—— (1996*a*). *Creating the Kingdom of Ends* (Cambridge, Cambridge University Press, 1996)

—— (1996*b*). *The Sources of Normativity*. Cambridge: Cambridge University Press.

Langford, G. (1981). 'The Nature of Purpose'. *Mind*, 90: 1–19.

Lenman, J. (1996). 'Belief, Desire and Motivation: An Essay in Quasi-Hydraulics'. *American Philosophical Quarterly*, 33, 3 (July): 291–301.

Lewis, D. (1973): 'Causation'. *Journal of Philosophy*, 70: 556–567; reprinted in Sosa and Tooley (1993).

Lyons, W. (1992). 'Intentionality and Modern Philosophical Psychology, III: The Appeal to Teleology'. *Philosophical Psychology*, 5, 3: 309–326.

McDowell, J. (1998). *Mind, Value and Reality*. Cambridge, Mass.: Harvard University Press.

McGinn, C. (1979). 'Action and its Explanation'. In Bolton (1979).

—— (1977). *The Character of Mind*. Oxford: Oxford University Press.

Mackie, J. (1974). *The Cement of the Universe*. Oxford: Oxford University Press.

—— (1977). *Ethics: Inventing Right and Wrong*. Harmondsworth: Penguin.

Malle, B. (2001). 'Folk Explanations of Intentional Action'. In Malle *et al.* (2001).

—— and Knobe, J. (1997). 'The Folk Concept of Intentionality'. *Journal of Experimental Social Psychology*, 33: 101–121

—— Moses, L. and Baldwin, D. (eds.) (2001). *Intentions and Intentionality*. Cambridge, Mass.: MIT Press.

Mele, A. (1992*a*). *The Springs of Action*. Oxford: Oxford University Press.

—— (1992*b*). 'Recent Work on Intentional Action'. *American Philosophical Quarterly*, 29, 3: 199–217.

—— (1995). 'Motivation: Essentially Motivation-Constituting Attitudes'. *Philosophical Review*, 104, 3 (July): 387–423.

—— (1996). 'Internalist Moral Cognitivism and Listlessness'. *Ethics*, 106 (July): 727–753.

—— (ed.) (1997). *The Philosophy of Action*. Oxford: Oxford University Press.

—— (1998). 'Motivational Strength'. *Nous* 32 (1): 23–36.

—— (2000). 'Goal-Directed Action: Teleological Explanations, Causal Theories, and Deviance'. *Philosophical Perspectives*, 14: 279–300.

Nagel, E. (1977). 'Teleology Revisited'. *Journal of Philosophy*, 74, 5 (May): 261–300.

Nagel, J. (2000). 'The Empiricist Conception of Experience'. *Philosophy*, 75: 345–375.

Nagel, T. (1970). *The Possibility of Altruism*. Oxford: Oxford University Press.

—— (1990). *The View from Nowhere*. Oxford: Oxford University Press.

Nesbit, E. (1999). *The Five Children and It*. New York: William Morrow; first published 1902.

O'Connor, T. (ed.) (1995). *Agents, Causes and Events*. Oxford: Oxford University Press.

O'Shaughnessy, B. (1980). *The Will*, 2 vols. Cambridge: Cambridge University Press.

Peirce, C. (1956). *Collected Papers*, ed. C. Hartshorne and P. Weiss, Vol 5. Cambridge, Mass.: Harvard University Press.

Platts, M. (1991). *Moral Realities*. London: Routledge.

Price, C. (1995). 'Functional Explanations and Natural Norms'. *Ratio*, (n. s.) 7 (September): 143–160.

Putnam, H. (1983). 'Why Reason Can't Be Naturalized'. In his *Realism and Reason: Philosophical Papers*, Vol. 3. Cambridge, Cambridge University Press, 229–247.

Quinn, W. (1993). *Morality and Action*. Cambridge: Cambridge University Press.

Rawls, J. (1970). *A Theory of Justice*. Cambridge, Mass.: Harvard University Press.)

Raz, J. (1975). *Practical Reason and Norms*. London: Hutchinson.

—— (1999). *Engaging Reason*. Oxford: Oxford University Press.

Robinson, W. (1999). 'Epiphenomenalism'. In E. Zalta (ed.), *The Stanford Encyclopedia of Philosophy* http://plato.stanford.edu/entries/epiphenomenalism.

Roth, A. (1999). 'Reasons Explanations of Actions: Causal, Singular, and Situational'. *Philosophy and Phenomenological Research*, 56, 4 (December): 839–874.

Russell, B. (1953). 'On the Notion of Cause'. In his *Mysticism and Logic*. Harmondsworth: Penguin.

Ryle, G. (1949). *The Concept of Mind*. New York: Barnes and Nobel.

Sayre-McCord, G. (1989). 'Functional Explanations and Reasons as Causes'. *Philosophical Perspectives*, 3: 137–164.

Scanlon, T. (1998). *What We Owe to Each Other*. Cambridge, Mass.: Harvard University Press.

Schick, F. (*1991*). *Understanding Action*. Cambridge: Cambridge University Press.

Schueler, G. F. (1989). *The Idea of A Reason for Acting*. Lewiston, Maine: Mellen.

—— (1991). 'Pro-Attitudes and Direction of Fit', *Mind*, 100, 277–281.

—— (1995*a*). *Desire*. Cambridge, Mass.: MIT Press.

—— (1995*b*). 'Why "Ought's" Are Not Facts'. *Mind*, 104, : 713–723.

—— (1996). 'How Can Reason Be Practical?', *Critica*, 28, 84 (December): 41–62.

—— (2001). 'Action Explanations: Causes and Purposes' in Malle *et al.* (2001).

—— (2003). 'Rationality and Character'. In Tenenbaum (forthcoming *a*).

Searle, J. (1964). 'How to Derive "Ought" from "Is" '. *Philosophical Review*, 73: 43–58.

—— (1983). *Intentionality*. Cambridge: Cambridge University Press.

—— (1991). 'Intentionalistic Explanations in the Social Sciences'. *Philosophy of the Social Sciences*, 21, 3 (September): 332–366.

—— (1992). *The Rediscovery of the Mind*. Cambridge Mass.: MIT Press.

—— (2001). *Rationality in Action*. Cambridge, Mass.: MIT Press.

Sehon, S. (1994). 'Teleology and the Nature of Mental States'. *American Philosophical Quarterly*, 31, 1 (January): 63–72.

—— (1997*a*). 'Deviant Causal Chains and the Irreducibility of Teleological Explanation'. *Pacific Philosophical Quarterly*, 78: 195–213.

—— (1997*b*). Natural-Kind Terms and the Status of Folk Psychology'. *American Philosophical Quarterly*, 34, 3 (July): 333–344.

—— (1998). 'Connectionism and the Causal Theory of Action Explanation'. *Philosophical Psychology*, 11, 4: 511–532.

—— (forthcoming *a*). 'An Argument Against the Causal Theory of Action Explanation'. *Philosophy and Phenomenological Research* (forthcoming).

—— (forthcoming *b*). *Teleological Realism: Mind, Agency and Explanation*. (forthcoming)

Smart, J. J. C. (1959). 'Sensations and Brain Processes'. *Philosophical Review*, 68, 141–156.

Smith, M. (1987). 'The Humean Theory of Motivation', *Mind*, 96: 36–61.

Smith, M. (1994). *The Moral Problem*. Oxford: Blackwell.

—— Pettit, P. (1990). 'Backgrounding Desire'. *Philosophical Review*, 99: 565–592.

Sober, E. (1993). *Philosophy of Biology*. Boulder, Colo.: Westview Press.

Sosa, E. and Tooley, M. (eds.) (1993). *Causation*. Oxford: Oxford University Press.

Stich, S. (1996). *Deconstructing the Mind*. Oxford: Oxford University Press.

Strunk, W. and White, E. B. (1959). *The Elements of Style*. New York: Macmillan.

Tanney, J. (1995). 'Why Reasons may not be Causes'. *Mind and Language*, 10, 1–2 (March/June): 105–128.

Tenenbaum, S. (1999). 'The Judgment of a Weak Will'. *Philosophy and Phenomenological Research*, 69, 4 (December): 875–911.

—— (2000). 'Ethical Internalism and Glaucon's Question', *Nous*, 34, 1: 108–130.

—— (ed.) (forthcoming *a*). *Pozman Studies in Philosophy of Science and Humanities: New Essays in Moral Psychology*. Amsterdam: Rodophi.

—— (forthcoming *b*). *Appearances of The Good: An Essay on the Nature of Practical Reason*.

Velleman, D. (1996). 'The Possibility of Practical Reason'. *Ethics*, 106, 4 (July): reprinted in Velleman (2000), pp. 694–726.

—— (2000). *The Possibility of Practical Reason*. Oxford: Oxford University Press.

Wallace, R. J. (1990). 'How to Argue about Practical Reason'. *Mind*, 99: (July): 355–385.

Watson, G. (1975). 'Free Agency'. *Journal of Philosophy*, 72, 8 (April): 205–220; reprinted in Watson (1982).

—— (ed) (1982). *Free Will*. Oxford: Oxford University Press.

Wiggins, D. (1998). *Needs, Values, Truth*. Oxford: Oxford University Press.

Williams, B. (1980). 'Internal and External Reasons'. In Harrison (1980); reprinted in Williams (1981).

—— (1981). *Moral Luck*. Cambridge: Cambridge University Press.

—— (1985). *Ethics and the Limits of Philosophy*. Cambridge, Mass.: Harvard University Press.

—— (1995). *Making Sense of Humanity*. Cambridge: Cambridge University Press.

Wilson, G. (1989). *The Intentionality of Human Action*. Stanford, Calif.: Stanford University Press.

Wright, L. (1973). 'Functions'. *Philosophical Review*, 82: 139–168.

Zangwill, N. (1998). 'Direction of Fit and Normative Functionalism'. *Philosophical Studies*, 91, 2: 173–203.

Index